AF659340

BUSINESS ADMINISTRATION

BUSINESS ADMINISTRATION

D.K. Sharma

CENTRUM PRESS
NEW DELHI-110002 (INDIA)

CENTRUM PRESS

H.O.: 4360/4, Ansari Road, Daryaganj,
New Delhi-110002 (India)
Tel: 23278000, 23261597, 23255577, 23286875

B.O.: No. 1015, Ist Main Road, BSK IIIrd Stage,
IIIrd Phase, IIIrd Block, Bangalore-560085 (INDIA)
Tel: 080-41723429

Email: centrumpress@gmail.com
Visit us at: www.centrumpress.com

Business Administration

© Reserved

First Edition, 2010

ISBN 978-93-80252-97-1

PRINTED IN INDIA

Printed at Balaji Offset, Delhi.

Contents

Preface

Administration, as a legal concept, is a procedure under the insolvency laws of a number of common law jurisdictions. It functions as a rescue mechanism for insolvent companies and allows them to carry on running their business. The process – an alternative to liquidation– is often known as *going into administration.* In business, administration consists of the performance or management of business operations and thus the making or implementing of major decisions. Administration can be defined as the universal process of organizing people and resources efficiently so as to direct activities toward common goals and objectives.

The word is derived from the Middle English word *administracioun,* which is in turn derived from the French *administration,* itself derived from the Latin *administratio* — a compounding of *ad* ("to") and *ministratio* ("give service"). Administrator can serve as the title of the general manager or company secretary who reports to a corporate board of directors. This title is archaic, but, in many enterprises, this function, together with its associated Finance, Personnel and management information systems services, is what is intended when the term "the administration" is used.

In some organizational analyses, management is viewed as a subset of administration, specifically associated with the technical and mundane elements within an organization's operation. It stands distinct from executive or strategic work. In other organizational analyses, administration can refer to the bureaucratic or operational performance of mundane office tasks, usually internally oriented and reactive rather than proactive.

Management characterises the process of leading and directing all or part of an organisation, often a business, through the deployment and manipulation of resources. Management is also called "Business Administration" and schools that teach management are usually called "Business Schools". The term "management" may also be used to describe the slate of mangers of an organisation.

This fast effective book helps you master core management concepts from the systems approach and decision making to organisational design. This book is designed to prepare a student to understand the principles of management. It contains a subject matter review and a sample test. This is the book you need if you want a clear, concise guide for the principles of management concepts.

— *D.K. Sharma*

1

Introduction

As an educational term, business administration has come to encompass an extraordinary number of academic study areas. As business has become more complex, so too has the oversight of companies: their management, their growth strategies, their personnel issues, their taxes and the role that taxes play in corporate economic strategy. Advertising has grown to include multiple media outlets and an assortment of targeted interest groups: new customers, repeat customers, stockholders, investors and new geographic markets. Marketing has become the term of choice for all of this strategically placed product exposure.

Defining business administration then means defining oversight roles for the assortment of internal specialties that every business of any size has come to include. That is why business administration degrees are now offered with a remarkable number of categorical specialties available as choices of study. Perhaps the best way to define business administration is to look at the types of courses offered in MBA curriculums and the specialties, or "majors," that one can opt for in an MBA program.

For a large corporation, business administration is going to include international and global business, as well as strategy and economics. In this instance, the definition of business administration will include requirements of certain cultural differences and an acute understanding of the global economy and its current fluidity. Also included in business administration at this scale is the art and science of acquisition: when to buy a company or property and why.

Business administration will always include the intangible quality of leadership; you can obtain an MBA that specializes in just that. Along with leadership comes the task of negotiation and conflict resolution, specifically with regard to personnel. Behavioural psychology plays an important role in business administration: a misstep in an adversarial situation with a union can take a company under, as it did Continental Airlines some years ago.

The definition of business administration will have to include marketing; you won't have a business to administer unless you sell your products. Ancillary to marketing is an understanding of the new tools available for product distribution, and that will involve understanding e-business and how it is rapidly evolving.

Whether you are working with distributors that are small businesses or you are starting your own business, administration includes an understanding of entrepreneurship: tax structures for small businesses along with personnel issues at that level, inventory and cash flow, and all the other small matters that make a big difference to a new or small business.

A critical part of business administration is the awareness of risk. This might include the risk of launching a new product, and the costs involved; the risk of an acquisition, the risk of a competitive strategy, the company's exposure in opting for this health plan instead of that one. There are risks involved in other personnel decisions and this area is of tangible importance: company morale is a key to productivity and the resultant profitability.

There are MBA courses taught in all of these areas, and MBA degrees that specialize in many of them. The definition of business administration includes whatever knowledge is required to make all of these components work productively, if not in complete harmony.

Business Administration

In business, administration consists of the performance or management of business operations and thus the making or implementing of major decisions. Administration can be defined as the universal process of organizing people and resources efficiently so as to direct activities toward common goals and objectives.

The word is derived from the Middle English word *administracioun*, which is in turn derived from the French *administration*, itself derived from the Latin *administratio* — a compounding of *ad* ("to") and *ministratio* ("give service").

Administrator can serve as the title of the general manager or company secretary who reports to a corporate board of directors. This title is archaic, but, in many enterprises, this function, together with its associated Finance, Personnel and management information systems services, is what is intended when the term "the administration" is used.

In some organizational analyses, management is viewed as a subset of administration, specifically associated with the technical and mundane elements within an organization's operation. It stands distinct from executive or strategic work.

In other organizational analyses, administration can refer to the bureaucratic or operational performance of mundane office tasks, usually internally oriented and reactive rather than proactive.

The world's first business school, the Ecole Supérieure de Commerce de Paris, France, was established in 1819. The first business school in the United States, the Wharton School of the University of Pennsylvania, was founded in 1881. Anecdotically, top French business school HEC was also created in 1881, while Harvard Business School, founded in 1908, was born just one year after France's prestigious ESSEC Business School.

Administrative Functions

Administrators, broadly speaking, engage in a common set of functions to meet the organization's goals. These "functions" of the administrator were described by Henri Fayol as "the 5 elements of administration" (in bold below).

- Planning is deciding in advance what to do, how to do it, when to do it, and who should do it. It maps the path from where the organization is to where it wants to be. The planning function involves establishing goals and arranging them in logical order. Administrators engage in both short-range and long-range planning.

Planning

Planning in organizations and public policy is both the organizational process of creating and maintaining a plan; and the psychological process of thinking about the activities required to create a desired goal on some scale. As such, it is a fundamental property of intelligent behaviour. This thought process is essential to the creation and refinement of a plan, or integration of it with other plans, that is, it combines forecasting of developments with the preparation of scenarios of how to react to them. The term is also used to describe the formal procedures used in such an endeavour, such as the creation of documents diagrams, or meetings to discuss the important issues to be addressed, the objectives to be met, and the strategy to be followed. Beyond this, planning has a different meaning depending on the political or economic context in which it is used.

Two attitudes to planning need to be held in tension: on the one hand we need to be prepared for what may lie ahead, which may mean contingencies and flexible processes. On the other hand, our future is shaped by consequences of our own planning and actions.

Overview

Planning is a process for accomplishing purpose. It is blue print of business growth and a road map of development. It helps in deciding objectives both in quantitative and qualitative terms. It is setting of goals on the basis of objectives and keeping in view the resources.

What Should a Plan be?

A plan should be a realistic view of the expectations. Depending upon the activities, a plan can be long range, intermediate range or short range. It is the framework within which it must operate. For management seeking external support, the plan is the most important document and key to growth. Preparation of a comprehensive plan will not guarantee success, but lack of a sound plan will almost certainly ensure failure.

Purpose of Plan

Just as no two organizations are alike, so also their plans. It is therefore important to prepare a plan keeping in view the necessities of the enterprise. A plan is an important aspect of business. It serves the following three critical functions:

- Helps management to clarify, focus, and research their business's or project's development and prospects.

- Provides a considered and logical framework within which a business can develop and pursue business strategies over the next three to five years.
- Offers a benchmark against which actual performance can be measured and reviewed.

Importance of the Planning Process

A plan can play a vital role in helping to avoid mistakes or recognize hidden opportunities. Preparing a satisfactory plan of the organization is essential. The planning process enables management to understand more clearly what they want to achieve, and how and when they can do it.

A well-prepared business plan demonstrates that the managers know the business and that they have thought through its development in terms of products, management, finances, and most importantly, markets and competition.

Planning helps in forecasting the future, makes the future visible to some extent. It bridges between where we are and where we want to go. Planning is looking ahead.

Types of Plans or Planning

- Architectural planning
- Business plan
- Comprehensive planning
- Enterprise Architecture Planning
- Event Planning and Production
- Family planning
- Financial planning
- Infrastructure planning
- Land use planning
- Life planning
- Marketing plan
- Network resource planning
- Strategic planning
- Urban planning.

Planning Basics

Essentials of Planning

Planning is not done off hand. It is prepared after careful and extensive research. For a comprehensive business plan, management has to:

1. Clearly define the target/goal in writing.
    1. It should be set by a person having authority.
    2. The goal should be realistic.
    3. It should be specific.
    4. Acceptability
    5. Easily measurable
2. Identify all the main issues which need to be addressed.
3. Review past performance.
4. Decide budgetary requirement.
5. Focus on matters of strategic importance.
6. What are requirements and how will they be met?
7. What will be the likely length of the plan and its structure?
8. Identify shortcomings in the concept and gaps.
9. Strategies for implementation.
10. Review periodically.

Applications

In Organizations

Planning is also a management process, concerned with defining goals for future organizational performance and deciding on the tasks and resources to be used in order to attain those goals. To meet the goals, managers may develop plans such as a business plan or a marketing plan. Planning always has a purpose. The purpose may be achievement of certain goals or targets. The planning helps to achieve these goals or target by using the available time and resources. To minimize the timing and resources also require proper planning.

In Public Policy

Planning refers to the practice and the profession associated with the idea of planning an idea yourself, (land use planning, urban planning or spatial planning). In many countries, the operation of a town and country planning system is often referred to as 'planning' and the professionals which operate the system are known as 'planners'.......

It is a conscious as well as sub-conscious activity. It is "an anticipatory decision making process " that helps in coping with complexities. It is deciding future course of action from amongst alternatives. It is a process that involves making and evaluating each set of interrelated decisions. It is selection of missions, objectives and " translation of knowledge into action." A planned performance brings better results compared to unplanned one. A Managers' job is planning, monitoring and controlling. Planning and goal setting are important traits of an organization. It is done at all levels of the organization. Planning includes the plan, the thought process, action, and implementation. Planning gives more power over the future. Planning is deciding in advance what to do, how to do it, when to do it, and who should do it. It bridges the gap from where the organization is to where it wants to be. The planning function involves establishing goals and arranging them in logical order.

- Organizing involves identifying responsibilities to be performed, grouping responsibilities into departments or divisions, and specifying organizational relationships. The purpose is to achieve coordinated effort among all the elements in the organization (Coordinating). Organizing must take into account delegation of authority and responsibility and span of control within supervisory units.
- Staffing means filling job positions with the right people at the right time. It involves determining staffing needs, writing job descriptions, recruiting and screening people to fill the positions.

Human resources is a term used to refer to how people are managed by organizations. The field has moved from a traditionally administrative function to a strategic one that recognizes the link between talented and engaged people and organizational success. The field draws upon concepts developed in Industrial/Organizational Psychology and System Theory. Human resources has at least two related interpretations depending on context. The original usage derives from political economy and economics, where it was traditionally called labour, one of four factors of production although this perspective is changing as a function of new and ongoing research into more strategic approaches at national levels. This first usage is used more in terms of 'human resources development', and can go beyond just organizations to the level of nations. The more traditional usage within corporations and businesses refers to the individuals within a firm or agency, and to the portion of the organization that deals with hiring, firing, training, and other personnel issues, typically referred to as 'human resources management'. This article addresses both definitions.

Development

The objective of human resources development is to foster human resourcefulness through enlightened and cohesive policies in education, training, health and employment at all levels, from corporate to national.

Management

Human resource management's objective, on the other hand, is to maximize the return on investment from the organization's human capital and minimize financial risk. It is the responsibility of human resource managers in a corporate context to conduct these activities in an effective, legal, fair, and consistent manner.

Key Functions

Human Resource Management serves these key functions:

1. Recruitment & Selection
2. Training and Development (People or Organization)
3. Performance Evaluation and Management
4. Promotions/Transfer
5. Redundancy
6. Industrial and Employee Relations
7. Record keeping of all personal data.
8. Total Rewards: Employee Benefits & Compensation
9. Confidential advice to internal 'customers' in relation to problems at work
10. Career development
11. Competency Mapping (Competency mapping is a process an

individual uses to identify and describe competencies that are the most critical to success in a work situation or work role.)

12. Time motion study is related to HR Function
13. Performance Appraisal.

Modern Analysis

Modern analysis emphasizes that human beings are not "commodities" or "resources", but are creative and social beings in a productive enterprise. The 2000 revision of ISO 9001 in contrast requires to identify the processes, their sequence and interaction, and to define and communicate responsibilities and authorities. In general, heavily unionized nations such as France and Germany have adopted and encouraged such job descriptions especially within trade unions. The International Labour Organization also in 2001 decided to revisit, and revise its 1975 Recommendation 150 on Human Resources Development. One view of these trends is that a strong social consensus on political economy and a good social welfare system facilitates labour mobility and tends to make the entire economy more productive, as labour can develop skills and experience in various ways, and move from one enterprise to another with little controversy or difficulty in adapting. Another view is that governments should become more aware of their national role in facilitating human resources development across all sectors.

Labour Mobility

An important controversy regarding labour mobility illustrates the broader philosophical issue with usage of the phrase "human resources": governments of developing nations often regard developed nations that encourage immigration or "guest workers" as appropriating human capital that is rightfully part of the developing nation and required to further its growth as a civilization. They argue that this appropriation is similar to colonial commodity fiat wherein a colonizing European power would define an arbitrary price for natural resources, extracting which diminished national natural capital.

The debate regarding "human resources" versus human capital thus in many ways echoes the debate regarding natural resources versus natural capital. Over time the United Nations have come to more generally support the developing nations' point of view, and have requested significant offsetting "foreign aid" contributions so that a developing nation losing human capital does not lose the capacity to continue to train new people in trades, professions, and the arts.

An extreme version of this view is that historical inequities such as African slavery must be compensated by current developed nations, which benefited from stolen "human resources" as they were developing. This is an extremely controversial view, but it echoes the general theme of converting human capital to "human resources" and thus greatly diminishing its value to the host society, i.e. "Africa", as it is put to narrow imitative use as "labour" in the using society.

In a series of reports of the UN Secretary-General to the General Assembly [e.g. A/56/162 (2001)], a broad inter-sectoral approach to developing human resourcefulness has been outlined as a priority for socio-economic development and particularly anti-poverty strategies. This calls for strategic and integrated public policies, for example in education, health, and employment sectors that promote occupational skills, knowledge and performance enhancement (Lawrence, J.E.S.).

Perceptions

Terms like "human resources" and "human capital" may be perceived as insulting to people. They create the impression that people are merely commodities, like office machines or vehicles, despite assurances to the contrary.

Corporate Management

In the very narrow context of corporate "human resources" management, there is a contrasting pull to reflect and require workplace diversity that echoes the diversity of a global customer base. Foreign language and culture skills, ingenuity, humour, and careful listening, are examples of traits that such programs typically require. It would appear that these evidence a general shift through the human capital point of view to an acknowledgment that human beings do contribute much more to a productive enterprise than "work": they bring their character, their ethics, their creativity, their social connections, and in some cases even their pets and children, and alter the character of a workplace. The term corporate culture is used to characterize such processes at the organizational level.

The traditional but extremely narrow context of hiring, firing, and job description is considered a 20th century anachronism. Most corporate organizations that compete in the modern global economy have adopted a view of human capital that mirrors the modern consensus as above. Some of these, in turn, deprecate the term "human resources" as useless. Yet the term survives, and if related to `resourcefulness', has continued and emerging relevance to public policy.

In general the abstractions of macroeconomics treat it this way-as it characterizes no mechanisms to represent choice or ingenuity. So one interpretation is that "firm-specific human capital" as defined in macroeconomics is the modern and correct definition of "human resources"-and that this is inadequate to represent the contributions of "human resources" in any modern theory of political economy.

Human Resources Management Trends and Influences

In organizations, it is important to determine both current and future organisational requirements for both core employees and the contingent workforce in terms of their skills/technical abilities, competencies, flexibility etc. The analysis requires consideration of the internal and external factors that can have an effect on the resourcing, development, motivation and retention of employees and other workers. The external factors are those largely outwith the control of the organization and include issues such as the economic climate, current and future trends of the labour market e.g. skills, education level, government investment into industries etc. On the other hand internal influences are broadly within the control of the organization to predict determine and monitor, for example the organizational culture underpinned by management behaviours (or style), environmental climate and the approach to ethical and corporate social responsibilities.

Major Trends

In order to know the business environment in which any organization operates, three major trends should be considered:

Demographics

the characteristics of a population/workforce, for example, age, gender or social class. This type of trend may have an effect in relation to pension offerings, insurance packages etc.

Diversity

the variation within the population/workplace. Changes in society now mean that a larger proportion of organizations are made up of "baby-boomers" or older employees in comparison to thirty years ago stankein advocates of "workplace diversity" simply advocate an employee base that is a mirror reflection of the make-up of society insofar as race, gender, sexual orientation, etc.

Skills and Qualifications

As industries move from manual to a more managerial professions so does the need for more highly skilled graduates. If the market is "tight" (i.e. not enough staff for the jobs), employers will have to compete for employees by offering financial rewards, community investment, etc.

Individual Responses

In regard to how individuals respond to the changes in a labour market the following should be understood:

Geographical Spread

how far is the job from the individual? The distance to travel to work should be in line with the pay offered by the organization and the transportation and infrastructure of the area will also be an influencing factor in deciding who will apply for a post.

Occupational Structure

the norms and values of the different careers within an organization. Mahoney 1989 developed 3 different types of occupational structure namely craft (loyalty to the profession), organization career (promotion through the firm) and unstructured (lower/unskilled workers who work when needed).

Generational Difference

different age categories of employees have certain characteristics, for example their behaviour and their expectations of the organization.

Framework

Human Resources Development is a framework for the expansion of human capital within an organization or (in new approaches) a municipality, region, or nation. Human Resources Development is a combination of training and education, in a broad context of adequate health and employment policies, that ensures the continual improvement and growth of both the individual, the organisation, and the national human resourcefulness. Adam Smith states, "The capacities of individuals depended on their access to education". Human Resources Development is the medium that drives the process between training and learning in a broadly fostering environment. Human Resources Development is not a defined object, but a series of organised processes, "with a specific learning objective" (Nadler,1984) Within a national context, it becomes a strategic approach to intersectoral linkages between health, education and employment.

Structure

Human Resources Development is the structure that allows for individual development, potentially satisfying the organization's, or the nation's goals. The development of the individual will benefit both the individual, the organization, or the nation and its citizens. In the corporate vision, the Human Resources Development framework views employees, as an asset to the enterprise whose value will be enhanced by development, "Its primary focus is on growth and employee development…it emphasises developing individual potential and skills" (Elwood, olton and Trott 1996) Human Resources Development in this treatment can be in-room group training, tertiary or vocational courses or mentoring and coaching by senior employees with the aim for a desired outcome that will develop the individual's performance. At the level of a national strategy, it can be a broad intersectoral approach to fostering creative contributions to national productivity.

Training

At the organizational level, a successful Human Resources Development program will prepare the individual to undertake a higher level of work, "organized learning over a given period of time, to provide the possibility of performance change" (Nadler 1984). In these settings, Human Resources Development is the framework that focuses on the organizations competencies at the first stage, training, and then developing the employee, through education, to satisfy the organizations long-term needs and the individuals' career goals and employee value to their present and future employers. Human Resources Development can be defined simply as developing the most important section of any business its human resource by, "attaining or upgrading the skills and attitudes of employees at all levels in order to maximise the effectiveness of the enterprise" (Kelly 2001). The people within an organization are its human resource. Human Resources Development from a business perspective is not entirely focused on the individual's growth and development, "development occurs to enhance the organization's value, not solely for individual improvement. Individual education and development is a tool and a means to an end, not the end goal itself". The broader concept of national and more strategic attention to the development of human resources is beginning to emerge as newly independent countries face strong competition for their skilled professionals and the accompanying brain-drain they experience.

Recruitment

Employee recruitment forms a major part of an organization's overall resourcing strategies which seek to identify and secure the people needed for the organisation to survive and succeed in the short to medium-term. Recruitment activities need to be responsive to the ever-increasingly competitive market to secure suitably qualified and capable recruits at all levels. To be effective these initiatives need to include how and when to source the best recruits internally or externally. Common to the success of either are; well-defined organisational structures with sound job design, robust task and person specification and versatile selection processes, reward, employment relations and human resource policies, underpinned by a commitment for strong employer branding and employee engagement strategies.

Internal recruitment can provide the most cost-effective source for recruits if the potential of the existing pool of employees has been enhanced through training, development and other performance-enhancing activities such as performance appraisal, succession planning and development centres to review performance and assess employee development needs and promotional potential.

Increasingly, securing the best quality candidates for almost all organizations will rely, at least occasionally if not substantially, on external recruitment methods. Rapid changing business models demand skills of experiences which cannot be sourced or rapidly enough developed from the existing employee base. It would be unusual for an organisation today to undertake all aspects of the recruitment process without support from third-party dedicated recruitment firms. This may involve a range of support services, such as; provision of CVs or resumes, identifying recruitment media, advertisement design and media placement for job vacancies, candidate response handling, shortlisting, conducting aptitude testing, preliminary interviews or reference and qualification verification. Typically, small organisations may not have in-house resources or, in common with larger organisations, may not possess the particular skill-set required to undertake a specific recruitment assignment. Where requirements arise these will be referred on an adhoc basis to government job centres or commercially run employment agencies.

Except in sectors where high-volume recruitment is the norm, an organization faced with an unexpected requirement for an unusually large number of new recruits at short notice will often hand over the task to a specialist external recruiter to manage the end-to-end resourcing programme. Sourcing executive-level and senior management as well as the acquisition of scarce or 'high-potential' recruits has been a long-established market serviced by a wide range of 'search and selection' or 'headhunting' consultancies which typically form long-standing relationships with their client organizations. Finally, certain organizations with sophisticated HR practices have identified there is a strategic advantage in outsourcing complete responsibility for all workforce procurement to one or more third-party recruitment agencies or consultancies. In the most sophisticated of these arrangements the external recruitment services provider may not only physically locate, or 'embed', their resourcing team(s) within the client organization's offices but will work in tandem with the senior human resource management team in developing the longer-term HR resourcing strategy and plan.

Modern Concept of Human Resources

Though human resources have been part of business and organizations since the first days of agriculture, the modern concept of human resources began in reaction to the efficiency focus of Taylorism in the early 1900s. By 1920, psychologists and employment experts in the United States started the human relations movement, which viewed workers in terms of their psychology and fit with companies, rather than as interchangeable parts. This movement grew throughout the middle of the 20th century, placing emphasis on how leadership, cohesion, and loyalty played important roles in organizational success. Although this view was increasingly challenged by more quantitatively rigorous and less "soft" management techniques in the 1960s and beyond, human resources development had gained a permanent role within organizations, agencies and nations, increasingly as not only an academic discipline, but as a central theme in development policy.

- Directing (Commanding) is leading people in a manner that achieves the goals of the organization. This involves proper allocation of resources and providing an effective support system. Directing requires exceptional interpersonal skills and the ability to motivate people. One of the crucial issues in directing is to find the correct balance between emphasis on staff needs and emphasis on economic production.
- Controlling is the function that evaluates quality in all areas and detects potential or actual deviations from the organization's plan. This ensures high-quality performance and satisfactory results while maintaining an orderly and problem-free environment. Controlling includes information management, measurement of performance, and institution of corrective actions.
- Budgeting, exempted from the list above, incorporates most of the administrative functions, beginning with the implementation of a budget plan through the application of budget controls.

Principals of Management

The Principles of Management are the essential, underlying factors that form the foundations of successful management. According to Henri Fayol (1841-1925) in his book *General and Industrial Management* (1916), there are fourteen 'principles of management'.

The Principles of Management

Management principles are statements of fundamental truth. These principles serve as guidelines for decisions and actions of managers. They are derived through observation and analysis of events which managers have to face in practice.

Division of Work

The specialization of the workforce according to the skills a person, creating specific personal and professional development within the labour force and therefore increasing productivity; leads to specialization which increases the efficiency of labour. By separating a small part of work, the workers speed and accuracy in its performance increases. This principle is applicable to both technical as well as managerial work.

Authority and Responsibility

The issue of commands followed by responsibility for their consequences. Authority means the right of a superior to give order to his subordinates; responsibility means obligation for performance. This principle suggests that there must be parity between authority and responsibility.. They are co-existent and go together, and are two sides of the same coin.

Discipline

Discipline refers to obedience, proper conduct in relation to others, respect of authority, etc. It is essential for the smooth functioning of all organizations.

Unity of Command

This principle states that every subordinate should receive orders and be accountable to one and only one superior. If an employee receives orders from more than one superior, it is likely to create confusion and conflict.

Unity of Command also makes it easier to fix responsibility for mistakes.

Unity of Direction

All those working in the same line of activity must understand and pursue the same objectives. All related activities should be put under one group, there should be one plan of action for them, and they should be under the control of one manager.

It seeks to ensure unity of action, focusing of efforts and coordination of strength.

Subordination of Individual Interest

The management must put aside personal considerations and put company objectives first. Therefore the interests of goals of the organization must prevail over the personal interests of individuals.

Remuneration

Workers must be paid sufficiently as this is a chief motivation of employees and therefore greatly influences productivity. The quantum and methods of remuneration payable should be fair, reasonable and rewarding of effort.

The Degree of Centralization

The amount of power wielded with the central management depends on company size. Centralization implies the concentration of decision making authority at the top management. Sharing of authority with lower levels is called decentralization. The organization should strive to achieve a proper balance.

Scalar Chain

Scalar Chain refers to the chain of superiors ranging from top management to the lowest rank. The principle suggests that there should be a clear line of authority from top to bottom linking all managers at all levels. It is considered a chain of command. It involves a concept called a "gang plank" using which a subordinate may contact a superior or his superior in case of an emergency, defying the hierarchy of control. However the immediate superiors must be informed about the matter

Order

Social order ensures the fluid operation of a company through authoritative procedure. Material order ensures safety and efficiency in the workplace.

Equity

Employees must be treated kindly, and justice must be enacted to ensure a just workplace. Managers should be fair and impartial when dealing with employees.

Stability of Tenure of Personnel

The period of service should not be too short and employees should not be moved from positions frequently. An employee cannot render useful service if he is removed before he becomes accustomed to the work assigned to him.

Initiative

Using the initiative of employees can add strength and new ideas to an organization. Initiative on the part of employees is a source of strength for the organization because it provides new and better ideas. Employees are likely to take greater interest in the functioning of the organization.

Esprit de Corps

This refers to the need of managers to ensure and develop morale in the workplace; individually and communally. Team spirit helps develop an atmosphere of mutual trust and understanding.

These can be used to initiate and aid the processes of change, organization, decision making, skill management and the overall view of the management function.

Science or Art

It depends on the institution and business department within the school as to which focus they prefer.

The BA has a broader scope, with a strong emphasis on the humanities, theoretical and general knowledge in a recognized discipline, interdisciplinary field, or of a professional study.

The BS is more of a focused approach with a science base to include a balance of liberal arts, technological knowledge, math and computer oriented skills, and practical skills needed for a particular discipline within the field.

Management – a Profession?

The traditional professions of law, medicine, and the clergy all have deep historical roots in another major institution of Western society, the university. Roman and canon law, medicine, and theology, in fact, constituted three of the four faculties of the medieval European university, and survive to this day in schools of law, medicine, and divinity, respectively, in the modern American university. The study of law in America today remains rooted in the centuries-old traditions of Roman and Anglo-American law as systematized and interpreted by the discipline of legal philosophy or jurisprudence. Law students now learn "the law" not as a collection of statutes but rather as a set of principles, doctrines, and rules that have evolved over the course of centuries and are said to constitute legal reasoning itself.

The study of medicine, for its part, has been continually transformed since the Middle Ages by the rise and ongoing progress of modern science, with the development of the germ theory of disease in the nineteenth century, for example, and of the science of genetics in the twentieth having gone into the formation of a theoretical structure that undergirds the body of knowledge every medical student is now required to master. The medical school curriculum proceeds from the premise that in order to diagnose and treat disease, the would-be physician must have a firm grounding in what science (or, perhaps more accurately, what is generally accepted as science) currently understands to be its causes.

Turning to the body of systematized knowledge underpinning the claim that business management, too, is a "profession," we find important differences between management as a "science" and the knowledge bases of the traditional professions. It is not just that the study of management was a latecomer to the university, which since the creation of the modern American research university in the last three decades of the nineteenth century has gained an effective monopoly over professional education. (The first university-based business school in America, the University of Pennsylvania's Wharton School of Finance, was not founded until 1881.) For even as management was being gingerly accepted as a subject deserving of inclusion within the university, the discipline of management—following close behind the occupation itself—was having to be invented *ex nihilo*. The professionalization of management, which was what business schools were founded to undertake, began as a quest to delve beneath the practice of business with its "rule of thumb" approach to business problems to discover a set of underlying principles that could explain effective practice. These basic principles were by no means evident to the pioneers of academic business education and, as we would suggest, they remain by no means evident today.

At the time that the first business schools were being constituted at the beginning of the twentieth century, "scientific management" was in the air, as Frederick Taylor's application of scientific methods to the study of physical labour had begun to be extended to the organization of industry as well as to spheres such as higher education and government. While Taylorism was quickly jettisoned as the core of the business school curriculum, it made scientific reasoning and method appear to be applicable to business, thus helping to legitimate the study of business as an activity within the university.

Yet what exactly a "science" of management should study would be puzzled over and debated for a great many years. Three curricular models emerged and competed with one another in the early decades of university business education. The first was a simple aggregation of courses taught elsewhere in the university and covering such obviously useful (if intellectually circumscribed) subjects as accounting and business law.

The second model attempted to organize business education around specific industries such as banking, transportation, merchandising, mining, and lumber. The third model—increasingly adopted by the 1930s, and still the basis of the business school curriculum today—was the functional approach, as the grouping of courses began to mirror the differentiation of finance, administration, operations, and marketing as the major activities of the firm. Thus the curricular structure evolved as a pragmatic response to the challenge of turning out graduates who could perform the tasks that would be required of them by employers.

It is not that there were no attempts, in the meantime, to discover an underlying general theory that would inform the tasks of a manager. But the search for a theoretical model capable of explaining effective business practice—which was actually a search for an existing discipline or set of disciplines from which such a model could be produced—foundered for many years on disagreements about the nature of business firms and the ultimate purpose of business. The decision (made very early in the history of university-based business education) to remove the study of business from economics departments stemmed from the recognition that economics, at the time, had no interest in one of management's most pressing concerns, namely, the internal organization of the firm.

When experimentation with disciplines including sociology, psychology, and even (at Harvard Business School's Fatigue Laboratory from the 1920s to the 1940s) physiology yielded results that were either too politically radical for the university's guardians and patrons (as happened at the Wharton School during the Progressive Era) or simply lacking in explanatory power and practical applicability, the resulting void at the centre of the business school curriculum eventually caused business educators to take a second look at the discipline of economics.

Economics, in the decades prior to World War II, had occupied a relatively weak position in the disciplinary pecking order. Yet as the growing acceptance of Keynesian theory in the postwar years gave the subject greater prestige, and the 1958 reports on the state of business education in America by the Carnegie Corporation and the Ford Foundation led to a greater emphasis on the social sciences and quantitative method in business schools, economics began to move into the position of dominance that it enjoys in the MBA curriculum today. Building on the foundational work of Adolf Berle and Gardiner Means on the separation of ownership and control in the large corporation, and of Ronald Coase on the significance of transaction costs, economists such as Michael Jensen and Oliver Williamson began, in the 1970s, to develop a new theory of the firm that treated it not as a "black box" that converted inputs into outputs but rather as an institution requiring and rewarding economic analysis.

It is undeniable that the works of these and other recent economic theorists have yielded important insights into the internal workings of firms that are applicable to managerial practice. Yet they have also left business education with a dominant theory that, in adhering to many of the individualist assumptions and methodologies of neoclassical economics, is unable to account for much of the social environment of business, the social and cultural factors that make themselves felt within organizations, and other essential aspects of the phenomenon it purports to explain.

System of Certification

Besides having failed to develop a body of knowledge and theory comparable to those of the true professions, management differs from these other occupations in lacking a set of institutions designed to certify that its practitioners have a basic mastery of a core body of specialized knowledge, and that they can apply it judiciously. In medicine and law, for example, there are institutions that specify the educational requirements (i.e., the MD or JD degree) that anyone desirous of practicing the profession must obtain. Beyond these educational requirements, aspirants to membership in the profession must obtain licenses to practice by passing a comprehensive exam designed to test mastery of the knowledge ostensibly acquired in professional school. Once the aspiring professional passes this test, he or she must invest in a certain amount of continuing education in order to stay abreast of evolving knowledge in the profession and maintain a license to practice.

Management differs from medicine, law, and other recognized professions in having neither a formal educational requirement nor a system of examination and licensing for aspiring members. Although the MBA has been the fastest-growing graduate degree for the last twenty years, it is not a requirement for becoming a manager. It is true that, for those seeking access to senior executive positions or work in the fields of investment banking or consulting, an MBA has become a de facto requirement. Yet even in these cases there is no requirement of passing a standard exam before being admitted to practice; nor are senior managers, investment bankers, or consultants required to participate in continuing education. There is no explicit obligation, for example, for experienced, high-level managers to know anything about investing in innovative new financial derivatives or special-purpose vehicles, even if they serve on boards that are required to approve such potentially risky transactions. In fact, data on enrollment in executive education programs offered by business schools suggest that those who already possess an MBA are least likely to return for such continuing education.

How would having a formal educational requirement and a system of certification and mandatory continuing education advance the practice of management? Although such barriers to entry would have the effect of closing managerial positions to some who now aspire to them, all true professions are, almost by definition, closed systems that tightly control and carefully restrict access to their own ranks. Closure in professions need not, as some might fear in the case of management, stifle innovation and progress; in the field of medicine, for example, the pace of discovery and creative progress rapidly accelerated in the wake of professionalization. In an open society, moreover, there will always be room for "rogue" entre preneurs to challenge the existing order, as practitioners of alternative medicine are challenging the medical profession today. From society's point of view, meanwhile, professional closure offers distinct benefits when the privilege of closure is granted in return for the commitments that true professionals make to serve the public good and forego certain forms of self-interested behaviour.

Commitment to Specialized Knowledge as a Public Good

Renunciation of Profit-Maximization

To be able to set and enforce standards of admission to a profession; determine how professional work is to be done; engage in self-regulation rather than be subjected to extensive regulation from without; and reap the economic benefits of a monopoly position in the marketplace—these are all privileges that society grants to professions in return for certain social benefits. The creation of these social benefits, in turn, places certain constraints on professionals. Because they possess specialized knowledge in areas of vital concern to society, genuine professionals are expected to place that knowledge at the disposal of all who require it and to provide services in a way that places the maintenance of professional standards and values ahead of the securing of individual advantage. The renunciation of unabashed self-interest that society expects of true professionals takes a very particular form: unlike actors in the marketplace as envisioned by classical and neoclassical economics, professionals engage in work out of more than merely economic motives, and eschew profit-*maximization* (as opposed to profit-*making*) as a goal. Indeed, because of the exemption they have been granted from certain laws of market exchange, professionals are specifically enjoined from using the laws of the market to reap economic gain at the expense of their professional obligations.

Implicit in this aspect of professionalism is the idea that, even when serving private clients, professionals are providing a public good; while the provision of public goods has been widely recognized in economics as a case that creates exceptions to the rules governing the provision of goods for purely private consumption. Lawyers serve private clients (be they individuals, corporations, or other private entities) but are understood to be providing a public good—if not justice in every case, then at least the implementation of the rule of law. Physicians also serve private individuals, but are understood, in so doing, to be providing the public good of health for the general population. That the advocacy system in American jurisprudence or the structure of the health care market in the United States (with its convoluted system of both private and public third-party payers) can tempt lawyers and doctors, respectively, to lose sight of professional obligations beyond serving the interests of particular clients does not invalidate this more general truth. Once a professional loses sight of the larger social benefit that his or her work is intended to provide, the line between professional services and commerce, in turn, becomes dangerously blurred.

The notion that those who lead and manage our society's major private economic institutions might provide, or be responsible for providing, a public good is quite foreign to our customary way of thinking about management. Yet this idea was often voiced by those who led American business schools in the early decades of their existence. For example, in a speech titled "The Social Significance of Business" that he delivered at Stanford University's School of Business shortly after its founding in 1925 (subsequently published as an article in *Harvard Business Review* of the same title), Wallace B. Donham, the second dean of the Harvard Business School, declared that the "development, strengthening, and multiplication of socially minded business men is the central problem of business." As Donham went on to say:

> *The socializing of industry from within on a higher ethical plane, not socialism nor communism, not government operation nor the exercise of the police power, but rather the development from within the business group of effective social control of those mechanisms which have been placed in the hands of the race through all the recent extraordinary revolutionizing of material things, is greatly needed. The business group largely controls these mechanisms and is therefore in a strategic position to solve these problems. Our objective therefore, should be the multiplication of men who will handle their current business problems in socially constructive ways.*

Haunted by a belief that scientific, technological, and material progress was outstripping society's capacity for moral self-governance, and that the professions that had traditionally provided social and moral leadership (i.e., law and the clergy) were no longer up to the task, Donham looked to a new "profession of business" for nothing less than saving modern, industrial civilization from itself. As the professionalization project that had provided the agenda for American business education from its founding up until the outbreak of World War II was abandoned in the postwar decades, expectations of what managers should contribute to society became, to say the least, rather more modest.

Today, in place of such notions as the "socializing of industry from within" and the business executive as an expert capable of, and responsible for, solving some of the most urgent problems facing modern societies, we find American business schools propagating the doctrine of shareholder primacy and the paradigm of the manager as the mere agent of the company's "owners." Taken in combination, these two concepts—both outgrowths of the intellectual domination of American business education by economics during the past three decades—render managers anything but the disinterested experts oriented toward the needs of society that we take to be part of the essence of professionalism. The doctrine of shareholder primacy has legitimized the idea that the benefits of managerial expertise may be offered for purely private gain and that this is equivalent to advancing societal interests. Having given rise to the notion of making managers "think and behave like owners" through equity-linked compensation, agency theory, in turn, can now be seen to have led directly to many of the worst profit-maximizing abuses unmasked in the recent wave of corporate scandals.

Now that the traditional professions have come under attack for providing refuge from the "disciplining" forces of the market, it is worth noting that a great many American business leaders who have enriched themselves spectacularly in recent years without engaging in actual malfeasance have managed to do so by insulating themselves from such fundamental market imperatives as "pay for performance"—meanwhile declining to accept the constraints that prevent legitimate professionals from engaging in profit maximization.

If the traditional professions are to be asked to accept a greater role for market forces, is it too much to ask business persons who enjoy exemptions from market discipline to accept a greater role for professionalism?

Code of Ethics

The fourth and final dimension on which, in our view, management differs significantly from the true professions is that its members are not governed by a shared normative code, reinforced by institutions that promote adherence to it. Such normative codes, whether known as a code of ethics or a code of con duct, are a central feature of almost any occupational group that desires to be seen as a profession.

Though normative codes exist among "professions" as diverse as librarianship and plumbing, the true professions go farther than simply having a written code by which members are encouraged to voluntarily abide. They teach the meaning and consequences of the code as a part of the formal education of their members. They test and verify this understanding during licensing exams. Once licensed, members are required to adhere to this code in order to maintain a license. A governing body, composed of respected members of the profession, oversees adherence to the code by establishing monitoring mechanisms, reviewing complaints, and administering sanctions, including the ultimate sanction of revoking an individual's license to operate as a professional.

Professions establish these codes and the institutions to enforce them as part of their implicit contract with society. "Trust us to exercise jurisdiction over an important occupational category," the profession asks. "In return, we will make every effort to ensure that the members of our profession are worthy of your trust, that they will not only be competent to perform the tasks with which they have been entrusted but will also adhere to high standards and conduct themselves with integrity." The privilege of self-regulation is granted out of society's recognition that, in cases involving the use of highly specialized knowledge, laypersons may not be in a position to pass accurate and fair judgment on the conduct of specialists.

Most normative codes, like the ancient Hippocratic oath for doctors, clearly articulate a profession's higher aims and social purposes and the manner in which these purposes must be pursued. Such role definitions have many benefits, among them that by establishing a normative standard for inclusion, they create and sustain a sense of community and mutual obligation among members of a profession as well as a sense of obligation to the profession as an abstract social entity. These bonds of membership create the social capital of a profession, which builds trust and significantly reduces transaction costs among members of a profession and between the profession and society. Since, as we began this paper by observing, trust in management as an institution could not be much lower than it is in American society today, the benefits of a true profession of management adopting a formal normative code would appear to be obvious—particularly in comparison with a regulatory regime that could all too easily stifle the innovation and risk-taking that have contributed so much to the success of American capitalism.

Legal and regulatory overreaction to the crisis currently afflicting American business and American management, however, is only one of the dangers that we now face. Another is that, heeding the cries for "integrity" and "ethics" that have gone up on all sides in the wake of the recent corporate scandals, business education and its supporting institution of management will succeed in allaying the public's skepticism by measures such as new ethics curricula and corporate ethical codes (Enron famously possessed one of the latter while its top managers were busy destroying the wealth of their shareholders and the livelihoods of their employees) that create an appearance of reform without delivering the genuine article.

For as phenomena such as the weak link between executive compensation and corporate performance, or the impotence of so many corporate boards, have recently shown us, American managers have become quite adept at decoupling the formal structures and symbols that give them legitimacy in the eyes of the public from their actual work activities.

Our speculations about a genuine professionalization of management as a remedy for the crisis of legitimacy now facing American business may strike some as radical. But assuming, once again, that increased regulation is not the whole or the best answer to the problem at hand, our idea of making man agement into a bona fide profession has the virtue, we believe, of asking a group that has seriously abused the public's trust to make a serious commitment to restoring it.

One way of looking at the problem with American management today, we would argue in closing, is that it has succeeded in assuming many of the appearances and privileges of professionalism while evading the attendant constraints and responsibilities. Although it is now fashionable in some quarters, as we have suggested, to denigrate professionals as elites enjoying shelter from the rough and tumble of the market, do we as a society really wish to surrender the benefits that we rightfully demand of professionals in return? And given the inevitable existence of elite knowledge workers, such as managers, in complex modern societies, ought we not to be concerned with producing elites who are motivated by something beyond the pursuit of self-interest under the laws of the marketplace, or the fear of punishment under the laws of the land? A self-interested, self-indulgent corporate leadership is not inevitable, and a model for something better lies at hand. We can find it in the flawed but durable institutions that serve society by meriting the name "profession."

Management – a Universal Process?

The more you understand something, the more you're able to develop and apply adequate concepts to explain it, the less complex and chaotic it becomes. This requires a fundamental understanding of what's being done, how it's being done, and why it's being done.

When understanding produces innovation, it's coupled with the ability to differentiate between seemingly similar objects, and/or finding similarities between seemingly unrelated objects. These are the core objectives of process management. When realized, these objectives enable companies to increase customer value, lower operating costs and differentiate themselves from the competition.

Many think of people as differentiators, because they're a company's costliest and most valuable asset. Over time, most companies attempt to improve the output of their people through technological advancements (hardware, software or other tools intended to change workflows). Unfortunately, many of these improvements fail to achieve optimal results, due to the absence of a structured, repeatable, reliable and flexible framework designed to optimize company performance levels, i.e., a process.

A standard process for optimization-combined with technology supporting people-forms a critical foundation for companies serious about calling themselves "world class" or "industry leader." However, processes are not only managed from the top-down. They're also managed from the bottom-up. To understand an organization's process and technology needs, three universal truths about the human condition should be acknowledged.

First, given a choice, people will almost always choose the action that's quickest, easiest and/or most familiar-from their perspective. In order to affect change, you need to change the perspective people have on their processes, as well as their choices for getting them done.

Change often introduces complexity and uncertainty. The more complicated an issue is, the more people are prone to oversimplify the solution, in an effort to find the quickest, easiest and/or most familiar path. Changing this mindset often requires an executive mandate, which can be easier said than done, because many executives do not excel at balancing strategic planning and tactical execution.

A mature process management program reflects an optimal balance of strategic planning and tactical execution. Simply stated, tactical execution is the process of getting things done. Strategic planning is the analysis needed to get things done better, faster or cheaper.

Strategic planning cannot be implemented without tactical execution, and tactical execution cannot be made optimally efficient without strategic planning. Put another way, a company cannot exist without tactical execution, but its organic growth will always be impeded without strategic planning. Unfortunately, many companies become so overwhelmed with the immediacy of fulfilling tactical requirements, they fail to plan (and execute) strategically.

This evokes the second universal truth. Many organizations are so internally focused, management cannot see the extent to which their processes are broken. In this environment, hard work is often mistaken for results, and it's exceedingly difficult to distinguish controllable objectives from those that can merely be influenced.

When these organizations finally notice the pieces of broken processes lying around them, the reaction is often a series of ad hoc attempts to patch things back together, because they don't know how to start over by applying a metrics-driven approach to root cause analysis. The end result is time, money and energy repeatedly wasted fixing things destined to break again.

The irony is that a company's resistance to change is often proportionate to the past success it's enjoyed with processes and business models that no longer work. This produces an organization lacking the agility and coordination to respond and adjust to changing technology demands, market conditions and personnel needs. This is the third universal truth. Understanding and accepting these truths is required, before the journey toward business process management optimization can begin.

Time Management

Time management can be defined as activities or tools which allow you to effectively manage your time. When you practice good time management, your productivity will increase, and if you are the owner of a business, it is likely that your business will experience larger profits.

Today, time management has been broken down into a number of categories, but they all basically seek to achieve the same objectives. When you hear most people talk about time management, they are generally referring to it on a personal level.

The idea of time management is that if you can spend more time doing things that are important, you are much more likely to be successful at whatever you are trying to accomplish. Once you have succeeded, you will be a happier person that will be able to get more out of life. To become skilled at managing your time, there are some skills you will need to develop, and these are setting goals, decision making, delegating, and prioritizing. Many people resort to using sophisticated tools such as PDAs to help them. While they can be helpful, the most important factor is the decisions you make. A machine can only take you so far.

Many people think that PDAs and other day planning devices will manage their time for them. This is incorrect. The machine will only hold the information that you put into it. It is your responsibility to make sure all the tasks are carried out. The ability to make quick decisions is very important. People who are indecisive will generally perform poorly when it comes to time management. Why? Because it takes them too long to make a decision. They "sit on the gate" trying to decide which option to go with, or they make a decision and then suddenly decide to do something else.

When it takes you a long time to make a decision, or you have to change your mind after you've made one, this is a sign that you are indecisive. Being indecisive can cause you to run into a number of problems. If you want to be successful with time management, you must learn how to quickly make a decision and stick with the decision you make. How do you do this? Generally, when you are presented with a decision, it will come in the form of two or more options. You must decide which option you will choose. The option that you pick can lead to your success or failure. The best way to quickly make the best decision is to look at the pros and cons of each option. Writing them down on a board can be helpful.

Once you write down the options, write down the pros and cons of each, and compare the number of pros and cons with each option. Pick the option that has the most pros with the least cons. This is a fast and simple way to make good decisions. The next skill you will want to look at is goal setting. It will be next to impossible for you to manage your time if you don't have goals. You should have a list of things that you need to get done each day. Your "goal" should be to get those things done. Anything that gets in the way of you achieving your goal will waste your time and stop you from being successful.

Being able to properly delegate tasks is important. If you have a business with employees, you should become skilled at delegating tasks to all of them. Everyone who works for you should know what they need to do. When you are not able to quickly delegate tasks to your employees, you are failing as a business owner. The next thing you will need to focus on is prioritizing tasks. When you write down a list of things you need to do each day, rate them by levels of importance. This is called prioritizing. Prioritizing is important because it allows you to put your energy into the most important tasks. If you have an unexpected situation, you don't want to be stuck doing things that are not important. Placing a priority on tasks based on their importance will allow you to work at a high level of efficiency.

Business and Its External Environment

A business does not function in a vacuum. It has to act and react to what happens outside the factory and office walls. These factors that happen outside the business are known as external factors or influences. These will affect the main internal functions of the business and possibly the objectives of the business and its strategies.

Main Factors

The main factor that affects most business is the degree of competition – how fiercely other businesses compete with the products that another business makes.

The other factors that can affect the business are:

- Social – how consumers, households and communities behave and their beliefs. For instance, changes in attitude towards health, or a greater number of pensioners in a population.
- Legal – the way in which legislation in society affects the business. E.g. changes in employment laws on working hours.
- Economic – how the economy affects a business in terms of taxation, government spending, general demand, interest rates, exchange rates and European and global economic factors.
- Political – how changes in government policy might affect the business e.g. a decision to subsidise building new houses in an area could be good for a local brick works.
- Technological – how the rapid pace of change in production processes and product innovation affect a business.
- Ethical – what is regarded as morally right or wrong for a business to do. For instance should it trade with countries which have a poor record on human rights.

Changing External Environment

Markets are changing all the time. It does depend on the type of product the business produces, however a business needs to react or lose customers.

Some of the main reasons why markets change rapidly:

- Customers develop new needs and wants.
- New competitors enter a market.
- New technologies mean that new products can be made.
- A world or countrywide event happens e.g. Gulf War or foot and mouth disease.
- Government introduces new legislation e.g. increases minimum wage.

Business and Competition

Though a business does not want competition from other businesses, inevitably most will face a degree of competition.

The amount and type of competition depends on the market the business operates in:

- Many small rival businesses – e.g. a shopping mall or city centre arcade – close rivalry.
- A few large rival firms – e.g. washing powder or Coke and Pepsi.
- A rapidly changing market – e.g. where the technology is being developed very quickly – the mobile phone market.

A business could react to an increase in competition (e.g. a launch of rival product) in the following ways:

- Cut prices (but can reduce profits)
- Improve quality (but increases costs)
- Spend more on promotion (e.g. do more advertising, increase brand loyalty; but costs money)
- Cut costs, e.g. use cheaper materials, make some workers redundant.

Social Environment and Responsibility

Social change is when the people in the community adjust their attitudes to way they live. Businesses will need to adjust their products to meet these changes, e.g. taking sugar out of children's drinks, because parents feel their children are having too much sugar in their diets.

The business also needs to be aware of their social responsibilities. These are the way they act towards the different parts of society that they come into contact with.

Legislation covers a number of the areas of responsibility that a business has with its customers, employees and other businesses.

It is also important to consider the effects a business can have on the local community. These are known as the social benefits and social costs.

A social benefit is where a business action leads to benefits above and beyond the direct benefits to the business and/or customer. For example, the building of an attractive new factory provides employment opportunities to the local community.

A social cost is where the action has the reverse effect – there are costs imposed on the rest of society, for instance pollution.

These extra benefits and costs are distinguished from the private benefits and costs directly attributable to the business. These extra cost and benefits are known as externalities – external costs and benefits.

Governments encourage social benefits through the use of subsidies and grants (e.g. regional assistance for undeveloped areas). They also discourage social costs with fines, taxes and legislation.

Pressure Groups Will also Discourage Social Costs

Businesses interact with the wider society they are part of. Businesses are affected by society, for example in the kinds of goods and services they are expected to produce, and businesses affect society by their activities. It is a two-way process.

Some of the ways in which businesses affect society are negative, and usually governments limit these activities by law. For example, some business activities damage the environment. In addition, there are ethical constraints set by the wider expectations of society. For example, it is legal to sack workers for some actions (eg ignoring a written warning), but society may think the sacking is unreasonable, and the business may feel pressured to not do it.

Groupings of people, such as Trades Unions, can be very effective at putting such pressure on businesses. The environment is a good example. The legal restrictions on environmental damage are relatively few, but society at large has increasingly strong views (orchestrated by some very effective groupings such as Green Peace) about what activities by business are acceptable and unacceptable. This produces pressure for businesses to change their behaviour, especially if sales and profits are threatened.

Many consumer businesses now produce 'green' versions of their products to attract environmentally conscious customers; their corporate advertising boasts (eg BP) that they have stopped doing this, or started doing that, in order to better look after the environment. Another good example is the way that some businesses (eg Nike) have changed their activities in some developing countries due to concerns by society over 'sweat-shop' labour.

The Case for Growth

A different argument says that the government should not stop businesses doing whatever it takes to create growth and employment.

This argument says managers are products of their society, and won't do anything that is against the interests of that society – managers have their standards, too, and won't work for an employer that asks them to take part in wrong actions.

Businesses are therefore self-regulating. A business that starts to behave in an unacceptable manner will find it increasingly hard to recruit workers, and to sell products, until the business decides to change its behaviour into a more acceptable form.

However, this argument tends to overlook the very great imbalance in power and information. Employees and customers don't always know or understand what businesses are up to. Employees (even managers) might feel they can't afford to lose their job, and so feel pressured to agree to behaviour they don't really approve of.

Businesses and Stakeholders

A business is owned by its shareholders. A traditional view is that the behaviour of the business is nobody's business but the owners', the shareholders who are interested in profit.

A more modern view is to consider all the groups of people that are affected by a business' behaviour – employees, customers, suppliers, the local community – and not just the shareholders.

The word 'stakeholders' is used to describe this wider community of interests. Some investment funds and pension companies refuse to invest in businesses whose behaviour they disapprove of eg arms manufacturers.

Business & Ethics

Ethical behaviour is morally 'good' behaviour. Businesses have always been ethical to the extent that their owners and managers have been interested in ethical behaviour (sometimes very little). There is now a new and strong interest from a growing number of businesses in ethical behaviour, especially in large MNCs which operate in different societies with different ethical standards. Some businesses even employ professional philosophers to help them understand the ethical consequences of their behaviour.

The main reason for this is that society at large takes more of an interest in ethical behaviour, and society has much bigger expectations of businesses. There are Different Reasons Given for This Development.

1. Employees (including managers) are better educated than they used to be, and so understand these issues better than they used to.
2. We have a less deferential society where 'ordinary' people are more willing to questions and challenge the decisions of their 'elders and betters'.
3. Competition for customers is fiercer, and any possible reason for losing customers has to be taken seriously.
4. The same issue is developing in employment, with employers increasingly dependent on attracting high quality staff who, with more choice than they used to have, are less willing to work for morally 'iffy' businesses.
5. The media have become very good at exposing questionable behaviour. Allied to this is that information is now so easy to get hold of, and the Internet makes it easier again.
6. Business decisions can be much more complex than they used to be., especially where very advanced technology is involved, and not all the consequences are known.
7. Businesses are entering new and morally more debatable areas. A good example of this is medical businesses where new knowledge about eg genes raises the possibility of products that pose fundamental moral questions; these were simply irrelevant until recently because no-one knew how to do it.

External environment of a business refers to all those factors that directly influence the working of the business. However, these factors are outside the control of the business.

External environment shapes the kind of business activity you can have. That is why it is extremely important for business. The factors that constitute the external environment include:

- Political and Legal factors
- Economic factors
- Social and Cultural Factors
- Technological Factors

- Competitors
- Demographics of consumers.

Now whatever the business might do, it can not control all the above factors. It can only plan its business by studying the trends in these factors closely. The Political and Legal factors define the government policies. These policies determine what kind of relaxation the business has. The Economy defines that kind of economic or business activity it can have. The Social and cultural factors along with the demographics of the society defines the acceptability and sales of that product. The technological factors define the technology and its affects on business. Lastly, competitors are also one of the influential factors.

All businesses and organisations operate in a changing world and are subject to forces which are more powerful than they are, and which are beyond their control. No business can survive without continued interaction with the external environment, just as a ship at sea is subject to powerful natural forces of which it needs to be aware and deal with, organisations are influenced by forces in their external business environment. Any business strategy needs to take account of all these forces so that opportunities and threats can be identified and the organisation can navigate its way to success by matching its internal strengths to external opportunities. (A SWOT Analysis can help here.) As an aid to identifying all these external forces, a couple of acronyms come in handy.

2

Nature of Business Activities

Definitions of Business

The term business has been defined by various au some of the Selected definitions are given below.

According to L. H. Haney, 'Business may be defined as human activity. Directed towards providing or acquiring wealth through buying and Selling's.

Urwick and Hunt describes 'Business as an enterprise which makes, Distributes or provides any article or service which the other members of The community need and are able and willing to pay for it."

According RN. Owen, business includes all the commercial and Industflal activities that provide goods and services to the people with an Objective to earn profit.

Characteristics of Business

The activities termed business has the following characteristics.

Deals in Goods and Services

Every business whether it is carried on a Small or on a large scale deals in goods and services. The goods may be Consumer goods like cloth, shoes, pensetc., or producer goods like machinery or it may take the shape of services like the supply of electricity, water, gas, transportation of goods, etc.

Economic Activities

The activities which are involved in the production or distribution of goods and services for economic motive are a part of business. Any activity undertaken for personal consumption or are exchanged free, fell outside the scope of business. For instance, if a shoemaker makes a pair of shoes and wears himself, it will not be business. However, if he makes shoes and sells them to the customers for money, it is then his business. So business covers only economic activities.

Series of Deals

When a firm takes up manufacturing or distribution of goods or providing of services for profit motive, there should be series of deals in it, It should be performed over and over again. A student, for instance, selling his books to the shopkeeper will not be doing a business. However, if he purchases the books and sells them in his spare time regularly to seek profit, it does constitute a business.

Profit

The primary aim of business is to earn profit If an enterprise is to exist for a longer period, it must yield profit. Profit thus is the driving force of every business activity.

Element of Risk and Uncertainty

There is an element of risk a uncertainty involved in every business. If an Signalization is not able to foresee or control or minimize the risk involved of business, it suffers losses, The main risks involved in a business operation are (1) Competition (2) Change in taste (3) Outmoding of a product (4) Theft (5) Flood (6) Earthquake (7) Fire (8) Marketing misjudgments (9) Customers disliking of a product (10) Strikes, etc.

Capital

Every business whether it is small or large cannot operate without capital. Money is required for investment in fixed assets such as land, building, machinery etc. Money is also needed for working capital such as purchase of raw material, payment of wages, electricity, gas bills etc.

Creation of Utilities

An important characteristic of business s the creation of utilities. The businessmen transports goods from a place where it is less needed to a place where it is more required place utility through transportation. He also converts raw material into semi finished and finished goods in order to make them useful for the cQnsumers (Form utility through processing). The businessmen, consumers and' the society all benefit by the creation of place, form and time utilities in goods. In short, business combines, human, material, technological and financial resources for profit.

All of us live in families and depending on the income, we have different standards of living. We require various types of goods and services to satisfy our needs and wants. Some members in your family have to work to earn and provide for the needs of the family. Thus, people engage in different activities which are known as economic activities. In ancient times, people had limited wants to satisfy. In modern times however, we need a large variety of goods and services to satisfy our needs and to raise our standard of living. On the one hand the supply of goods and services has led to various activities. On the other hand, activities of different types are undertaken by people to earn sufficiently to fulfil their increasing wants. Thus we find large numbers of people engaged in business, industry, and profession. Such economic and business activities satisfy various needs and demands for goods and services.

Human Activities and Business

You know that man always keeps himself engaged in some kind of activity to satisfy his needs and wants. All human activities may be broadly divided into two categories: (i) economic activities, and (ii) non-economic activities.

The work of a farmer, manufacturer, teacher, doctor, trader etc. are some examples of economic activities. They are primarily concerned with the production, distribution and consumption of goods and services. Economic activities are undertaken to earn one's living and for the production of wealth. Besides economic activities, people also undertake a number of activities for mental satisfaction. They engage in charitable work, practice religion, undertake recreational activities and also do many things out of love for others or out of patriotic feelings. These activities are known as non-economic activities.

These activities are undertaken not for any material reward or gain but for one's happiness, pleasure or satisfaction which can not be measured in terms of money.

Distinction Between Economic and non-economic Activities

Following are the points of distinction between economic and non-economic activities.

Economic Non-economic

1. Economic activities are motivated Non-economic activities are by economic gain motivated by a desire to achieve mental satisfaction or happiness.
2. Monetary gain is expected from There is no such satisfaction from economic activities non-economic activities.
3. Economic activities lead to Non-economic activities lead to creation of wealth personal satisfaction.

However, a particular kind of activity which is non-economic in one case may be economic in the other. Cooking by a housewife is non-economic but cooking in a hotel is an economic activity.

Types of Economic Activities

When a person is regularly engaged in a particular economic activity, it is known as his or her occupation or vocation. Occupations may be classified into three categories —

(i) Business,

(ii) Profession and

(iii) Employment (Service).

Business

Activities connected with the production or purchase and sale of goods or services with the object of earning profit are called business activities. Mining, manufacturing, trade, transportation, insurance, banking are business activities. Thus business may be defined as an economic activity involving regular production or purchase and distribution of goods and services with the object of earning profits.

Profession

Any activity which requires special knowledge and skill to be applied by an individual to earn a living is known as profession. For example doctors, teachers, lawyers, engineers and accountants are engaged in profession. Profession involves intellectual activity. It is not a mechanical or routine operation.

The main characteristics of profession are:

(i) Every profession requires special knowledge and training.

(ii) The primary objective is to render service.

(iii) The service cannot be substituted by another individual.

(iv) Every profession is regulated by a professional body. For example the profession of Chartered Accountants is regulated by the Institute of Chartered Accountants of India.

Employment

When a person works regularly for others and gets wages/salary in return, he is said to be in employment. Thus factory workers, office assistants and managers are said to be in employment.

Those in employment are called employees. Employment may be in government department or in private organisation. It may be full-time or part-time, permanent or temporary. The main features of employment are :

(i) Employees always work for others.

(ii) There are certain terms and conditions of work.

(iii) The people involved earn fixed income.

Vocation

Vocation means an occupation which involves the use of some basic skills which can be developed by practice. Type-writing, tailoring, laundering, carpentry etc. are some examples of vocation. Those who wish to get employed after completing secondary education may acquire the basic skills required for any vocation.

Distinction between Business, Profession and Employment

Basis Business Profession Employment

1. Primary Earning Rendering Earning Objective profit paid service wages/salary
2. Reward Profit Professional fee Salary/wages
3. Nature of Production of Expert Job work purchase and sale serve performance
4. Qualification Undefined Professional As per the need training of the employer.

Nature and Purpose of Business

Nature of Business: The nature of business is best understood on the basis of its characteristics or features which are as follows:

1. Business is an economic activity
2. It includes the activities of production or purchase and distribution.
3. It deals in goods and services.
4. It implies regularity of transactions.
5. It aims at earning profits through the satisfaction of human wants.
6. It involves risk; it is not certain that adequate profit will be earned.
7. It creates utilities.

It serves a social purpose by improving people's standard of living.

Objectives of Business

Success in business depends on proper formulation of its objectives. Objectives must be clear, and attainable. Objectives may be divided into two parts-

(i) economic and

(ii) social.

Economic Objectives

Economic objectives of business include earning adequate profit or satisfactory return on capital invested, survival in the case of competition and growth to maintain progress.

Social Objectives

Social objectives include providing employment opportunities, supply of quality goods and services at reasonable price, improving the standard of living and contributing to environmental protection. It also includes justice to workers in terms of wages, welfare amenities, improved service conditions and professional growth.

Significance of Business in Modern Society

Business is an integral part of modern society. It is an organised and systematised activity for profit. It is concerned with activities of people working towards a common goal. The modern society can not exist without business. The need and importance of business in society can be described as follows:

Improvement in Standard of Living

Business helps people in general to improve their standard of living.

Proper Utilization of Resources

It leads to effective utilization of the scarce resources of society. It provides facility of mass production.

Better Quality and Large Variety of Goods and Services

It involves production, purchase and sale of goods and services for price. Customer' satisfaction is the backbone of modern business. Services such as supply of water, electricity etc. may be considered highly significant for the community.

Creates Utilities

Business makes goods more useful to satisfy human wants. It adds to products the utilities of person, time, place, form, knowledge etc. Thus, people are able to satisfy their wants effectively and economically.

Employment Opportunities

It provides employment opportunities to large number of people in society.

Workers' Welfare

Business organisations these days take care of various welfare activities for workers. They provide safer and healthier work environment for employees.

Classification of Business Activities

Business activities are undertaken to satisfy human wants by producing goods or rendering services.

We may classify business activities on the basis of functions into two broad categories

(a) Industry and

(b) Commerce.

Industry is concerned with the production and processing of goods. This type of business units are called 'industrial enterprises' which produce consumer goods as well as machinery and equipments. On the other hand, 'commerce' includes all those activities which are necessary for the storage and distribution of goods. Such units are called 'commercial enterprises' which include trading and service activities like transport, banking, insurance and warehousing.

Let us examine the characteristics of industry and commerce.

Industry and its Types

Industry means production of goods for sale by the application of human or mechanical power. In other words, industry refers to economic activities which are connected with raising, producing and processing of goods and services.

Characteristics of Industry

The main characteristics of industry are as follows:-

- Industry refers to the productive aspect of business.
- Production is done by the application of human or mechanical power.
- It creates form utility to natural or partly processed goods.
- It is concerned with the production of both producer and consumer goods.
- Industrial activities are regulated by different laws.
- It involves continuous operation.

Types of Industries

Industries are divided into two broad categories:

(i) Primary industries

(ii) Secondary industries.

Primary industries include all those activities which are connected with extraction, producing and processing of natural resources. These industries may be further subdivided into two types: (a) extractive and (b) genetic.

Secondary industries are concerned with the materials which have already been produced at the primary stage. For example, mining of iron ore is a primary industry, but manufacture of steel is a secondary industry.

a) Extractive Industries: Extractive industries are concerned with the extraction of materials from the earth, sea and air such as mining, farming, fishing and hunting etc. Products of these industries are used either directly for consumption such as food grains, fruits and vegetables or as raw materials such as cotton, sugar-cane, etc.

b) Genetic Industries: Genetic industries include activities connected with rearing and breeding of animals and birds and growing plants. Reproduction and multiplication is the main activity in these industries, such as, agriculture, animal husbandry, dairy, poultry, pisciculture etc. Main products are milk, wool, butter, cheese, meat, egg, fish, seeds of plants, etc.

Secondary industries may also be of two types: (a) manufacturing, and (b) construction.

a) Manufacturing Industries : Industries engaged in the conversion of raw materials or semi-finished products into finished product are called manufacturing industries. Cotton is converted onto textiles and iron one is converted into in these industries. It creates a form utility of the product.

b) Construction Industries : The activities of Construction industries include erection of buildings, bridges, roads, railways canals etc. Their output do not consists of movable goods. It makes use of the output of other industries like brick, cement, steel etc. Characteristics of Commerce is the sum total of all the activities connected with the placing of the product before the ultimate consumer. It provides the necessary link between the producer and the consumer of goods.

Commerce is defined 'as activities involving the removal of hindrances in the process of exchange'. Commerce includes all those business activities which are undertaken for the sale or exchange of goods and services and facilitates their availability for consumption and use-through trade, transport, banking, insurance, and warehousing. Thus commerce includes trade and auxiliaries to trade, that is transport, banking, insurance and warehousing.

The Main Characteristics of Commerce are as Follows

(i) Commerce is the sum total of activities which facilitate the availability of goods to consumers from different producers.

(ii) It aims at ensuring proper distribution of goods.

(iii) It adds different type of utilities to the goods by making goods available at the right time and the right place to the people who need them.

(iv) It includes trade and auxiliary to trade.

Trade and its Types

Trade is an integral part of commerce and refers to sale and transfer of goods. It involves actual buying and selling of goods. It means exchange of goods and services for cash or credit. Traders help in directing the flow of goods to the most profitable market. They also bring about equitable distribution of goods on a national and international scale. It is because goods are produced on a large scale and it is difficult for producers to reach individual customers, that trade is said to remove the hindrance of persons through traders. Goods acquire place utility through trade.

Characteristics of Trade

The main characteristics of trade are as follows:

(i) Trade is regarded as the primary activity in commerce;

(ii) It means exchange of goods and services for price;

(iii) It helps in directing the flow of goods to the most profitable market;

(iv) It helps to equalise the supply of and demand for goods in different markets both national and international.

Classification of Trade

Trade may be classified into (i) Home Trade or Internal Trade and (ii) Foreign Trade or External Trade.

i) Home Trade: Home Trade means trade carried on within the boundaries of a country. The primary object of home trade is to bring about proper distribution of goods within the country. It may be divided into two types (a) Wholesale Trade and (b) Retail Trade

(a) Wholesale Trade: Wholesale trade involves buying goods from producers and selling them in small quantities to retailers. The wholesaler generally deals in large quantities of goods of a limited number of varieties. He serves as a connecting link between the producer and the retail dealer.

(b) Retail Trade: A retail trade consists of selling goods directly to the consumers in small quantities. A retailer usually purchases goods from wholesalers or manufacturers and deals in a variety of goods of different manufacturers.

ii) External Trade: External trade refers to trade between two countries. It implies buying and selling of goods by traders of two different countries. It creates a very wide market for goods produced in different countries. External trade involves (a) Export and (b) Import.

Export is concerned with the sale of goods to foreign countries. Import trade relates to the purchasing of goods from other countries.

Distinction between Industry, Commerce and Trade Basis of Industry Commerce Trade Difference

1. Meaning Production of Sum total of Exchange of goods and activities for price through services for connected with buying and selling sale transfer of goods from producers to consumers
2. Utility Creates form Creates time Creates time and utility and place utility and utility removes hindrance of persons
3. Broad Four types: Two types: Two types: classifigenetic, Trade and internal and cation extractive, auxiliaries external manufacturing to trade and construction Interrelationship between Industry, Trade and Commerce All the three branches of business are closely related to each other. Each depends upon the other for the achievement of aims and objectives of business.

For example, industry is concerned with the production of goods and services, trade is related with sale and purchase of products, and commerce arranges for their distribution. Industry can succeed only if goods are marketed and without production of goods, there cannot be commerce and trade. Hence, trade provides necessary support to industry and commerce. Thus, industry, trade and commerce are inter-dependent and cannot operate in isolation. Service facilities also provide necessary support to trade.

Transport and Communication

Transport: It is one of the most important auxiliaries to trade. Transportation helps trade by facilitating the movement of goods and passengers from one place to another. Transport creates 'place utility' of the goods and remove the problem of distance. All kinds of goods can be transported in large quantities over long distances.

A business can depend upon a number of modes of transportation-land transport (road, railways, and pipeline), water transport (inland waterways, coastal and sea) and air transport (domestic and international).

Communication: Nowadays it is not possible to have business without communication. Communication implies transmission of information, ideas, opinions, etc. between two or more persons. It is a systematic and continuing process of telling, listening and understanding. Communication may be of two types-(i) internal and (ii) external. Internal communication refers to transmission of information by a person to another of the same organisation. External communication refers to transmission of information by persons to others outside the organisation. Methods of communication may include face to face, by telephone, postal mail, etc. On the basis of means of communication, there are two types of communication –oral and written.

Banking and Finance

Banking provides safe, efficient and convenient mode of payment for goods in inland trade as well as in foreign trade. Banking helps business firms to overcome the problem of finance by lending money as and when required. Banks accept deposits and lend money. The other services of banks are: discounting of bills, collection of cheques, acting as agent. A bank accepts deposits on various accounts such as fixed deposit, savings, recurring deposit, and current. Loans are granted through overdraft, cash credit, loans and advances, discounting of bills. Other services of banks include collection of payments on cheques, bills, drafts etc., sending money from one place to another, buying and selling securities, payment of insurance premium, issuing travellers cheques, providing locker system, and providing information on credit worhtiness. Banks are of various types: commercial, agricultural, indigenous, rural, cooperative, exchange, central, etc. In fact banking is the lifeline of business.

Finance: Finance is the life blood of business. It implies provision of money at the time it is required by business. Provision of funds is essential for every type of trade. Finance needed by business is called "Business Finance".

It means arrangement of cash and credit to carry out business activities. Types of finance required by business are long–term, medium–term and short–term. Long–term finance (more than 10 years) is required for buying fixed assets; medium–term finance (one to 10 years) is required for modernization and expansion of business, and short-term finance (upto one year) is needed for working capital. Sources of finance may be owned funds and borrowed funds. Special financial institutions which provide finance to business are IFCI, SFCs, ICICI, IDBI, SIDBI, and IRBI. They provide long-term and medium-term finance.

Warehousing: Warehousing refers to storage of goods which are generally produced on a large scale in anticipation of demand. Goods have to be stored for some time before transportation by manufacturers, wholesalers and retailers. Thus warehousing creates 'time utility'.

Insurance: Insurance occupies a prominent and valuable place as an aid to business and commerce. Insurance provides security against risks. It makes trade and business secure by making provision against all probable losses. Insurance is based on the principle of 'pooling of risks'. Insurance helps the businessman to conduct his business with confidence and peace of mind.

There are two major types of insurance coverage-(i) insurance of life of people and (ii) insurance of property.

Business and Economic Structure

Some of the common, legally recognised business structures discussed in this section are:

- sole proprietorships/sole trader;
- partnerships;
- companies;

- cooperatives;
- Franchises
- trusts; and
- joint ventures.

Incorporated and Unincoprorated Business Structures

The legal forms of Business Structures fall into two Categories: unincorporated forms and incorporated forms. For example, sole proprietorship, partnership, joint venture, trust and franchises are unincorporated business structures, whereas company and cooperatives are incorporated business structures.

The basic difference between these forms of business structures is the legal *liability* of its operator/owner. For unincorporated business structures, the liability is unlimited. It means that the owner of the business may be personally liable for all the debts of the business and the *creditors* can personally sue the owner of the business. For incorporated business structures (i.e. cooperatives, company) the legal liability is limited. It means that in case of *bankruptcy* or debts of the business, the shareholders/operators will not be personally liable. The extent of their liability is limited to their shares in the company.

There are advantages and disadvantages of each business structure. Before you embark upon selecting a particular form of business structure, you may need to speak to your financial adviser or accountant as to which business structure may suit your personal needs and gives you maximum financial benefits and legal protection.

Some of the issues to consider when choosing an appropriate business structure include:

- purpose, nature and objectives of the business
- Credit and capital requirements for the business
- limiting your liability for business debts;
- ease of operating the business;
- management and control on the business (i.e.flexibility to review your business operation should your objectives change in future;
- simplicity and cost reduction;
- minimising your taxation liability and

- ease with which the interest in the business may be transferred to others in case you want to bind up your business

Whether your business needs the simplicity of the sole proprietor or partnership, or the more complex, more public but-for the members-more secure company structure will usually be a matter for you to decide in conjunction with your professional advisors. Whatever you do, it is important to get professional advice from your lawyer and accountant before you make the choice-it may save you a lot of heartache in the long run.

In certain circumstances you may decide that none of the available structures alone fits the bill for your particular business. A combination of structures may be necessary to cover all eventualities. It is common to find a rural property structured this way. For example, the land could be owned by the family company while the stock is owned by a partnership comprising the husband and wife. To avoid tax they may have created a trust with various members of the family-including the children-as beneficiaries, and with the family company appointed trustee.

Does life have to be this complex? Very often the simpler structures have the greater benefits.

Sole Proprietors/Sole Trader

Registering a Business Name

Many small businesses start with the owner as sole proprietor. This is the oldest and simplest form of business structure. Basically, it means the owner is the manager.

If you are a sole proprietor, the business debts are yours in the same way as the profits, and your *creditors* can pursue you and seize your personal assets to pay your business debts. This is called having 'unlimited liability'.

These days a sole proprietor can incorporate-that is, become a one-person company. For more on the advantages of forming a company.

There is no particular law covering sole proprietors, other than the requirement to register your business name if it is different from your personal name. You are taxed as a single person and your business and personal assets are not distinguished as separate entities. Generally, the more you earn, the higher the rate of income tax you pay. Therefore, if you split your income between two or more people who pay tax at a lower rate, you can pay less tax.

Taking holidays may also be difficult if you are a sole proprietor as it's often necessary to find someone to run the business while you are away, and delegating the full responsibility to someone else may not be easy for you if you are used to controlling everything yourself. It might also be difficult to find someone who is able and willing to fill in for you.

As the business grows, many sole proprietors start to recognise the need to:

- share the responsibility;
- have a second opinion on management decisions;
- find a way to pay less tax; and
- avoid the worry of losing everything if the business fails.

If you are ready to share your management control and responsibility for decision-making, you may consider to set up your business in a partnership.

It is usually a good idea to get legal and financial advice first to work out which structure would suit you best.

Sole trader, like other forms of business structures, is subject to a vast variety of laws and regulation (i.e. laws relating to occupational health and safety; environmental protection, banking and finance, consumer protection, taxation laws and *liability* under the Trade Practices Act (Commonwealth) and Fair Trading Act (of relevant state).

- Partnerships
- Partnership agreements
- Partnership agreement checklist
- Liability for partnership debts
- Duties to the other partners
- Dissolving a partnership
- Assets and debts after a partnership is dissolved.

In many ways the partnership is the logical next step from the sole proprietor. The Victorian *Partnership Act 1958* defines a partnership as the relationship that exists between people who are 'carrying on a business in common with a view of profit' (s. 5). As a business structure a partnership is simple, flexible and, if properly set up, an effective arrangement. Whether it suits your business needs will depend on your circumstances and requirements.

The Advantages of a Partnership Arrangement are :

- it is a simple structure both legally and financially;
- flexibility-many of the provisions of the Act can be changed to suit your particular needs;
- that each partner can bind the other partners in contract;
- the partnership pays no tax though it must still lodge a tax return;
- profits are shared among partners in whatever proportion they decide and each pays tax on them at the personal rate;
- no special partnership reports or returns other than a partnership tax return are required; and
- that it only has to be registered if its official name is different from the names of the partners.

The Disadvantages of a Partnership are:

- the *liability* of the partners for the debts of the business is unlimited, as it is with sole proprietorships;
- each partner is 'jointly and severally' liable for the partnership's debts;
- sometimes the law can decide that a partnership exists even though you haven't intended to form one;
- if partners join or leave, you will probably have to value all the partnership assets, which can be costly; and
- if partners join or leave, the Taxation Office treats the partnership as having terminated and requires a special tax return to be lodged.

Partnership Agreements

Partnership agreement can be verbal, in writing or may be implied by the conduct of the partners. There is no legal requirement for partners in a business to draw up a partnership agreement, but it is advisable to have the partnership agreement in writing if the partners intend to operate the business over an extended period. Your accountant or legal adviser may be able to draw up a partnership agreement for you.

It is a valuable exercise for partners to sit down together and draft, in plain and simple language, how they want the partnership to work. In the absence of such agreement the Partnership Act 1958 (Vic) provides fallback provisions of what should be included in the agreement. These may not always be things you want in the partnership agreement. For example, the Act expects the profits and losses to be shared equally among partners but you may want a different arrangement. Similarly, where the Act expects all partners to share in management, your partner may live a long way from your operation, making shared management impractical.

Partnership Agreement Checklist

The checklist below provides a good example of what you should have in your partnership agreement. If you use it, remember to state exactly what has been agreed to. The clause on bank accounts, for example, should say 'the partnership bank account shall be kept at the — Bank at —. Any partner may sign cheques for up to $ — but at least two partners together must sign a cheque for a greater amount', and so on.

It is wise to avoid woolly statements like 'the partnership bank account shall be kept at any bank that the partners agree upon'. It's much more useful to explain what you actually decided.

These days, it is very simple to call up the agreement on a word processor and print out a new agreement whenever you want to change a clause, which you can do at any time. The only people who need to know of this are yourselves-the partners. A copy of the agreement should be signed and dated by both (or all) partners, and everyone should be given a copy. You can change it whenever you like, but you'll need to get the amended document signed and dated by all the partners, each time a change is made.

A point to be careful about is that the Act provides that death or *bankruptcy* will end the partnership. This may not suit you as you may prefer to be able to buy out the bankrupt or deceased partner so the partnership can continue to operate. If you and your partners decide to do this, it would be wise to have the agreement checked by a lawyer to ensure that you have covered the necessary legal angles.

You can of course choose to have the whole agreement drawn up by your lawyer but this deprives you of the personal involvement of drawing it up yourselves. Sometimes it is this personal involvement that produces a personal commitment from partners to abide by the agreement.

Liability for Partnership Debts

Unlimited Liability

In a partnership the partners' *liability* for the debts of the operation is unlimited. As with a sole proprietor, this means that if the business fails, the *creditors* can take your personal assets to pay the partnership's debts.

Joint and Several Liability for Contracts, Civil Wrongs and Crimes

Partners are 'jointly' liable for all the debts of the business. They are 'jointly and severally' liable for the partnership's civil wrongs and crimes along with the individual partner who commits them. This means that a *creditor* can either sue all the partners jointly for the debts of the firm, in which case you will have to contribute towards those debts in the same proportion as you have chosen for profit sharing. Alternatively, the creditor(s) can sue you personally for the entire debts of the partnership. Where you are the only partner with assets, or the easiest to find, you may well receive the entire attention of the creditors.

Limited Partnerships

One way of avoiding the burden of unlimited *liability* is to form a 'limited partnership'. This is particularly suitable for partners who want to invest in the business but are not concerned about being involved in management. It may work well for partners who live some distance from the farm or other business base of the partnership. (Limited partnerships are explained in Part 3 of the Partnership Act.)

A limited partnership must be registered with Consumer and Business Affairs Victoria. This costs $500 (as at Sept, 04) and can give the 'limited partners' (the investors) liability limited to the amount of their investment. They could lose this if the partnership becomes *insolvent* and is wound up, but their personal assets are not seizable by *creditors*. You will have to draw up a special agreement showing the limit of liability of each limited partner. Be aware that this will not affect the unlimited liability of the other, or general partners.

Any documents (i.e. letters, notices, *contracts* or cheques) issued by or on behalf of limited partnership in connection with carrying out the partnership business must contain in clear and legible words 'A Limited Partnership' immediately adjacent to its firm's name.

It should be noted that a partnership ceases to a limited partnership if none of the partners is a limited partner or the other partners agree they would like to carry out their partnership business as normal partnership.

A further alternative to the limited liability partnership has been introduced in the laws of New South Wales, Victoria and Queensland. This form of partnership is called the 'incorporated limited partnership'. In this partnership structure, the general partner manages the business on behalf of the company. Because the business is incorporated, there is no risk to limited partners. The limited partners, therefore, will not be held liable to the breaches of duty by the general partner. (Incorporated Limited Partnerships are explained in Part 5 of the Partnership Act 1958 (Vic).

A limited partnership is taxed as a company, and the profits are taxed as dividends in the hands of the partners. If you decide to form a limited partnership, make sure you get advice from a lawyer or accountant on what records you need to keep.

A Family Farm Partnership

A family farm partnership could comprise a husband and wife as working partners, and parents who want to be involved in running the place, but are content to leave day-to-day decisions to the younger generation. The profit sharing could reflect this arrangement. The partnership could also involve an uncle living in the city who has invested substantial capital in the farm but doesn't wish to be involved in the management and wants to be sure that his private assets are secure from creditors.

In this situation, the husband and wife and the parents would probably be general partners while the uncle could be a limited partner. Alternatively, the husband and wife could be the only general partners with all the others being limited partners.

Limited partners are a relatively new introduction in Victoria, as in New South Wales and have not been widely adopted as a business structure, perhaps because forming a company has been simplified recently (companies provide limited liability for business debts).

Duties to the Other Partners

In any partnership, each partner has a 'fiduciary' duty to the other. This is a duty of utmost good faith, trust and mutual confidence that allows each partner to act as an agent for the other in matters relating to the partnership. In other words, each partner can bind all the others in a *contract* with a third party. For this to work, partners must have confidence and trust in each other, and fully disclose to each other their activities in relation to the partnership. A partner who makes a personal gain out of partnership activities must account for it to the other partners (Partnership Act s. 33), and partners must not set up a business in competition with their partnership. If they do, they must hand over all profits made in that business (s. 34).

Every partner has a right to inspect and copy the partnership accounts (s. 28(9) and render true and full accounts to other partners (s. 32).

These legal responsibilities emphasise the need for the *fiduciary duty* to be observed at all times by all partners and to be continuously stressed as the cornerstone of the partnership.

Dissolving a Partnership

Subject to any agreement between the partners, ss. acirc; of the Act provides basic rules on how to end a partnership.

If your partnership was formed for a specific term (say five years) or for a specific venture, it is automatically dissolved when this term expires or when the venture has been completed. If the partnership is formed for undefined time, any partner can give notice to others of his/her intention to dissolve the partnership. Such a notice must be in writing. The dissolution will take place from the date mentioned in the notice. If no date is mentioned in the notice, the dissolution of partnership will take place from the date when the notice is received by other partners. In other cases a partnership will be dissolved by one of a number of events, listed below:

- the death or *bankruptcy* of any partner (s. 37);
- any partner's notice of their intention to dissolve it (s. 36);
- by becoming unlawful for the business if the partnership continues (s. 38); and
- by a court if it has just and equitable reasons for doing so (s. 39).

You should recall that although the agreement can provide for the partnership to continue in most of the situations outlined above, the Income Tax Assessment Act (Cth) will still require a taxation return to be lodged because it considers the partnership to have ended. It should be noted that partners still are liable for the debts of the business and the acts or omissions of the other partners even after they leave the partnership. They need to follow the proper legal requirements laid down under s. 40 of the Partnership Act.

For example, the Partnership Act 1958 (Vic) requires an advertisement in the Government Gazette and in at least one newspaper circulating in each district where the firm carries on business. This notice is for those who may deal with the firm after its changed constitution. For regular customers of the firm an actual (verbal or written) notice must be given advising them about the dissolution of the firm. An agreement that is well thought out can minimise the damage done to the partnership by the events above. For example, it could stipulate the type of notice a retiring partner should give or the notice required of a partner wishing to dissolve the partnership.

Assets and Debts after a Partnership is Dissolved

Basically as a partner you share in the liabilities and in the division of assets after all debts have been settled, in the same proportion as that in which you shared the profits (s. 44). This arrangement can be changed by agreement between the partners, but the change can only be binding on the partners and does not affect the rights of the *creditors.*

If the debts exceed the assets, you will have to pay them out of your own, non-partnership resources. For this reason, it is important to get proper financial advice on your assets and liabilities before you dissolve the partnership.

What is a Company?

A company or corporation (the words have the same meaning) is a legal entity that is separate from its members. When you form a company, you form an imaginary legal person which can hold and dispose of property, take legal action and sign documents. Because of this separate legal entity a company can have assets and liabilities and make profits and losses quite separately from its members. You may form, or already be in a company for a number of reasons including:

- to protect yourself against *liability* for business debts;
- to take advantages of company taxation rates; and
- the flexibility of membership that is provided by a company structure.

So what exactly is a company, and what are its advantages compared to those of a sole proprietorship or partnership? A company is a legal entity separate from its members. It can acquire and dispose of property, take legal action against people or other bodies, and-through its human managers-conduct its business as a human would.

The federal *Corporations Act 2001*-a lengthy and complex *statute*-controls the operations of all companies in Australia. It is administered by the Australian Securities and Investment Commission (ASIC) which displays a great deal of useful company information on its website (link to website: www.asic.gov.au). In the course of simplifying company law, a Small Business Guide was introduced as Part 1.5 of the Corporations Law. It is available through the ASIC website. It is easy to read and is a very good introduction to the principles and operations of our current company law.

Types of Companies

There are a number of different types of companies that can be formed in Australia. There are only two types of proprietary companies and four types of public companies that can be registered under the Corporation Act.

The basic difference between a public and proprietary company is explained below:

Public Companies

Public companies are permitted by law to raise money from the public by offering their shares for sale, usually by listing them on the share market. Some public companies are not listed on the share market, but most are. You can recognise a public company because it must put the word 'Limited' or the abbreviation 'Ltd' after its name.

Public companies need only have one shareholder, but they must have three directors.

Proprietary Companies

A proprietary company is usually smaller than a public company. It can have between one and 50 shareholders. Proprietary companies are not permitted to raise money by selling shares to the public (although they can convert to public company status by 'floating' their shares). You can recognise a proprietary company by the abbreviation 'Pty Ltd' that comes after its name.

Companies for Rural Business

Most companies in the rural sector are proprietary companies except for the rural supplies companies and other large trading groups.

If you are involved in a small company it will probably be a proprietary one, and a small proprietary company at that. This type of company has assets of less than $5 million, an annual gross income of less than $10 million and less than 50 employees. If in any year your company exceeds two of these criteria, it becomes a large proprietary company and has more legal and accounting obligations.

Some companies are formed for community reasons rather than profit motives. The local RSL club and a supported employment organisation are two examples. This type of company does not issue shares, but its members *guarantee* a sum of money should the company need it. It is therefore called a company limited by guarantee and is a special sort of public company.

Advantages of Forming a Company

The advantages of incorporating (forming a company) compared with a partnership are:

- your *liability* for the company's debts is limited;

- changes in membership do not affect the company; (this is called perpetual succession);
- members can be employed by the company; and
- taxation rates are more favourable (though you will have to consult your accountant about whether this provides an overall benefit).

These advantages will vary in significance depending on the particular company you have chosen.

Disadvantages of Forming a Company

Because of the complexity of the Corporations Act, running a company does have some disadvantages. These could be:

- the expense of forming and registering (about $1000);
- the requirement to provide annual and other returns to the ASIC;
- public scrutiny of your affairs;
- prosecution and heavy fines for failing to comply with the Corporations Act;
- scrutiny of directors' activities by the ASIC; and
- lack of control in day-to-day management of the company's affairs.

Forming a Company

Once you have decided on the name of your company there are two ways of forming it: by applying to ASIC and completing the required forms (you can do this through the ASIC website www.asic.gov.au); or buying a shelf company and changing its details to those of your new company.

You can apply for incorporation to the ASIC yourself, by following their requirements. Alternatively, you can ask a lawyer to do it for you.

A quicker, but slightly more expensive way of incorporating is to buy a shelf company. This is the husk of a former company that has never been de-registered. It is called a shelf company because it can literally be bought off the shelf. A number of organisations-including your lawyer or accountant-will arrange this for you if you wish by re-activating the company on the ASIC files, changing the details of members and directors, its name, and supplying you with all the details. The cost of shelf companies varies. You can see them advertised for as little as $800. Before you commit yourself to one, however, make sure you know if there are any hidden costs-in other words exactly what the fee covers and what it does not.

Duties of Company Directors

A primary producer may be a director of either their own company, or of a cooperative, or of another company. The general duties of directors are set out in the Corporations Act. Directors are required to:

- disclose any conflict between their personal interests and those of the company (s. 191);
- act in good faith in the interests of the company, and for a proper purpose (s. 181);
- exercise the degree of care and diligence that a reasonable person in a similar position would exercise (s. 180); and
- not make improper use of information or improper use of position (ss. 182Â–3).

These duties are deliberately worded loosely to accommodate changing meanings, standards and circumstances.

Recent cases are important in showing that the duties and obligations of directors are treated seriously under the law. Directors who breach their duties under the Corporations Act can face severe penalties of up to $200 000 or disqualification from managing a company or both.

Ignoring Directors' Responsibilities

A Melbourne family owned a string of tobacconists that were very profitable. When the husband, who was the working director, died, his widow — also a director — asked her son to carry on running the business. In the son's hands the business went rapidly downhill and ended up in liquidation. The widow was sued personally by the principal creditor because she had allowed the company to trade while insolvent and had thus breached her duty to act with care and diligence. Even though — indeed because — she had no hand in running the company and had taken no interest in its fortunes, she was found personally liable for the debt to that creditor — about $250 000 — a decision which was confirmed on appeal to the Victoria Supreme Court. (*Morley v.*

Statewide Tobacco Services Ltd (1992) 8 ACSR (305) Insolvent trading today— the duty imposed on directors.

Trading While Insolvent

Section 588G imposes one of the most stringent duties on directors. It requires you as a director to 'prevent' the company trading while it is *insolvent* or becoming insolvent.

The duty requires director/s to avoid incurring further debts when the company is insolvent including: Paying a dividend, reducing the share capital, buy back shares, redeeming prefences shares, financially assisting other persons to acquire shares or entering into an uncommercial transaction.

To start with, this implies that you must be sufficiently informed about the company's financial state to know when it is approaching insolvency.

'Prevent', in this context, means you must do everything reasonable to stop the company incurring the debt. This means, for example, arguing against it at a board meeting, having your dissent recorded and even resigning from the board if you feel this is necessary.

If the company insists on incurring the debt, and is subsequently placed in liquidation, two things may happen. First, the directors who were responsible could be prosecuted by the ASIC and incur a civil penalty of up to $200 000. Secondly, each of the directors-except those who could show that they had acted responsibly (s. 588H)-could be sued personally for that debt. In 2003, the ASIC introduced a National Insolvent Trading Program to, among other things, ensure directors are aware of their company's financial position, and make directors of potentially insolvent companies aware of their responsibilities and the implications of continued trading if they know they're insolvent.

Directors' Liability in Insolvent Trading

Water Wheel Mills Pty Ltd. and Water Wheel Holdings Limited (collectively 'Water Wheel') entered the business of purchasing and milling of wheat and paddy rice and the distribution of the resulting product in 1997. By October 1998, Water Wheel was experiencing difficulties in paying creditors on time. In February 1999, the company's auditors reported to the Board that for 11 months to 31 October 1998, the company recorded a large loss of $1.5m, rather than a $1m profit which was expected. At a board meeting in March 1999, Water Wheel's financial officer raised concerns with the Board about the company's insolvency. However, the company continued to order supplies, and experienced further difficulty paying creditors. It was not unusual for creditors to be paid over 120 days late. The Board believed that the group was still solvent, as it had assets (in the form of certain businesses) which it could sell if needed to meet debts. In September 1999, the company's bank ceased its relationship with the group, and demanded that the proceeds of any sale of assets be used to pay off its debt to the bank. The company continued to incur debts until February 2000, when it was placed under voluntary administration. ASIC commenced proceedings against Water Wheel's directors, including its non-executive director, John Elliott.

In the Victorian Supreme Court, Mandie J held that Water Wheel had continued to trade and incur debts whilst it was insolvent. According to Mandie J, Water Wheel was insolvent at least since September 1999 when the bank ceased its relationship with the company. A reasonable person in the position of each of the company's directors, including the managing director, and the non-executive director Elliott, would have suspected on the facts that the companies were insolvent in September 1999, and probably well before this time. Neither Water Wheel's managing director, nor Elliott as the non-executive, took any steps to prevent the companies from continuing to trade whilst insolvent. In relation to Elliott, Mandie J said he had 'turned a blind eye' to the details of Water Wheel's liquidity crisis in the hope that 'something would turn up'. Due to breaching section 588G, the managing director was disqualified for 10 years, Elliott for 4 years, and both were required to pay pecuniary penalties and compensation.

This decision was upheld on appeal, with the exception that the disqualification period for the executive director was reduced from 10 years to 7 years. On appeal, it was also held that a non-executive director will still breach section 588G even if they do not have a particular power to prevent the company incurring a particular debt when the company is insolvent, or which makes the company insolvent. Even without such a particular power, directors, including non-executives, are expected to do all that is reasonable to prevent the company trading whilst insolvent.

3

Business Structure Task

The organisation structure of a traditional business and the structure of the business processes often differ.

Suggested Step Flow

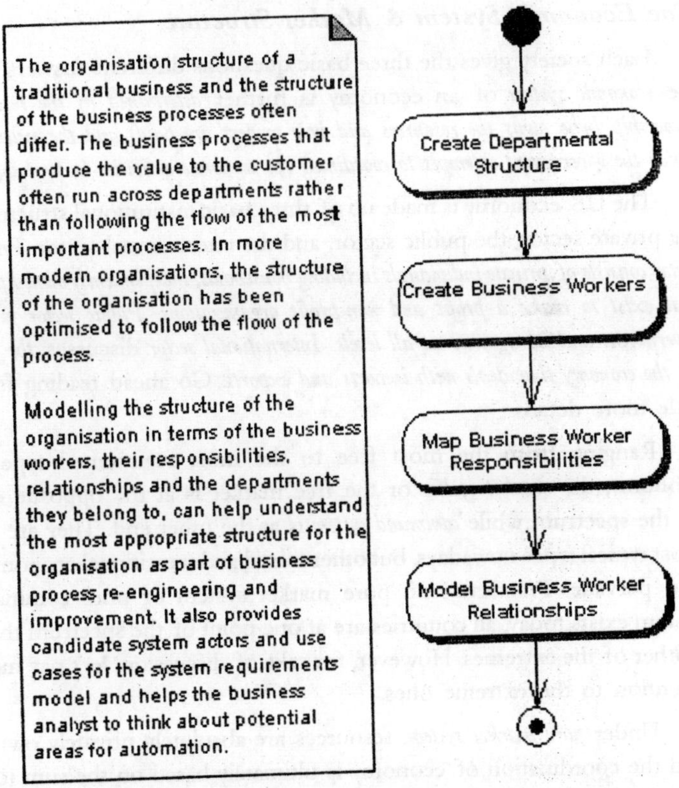

The business processes that produce the value to the customer often run across departments rather than following the flow of the most important processes. In more modern organisations, the structure of the organisation has been optimised to follow the flow of the process.

Modelling the structure of the organisation in terms of the business workers, their responsibilities, relationships and the departments they belong to, can help understand the most appropriate structure for the organisation as part of business process re-engineering and improvement. It also provides candidate system actors and use cases for the system requirements model and helps the business analyst to think about potential areas for automation.

Economic System

The Economic System & Market Structure

Each society gives the three basic questions different answers, but the *economic system* of an economy is further *determined by the resource ownership (who owns the resources and how owners are paid) and the extent to which the government attempts to coordinate the economic activities in that society.*

The U.S. economy is made up of three basic institutional structures, the private sector, the public sector, and the international sector. *Private sector consists of private individuals including households, independently owned firms that exist to make a profit and non-profit organizations. Public sector* is *the government and its agencies at all levels. International sector* discusses *the part of the economy that deals with imports and exports.* Go ahead reading for a little more details.

Ranging from the most free to the most regimented type of economy, the *market system* or the free market is at the opposite end of the spectrum while *command system* is at the other end. They are the most typical types nowadays, but other mixed and transitional economies also pervade. Practically, no pure market system or pure command system exists today, all countries are at one point of the spectrum that's neither of the extremes. However, for sake of discussion, let's pay more attention to the extreme ones.

Under *pure market system,* resources are absolutely privately owned and the coordination of economy is ultimately based on the sum total decisions of millions of individuals who pursue their own self-interest without any central direction or regulation. Government is left out, and the *market* is the exclusive central institution in which the three basic questions are answered. Buyers and sellers of goods and services, resource owners and bidders interact in no way affected by other force like the government regulation. Their decisions are dependent only on the interest of their own. Consumers dictate what is produced (or the *consumer sovereignty*) and producers have to produce the goods and services people want, so is the resources allocation process. The distribution of output is also determined in a decentralized way. The amount that any one household gets depends on its income and wealth. The income and wealth are determined by their capabilities and skills as well as the choice whether to go to work or not. In a word, in a pure market system, while non-government members of the society determine their individual actions, they ultimately determine the whole economy.

In a *pure command system*, resources are directed and production is coordinated based on the command, or central plan, of government rather than by markets. A central authority or agency establishes what will be produced and when, sets production goals, makes rules for distribution and determines how much compensation workers are to receive for their labours. In theory, a pure command system incorporates individual choices into collective ones. In practice, however, it has flaws, most notably are:

1. Since nobody in particular owns resources, people have less incentive to employ them in their highest-valued use; so some resources are wasted.
2. Central plans may reflect more the tastes and preferences of central planners than those of society.
3. Since the central government is responsible for all production, the diversity of products is much more limited than that in a competitive economy.
4. Each individual has less personal freedom in making economic choices.

Because of these limitations, countries have modified the pure command system to allow a role for markets. North Korea is perhaps the most centrally planned economy in the world today.

The Institutional Structure of the U.S. Economy

The U.S. economy is made up of three basic institutional structures, the private sector, the public sector, and the international sector. *Private sector consists of private individuals including households, independently owned firms that exist to make a profit and non-profit organizations. Public sector* is *the government and its agencies at all levels. International sector* discusses *the part of the economy that deals with imports and exports.* Go ahead reading for a little more details.

The Private Sector

The *private sector* of a nation's economy *consists of enterprise that is outside the state.* It includes a variety of for-profit entities such as private limited companies, partnerships, corporations, banks (other than central banks), as well as individuals not employed by the state. In this sector, different factors of production in various production activities are owned and managed privately by individuals or private corporate bodies. The aim of the enterprise is to make a profit for the owner, by producing goods or services that can be sold to customers.

The International Sector

International sector is *the part of an economy that deals with the other economies, or the rest of the world.* Basically, from a certain country's perspective, international sector consists of *imports and exports with all other countries.*

Not only the U.S., but also many other countries have become more and more serious about the international sector of their economies, especially since the great economic lessons of the 1970s and 1980s when all economies, regardless of the sizes, depend to some extent on other economies and are affected by events outside their borders. The U.S. economy is in no way closed or self-sufficient. In the light of the theory of comparative advantage, every country can benefit from participating in the global trading, even if it is absolutely inferior in productivity in every domain. And we are used to it now; none of us solely produce everything we need, instead, we specialize. However, specialization leads to interdependence, which in turn, results in growing exposure of domestic economy to the international sector.

This is one of the reasons that arouse such international economic treaties or organizations as NAFTA (North American Free Trade Agreement) and APEC (Asia-Pacific Economic Cooperation). Because conflicts arise and everyone of the international community is trying solve the problems on an equal and mutual-benefiting basis.

The Four Main Economic Systems

Four main economic systems shaped the economic development of various countries in the world.

An economic system is the system of manufacturing products and services, distributing the goods and services, and consumption of goods and services.

Whenever there are two persons making a trade, it is an economic system. For example, a young kid is negotiating with his neighbour. The young kid wants to make some money, so he wants to cut the lawn for his neighbour. That is a trade. That is an economic system in very small scale.

When we talk about economic systems at national level, there are basically four main economic systems.

The first economy system is the Free Market Economic System. Most developed countries use free market economic system. The governments provide oversight and guidance for the free market economic system. The governments generally do not try to control the expenditure of individuals.

The free market economic system uses demand and supply mechanism. The demand of the consumers will determine the price and output of the manufacturers. The consumers have freedom to choose what they want, and decide how much to pay for the service. The manufacturers have to decide on the quantity and quality of the product, as well as determine the selling price.

The second economy system is the Centralized Economic System. Some communist countries use central economic system. In centralized economic system, the governments do the planning for the economy. The governments decide on the kind of industries for the economy, the quantity, and quality of products and the pricing of the products. The governments decide on the salary scale of the individuals.

Many countries switch from centralized economic system to free market economic system. The transition is rather painful in the beginning. People no longer enjoy job security. Massive layoffs become a feature of the transition from centralized economic system to free market economic system.

The third economy system is the mixed economic system. The government has more control over certain aspect of the economy. The governments in many countries do not allow 100% free market economy system. Some governments use subsidy and quotas to control the economy. Some governments have monopoly in certain industry.

The last economy system is the traditional economic system. The barter economy is an example of traditional economic system. Many developing countries practice the traditional economic system. In a smaller scale, the barter system is still active in all parts of the world.

When you use a carton of milk to exchange for the apples with your neighbour, you are utilizing the barter economy.

The study of Economics usually focus on the free market mechanism.

There are vast differences between the economies of isolated, small, self-sufficient societies and large-scale ones that are integrated into the modern system of global commerce. These differences are not only in terms of the scale of the economies. Their systems of production, distribution, and exchange as well as concepts of property ownership are often radically different.

Systems of production refer to how food and other necessities are produced. In other words, they are the subsistence patterns discussed in the last tutorial of this series—i.e., foraging, pastoralism, horticulture, and intensive agriculture. Systems of distribution and exchange refer to the practices that are involved in getting the goods and services produced by a society to its people. Regardless of the type of subsistence base, all societies need to have mechanisms of distribution and exchange. These mechanisms, along with ownership concepts, are the focus of this tutorial.

All of the large-scale societies of the world today have market economies. These are very impersonal but highly efficient systems of production, distribution, and exchange that are principally characterized by:

1. the use of money as a means of exchange
2. having the ability to accumulate vast amounts of capital (i.e., wealth that can be used to fund further production)
3. having complex economic interactions that are ultimately international in scale.

A trip to buy a loaf of bread in an American supermarket typifies the nature of market exchanges. An individual who speaks no English and who is a total stranger to all of the people in the store can walk in, look around without any assistance, and find the bread. Taking it to the check-out stand, the price is registered automatically with a bar code reader and appears on the cash register display screen. Without saying a word, the purchaser can hand over the money, pick up the bread, which is usually now in a plastic bag, and walk out of the store. The exchange is quick, efficient, and did not require talking. The purchaser did not need to personally know the people working in the store, the baker, the miller, the farmer who produced the wheat, or the truck drivers who carried the product from one stage of production to another and ultimately to the point of distribution. Likewise, the purchaser did not need to even think about the fact that the plastic bag that enclosed the loaf of bread was created mostly out of petrochemicals that very likely started out as crude oil on the other side of the planet. Likewise, the money that was given in exchange for the bread was made with machinery that was created out of a number of different materials that probably were acquired from several different countries. On close examination, almost any simple market exchange involves the interaction of people all over the world and elaborate technology used in production and distribution.

This kind of complex market exchange system does not usually exist in small, isolated economies, such as those of indigenous foragers, small-scale horticulturalists, and nomadic pastoralists. These societies rarely use money and most people produce their own necessities. Their very different non-market economies are described in the next section of this tutorial.

What is Money?

Before exploring the nature of non-market economies, it is of value to compare the two broad types of money that people have used around the world. Anthropologists refer to them as general purpose and special purpose money.

General purpose money is a portable, arbitrarily valued medium of exchange. All market economies today use this form of money. It can have a variety of physical forms—e.g., coins, paper money, or bank checks. It can also be simply a digital transmission from one computer to another that occurs with the use of credit cards or the electronic transfer of funds. The key point about general purpose money is that anything that is for sale can be bought with it—everyone accepts it. General purpose money is also referred to as "standardized currency."

Special purpose money consists of objects that serve as a medium of exchange in only limited contexts. In societies that have it, usually there are certain goods and services that can be purchased only with their specific form of special purpose money. If you don't have it, you cannot acquire the things that it can purchase. You may not be able to easily obtain the special purpose money either. The Tiv people of central Nigeria provide an example.

In the past, they used brass rods to buy cattle and to pay bride price. These rods were acquired by trade from Sahara Desert tribes who ultimately obtained them from the urbanized societies of North Africa. If a man could not acquire brass rods by trade or borrowing them, he would be prevented from acquiring cattle and getting married. This was potentially a critical problem because having wives and cattle identified a man as being important and worthy of respect.

Traditional pastoralists commonly measure wealth in terms of numbers of livestock. In a very real sense, their animals are their form of special purpose money. They usually make exact equivalences in terms of relative value—e.g., so many sheep equal so many head of cattle which in turn equal the cost of a gun or something else of value. If a man does not have livestock in such societies, he usually cannot trade for high prestige items nor can he get married since animals must be given as the bride price. Using animals as currency has distinct disadvantages and advantages. Animals can die of diseases and must be actively cared for and guarded. This makes herding a risky business. On the other hand, animals reproduce so that an individual's wealth can grow rapidly. This is like getting a very high interest rate on money in a bank.

When general purpose money is introduced into an economy that previously only had special purpose money, the effect most often is dramatic for the social order. Among East African cattle herding cultures, it is now possible for a young man to get a job outside of his local community and to earn general purpose money. In these pastoralist societies in the past, young men had little hope of obtaining wealth before they were in their early middle age. They usually had to delay marriage for years because of the inability to accumulate a sufficient number of cattle to pay a bride price. Typically, a man in his late 20's or early 30's had to obtain a loan of cattle from elder men in his family for this purpose. The continuing obligation to pay off such loans reinforced the traditional authority of older men and the dependence of younger men. Now it is possible for a young man to accumulate enough general purpose money to purchase cattle and bring them back to his tribal homeland. He can then use them to pay a bride price. As a result, he will not be in financial debt to his elder kinsmen. The result is greater economic independence for young men. This is likely to be seen as good from the perspective of democratic, achievement oriented cultures, such as those of North America and Europe. However, from the perspective of the pastoralist societies in which these changes are occurring, it can be seen as being bad because it undermines the traditional authority of elders. This authority has been a key part of their cultural value system. A major concern of these societies often is that erosion of the value system will result in social chaos and the destruction of their traditional culture.

It is clear that the introduction of general purpose money has had a powerful effect on previously isolated small-scale societies. It facilitates trade and gives individuals the ability to accumulate wealth. Paradoxically, however, as the use of general purpose money draws a society into the global economic system, it does not result in economic independence for the society as a whole. In fact, it usually results in less self-sufficiency.

The study of economic systems includes traditional, market, command, and mixed economies. All of these systems attempt to answer the same questions. What should be produced? How much?

How should goods be produced? And, for whom? Tradition economies rely on farming and very simple barter trading. Examples include Neolithic farming villages and the first river civilizations. A market economy is controlled by the forces of supply and demand. Market economies, such as those run by the Western European democracies have allowed these countries to grow large and strong. A command economy is run by a strong centralized government and tends to focus on industrial goods. The Soviet Union and Communist China in the 20th century operated under this economic system. While short term gains did occur, the majority of people suffered under system that paid little attention to food production or consumer goods. A mixed economy is a combination of market and command. The United States and many nations in the European Union operated under this system today.

Economic Systems

Traditional	• Based on agriculture • Limited barter trade • Neolithic Civilizations • Early River Valley Civilizations
Market	• Based upon Supply and Demand • Usually focus on consumer goods • Little government control
Command	• Controlled by strong, centralized government • Usually focuses on industrial goods • Little attention paid to agriculture and consumer goods
Mixed	• Combination of Market and Command economic systems • Market forces control most consumer goods • Government directs industry in need areas.

Included in this theme are factors of production, which are the resources necessary to produce goods and services. These factors include human resources, natural resources, and capital or money resources. Human needs and wants also must be balanced within an economic system. Attention must be paid to the resources humans need to survive, and to those goods and services that serve to enhance living. Finally, the concept of scarcity must be explored and balanced. Scarcity is the conflict between limited resources and unlimited need. When scarcity of any resource occurs, new factors of production must be explored for humans to continue to survive.

As the important condition of the analysis transformation economy search of new tools of research of essence of modern economic systems, specificities of mechanisms and laws of their functioning acts on the basis of those approaches which exist in other sciences for the analysis of any systems. It is considered, that the general theory of systems as a scientific direction has appeared in the beginning of XX century. Russian scientist A.Bogdanov has put in pawn a ba sis of this direction in work "Tektology, or a general organizational science" (term belongs to L. Bertalanfi-"the General theory of systems" (1926ã.)). According to this theory, system in general name complete object which supports the existence and carries out the certain functions on the basis of interaction of its elements. The system is always considered as process. As systems cooperate with their environment, it is necessary to study also organizational mechanisms-positive and negative feedback. In fact, as writes A. Bogdanov, exists tektological the law: if the system will consist of subsystems of the supreme and lowest organization its behaviour is determined by the second subsystem [quo. For 2, c.15-16].

The system is a complete object which supports the existence and functions thanking interactions between elements. The system has own characteristics: 1) the behaviour of systems depends on the law of a composition; 2) a principle system hierarchy: the system will consist of subsystems and most is a subsystem of system more a high rank; 3) dynamic complexity: different conditions of elements can change properties of system; 4) a principle of conformism: laws of behaviour of systems-universal. It means, that studying system of the certain type, results of this research can be distributed to all systems of similar type.

Traditionally economic science studied linear systems which properties do not change for the period of change of their qualitative conditions. In linearly organized (promodelled) system structural elements have rights only on those qualities and properties which are del egated by it system as whole. "The world of linear systems is the world without alternative realism, the world without a choice. Such the social validity from positions of totalitarianism for which and the analytics, accordingly, is not necessary " also is imagined,-Ukrainian philosopher M.A.Ozhevan marks. At the same time, value of linear modelling is hard for overestimating, as it enabled to analyze critical modes of functioning of difficultly organized systems. Linearity very important when is kept in time the certain structure where communications between its elements are counterbalanced. And on the contrary, the more the system comes nearer to conditions of a unbalance, in it nonlinear characteristics and the less in it of attributes lines especially accrue.

In second half XX item "the theory of chaos" or a nonlinear science which has received practical application in parallel in many areas of a science (A.Puankare, A.Andronov, Kh.Uintni – in mathematics began to develop so-called; I.Prigozhin-in thermodynamics; E.Janch and M.Moiseev-in a history; L.Leskov-in modelling welfare processes). Scientists have understood, that the knowledge of the social validity should be enriched due to accumulation of the knowledge extracted in other sciences. In dialogue of sciences the new research paradigm is under construction today.

Nonlinear there are those systems which properties significally depend on processes which in them occur. The essence of nonlinearity will consist in because at change of the certain managing parameter there can be determined its critical condition, beginning from which the behaviour of system essentially changes. There is a line of characteristics of such systems:

1) Nonlinear systems provide not simply different, and alternative decisions which cannot be realized simultaneously;
2) even minor alterations around of such points can lead to significant changes in behaviour of system;
3) qualitative the characteristic (attribute) of nonlinearity and criticality are shown in situations nonbalans;
4) in open systems possible evolutionary no equilibrium processes which occur alternatively;
5) at the analysis socioeconomical systems the problem becomes complicated also that their development submits influences of subjective decisions.

The behaviour of dynamic systems supposes instability, that is why presence of a problem of unpredictability. An interval of time during which movement remains expected, name horizon of vision. In conditions of instability the horizon of vision becomes finished. " Final horizon of vision and own time inherent not only to chaotic systems. They characteristic for any difficult objects, including what concern to socioeconomical spheres "-are rebuked by V.M.Kostjuk [2, 14-17].

Scientists attach great importance to functions of chaos during self-organizing and selfmanagement.

It consider as: à) the factor of updating of the difficult organization; б) the mechanism of an output on one of tendencies from a spectrum potentially possible; B) a way of synchronization of rates of evolution of subsystems inside difficult system and by that a way of preservation of its integrity; г) the factor of the adaptation to change of an environment; д) a way of preparation to different to variants of the future development [3, 146]. In connection with these characteristics allocate rules which it is necessary to adhere at management in conditions of chaos: 1) the indignation should not be strong; 2) management should be extremely sensitive to a condition of system; 3) it is important to establish, as far as freedom of actions should be limited during instability and, at last; 4) integrity of system should not be destroyed. The ratio between the order and chaos, harmony and disharmony all time changes. Sometimes people accept the order more, but for the majority of the human purposes the most useful is a degree of a muddle which changes. The task of management consists not in eradicating chaos, and in achieving a convenient ratio between the order and a muddle.

As modern method of the analysis of the self-organized nonlinear systems the social synergetrics acts. Synergetical the approach develops at different schools which concern to different areas of scientific knowledge.

The main idea of use sociosynerhetical the approach consists that the society is ex amined as open system, but such, that has one real and many potential conditions. The society can pass from real in one of potential conditions. For its analysis bifurkatsy-a branching when the system is in a critical nonequilibrium condition, and the further development can result very important condition or in the new order, or to disintegration of the system. It is important to take into account also intermediate conditions and processes which very much complicate procedure of forecasting of development of social systems. If during the stable periods as the main tendency the determinism in transformation the periods the role of fluctuation (casual changes) very grows acts, and bifurkatsia casual character has. Sociosynergetics brings to a focus to those aspects of a social reality which in classical theories are examined as minor and to a case though, for example, in crisis situations they can play a leaguing role. The social synergetrics today is the most substantial and promising direction of research of social systems as opens new aspects and new mechanisms of their research.

Statement of a Task

Using general scientific approaches, each science including the economic theory, not should is artificial to search and garble the facts, aspiring to confirm presence of all characteristics of system in objects of the research. Such approaches give an analysis algorithm of systems and allow to understand internal interrelations and mechanisms of their development with the purpose of studying ways of effective influence on this development and its possible alternatives as influence of various internal and external factors. In economy such approaches should underlie economic thinking both on the equal states, and at a level of separate economic subjects. The purpose of the given research is revealing features of internal structure and mechanisms of development of modern social and economic systems on the basis of use of methods sociosunergetics.

Results

Structural-sunergetical thé approach enables to connect long-term tendencies and nonlinear changes which have temporary character in research. During modernization the society receives new qualitative characteristics which change the previous structures and mechanisms of functioning of political institutes. If during the evolutionary periods prevail transhistorical tendencies during the periods bifurcatsy there are processes of self-organizing.

Any social system inherently represents concrete historical education which functions with a definite purpose or assignment. Distinguish economic, political, information, ideological and other systems which are formed at a level of public ability to live. Each of them acts as set of the ordered and structured elements and communications which have the different purposes of the existence. It is very important to analyze internal logic of system, proceeding from definition of its structural elements and the mechanism of their interaction. For stationary systems (during balance) as standard characteristics of system act: integrity or existence of such features which are not reduced to the sum of characteristics of separate elements; structure, presence of organizational structures which coordinate interrelation of separate elements; the self-regulation directed on preservation of a proof equilibrium condition; Complexity, i.e. presence of feedback; information or presence of liaison channels and signaling between elements of system; dynamism, ability to adaptation in new conditions and also to development.

In an opposition of tendencies of conservatism and dynamism there is a development or change of a society. Provide integrity of system its organizational structures, their coordination and coordination. In case of disorganization of social system its integrity is lost, deepen disproportions, social disagreements become aggravated, there a re conflicts which can lead to significant updating or replacement of system.

In functioning any society there is a system of norms, rules, procedures, and also mechanisms of their realization, which structuring relations between people and the organizations.

These are political and social and economic institutes which act as forms of social integration, determine "game rules", the order in a society. They authorize norms and structures of social relations, functions of the state structures, a range of the rights and duties of individuals, the mechanism of interaction of manufacture and consumption, sadly developments and forms of coordination of public processes. At the same time, institute s in the certain measure pawn borders of stability of the system, scales of possible changes, act as intrasystem "terminator" of social changes. The majority of scientists count, that specificity institution environments is determined by material conditions of existence of a society. " Any social generality can be examined as the industrial or economic mechanism which structure will consist that refers to as social and economic institutes. Such institutes are usual ways of realization of process of a public life in its communication with a material environment in which the alive society ",-writes T.Veblen [2, 204].

In a modern science more popular opposite approach. For example, F.Fukujama, the known American sociologist, considers, that various social institutes are built on above family as the primary tool socialization. " In family the person receives culture and habits which values allow to exist normally to it in a society and because of which and experience of this society are transferred from generation up to generation ",-it writes [6, 17].

Historically informal rules of public behaviour were gradually supplemented with artificial, formal institutes. Legislative norms, and also establishments, mechanisms, the organizations which create with the purpose of the control over observance of these rules, act as result of subjective activity of people.

They rather mobile in space and time, and their efficiency as historical experience testifies, depends on a measure of conformity to informal institutes. So, formal and informal institutes behave differently-at different levels and with different rates. As writes D.Nort, " if formal rules can be changed for one night informal norms usually change only gradually. But norms give "legitimacies" to system of rule s and consequently revolutionary changes never are so revolutionary as that their supporters "[7] would aspire.

Structure of Industry

Industry Structure Analysis

A business needs to understand the industry in which it competes. The question is how? The best answer is to use Michael Porter's industry model. This analysis is a useful way of analysing any industry.

The analysis views the industry along the following five dimensions:

1. Industry competitors. Existing competitors should be analysed in terms of competitive advantages and disadvantages, as well as likely shifts in strategy.
2. Potential entrants. New entrants into the industry will increase competition and potentially bring new strategies that alter the basis of competitive advantage.

3. Buyers. Buyers are not all alike and should be analysed based on their needs.
4. Substitutes. Substitutes represent products and services that could be used instead of the industry's products. For example, contact lenses and eye surgery are substitutes for eyeglasses. Ignore substitutes at great peril.
5. Industry suppliers. Suppliers affect costs and the ability to differentiate.

According to Porter, "the collective strength of these five competitive forces determines the ability of firms in an industry to earn, on average, rates of return on investment in excess of the cost of capital." The relative strength of each of these five forces is different for each industry, and changes over time.

Industry Segmentation

For a given industry, not all buyers are alike. Whether a firm's customers are individuals, corporations, or government entities, a firm cannot equally satisfy the different needs and purchase criteria of all types of buyers. For example, corporate customers may differ by geographical location, industry, company size, and a host of other variables, any of which may be relevant for understanding how to best group customers based upon common needs.

A firm needs to clearly articulate which set of customers it will serve, and which customers it will not serve. It is also important to understand how the needs of customers will likely change, and how to take advantage of those changing needs.

The basic theme, however, is that strategy is deciding which segments to focus on, and which segments to leave for other competitors.

Each industry segment (a given buyer type-for a given product variety) can be discussed in terms of: current and future competitors; current and future customers; current and future revenue and profitability; etc. In practice, developing an industry matrix is an excellent team building task that greatly facilitates a common understanding of the industry structure and industry dynamics. (It's the next step, choosing which industry segments to target, that sometimes leads to not-so-subtle differences of opinion.)

Target Marketing

It is important that each business within a corporation develop its own industry matrix, including its own view of how to segment buyers. For example, the top ten U.S. banks, each of which competes in 75 to 150 businesses, should not expect each business to segment its customers the same way.

Different criteria are relevant for each business unit depending upon the particular products or services provided and how customers purchase and use them.

For example, the retail credit card business may segment its customers based upon income, or language spoken, or age, or credit history, or dining or travel habits, or even on favourite sports team or charitable cause.

The wholesale funds transfer business, however, should segment its customers quite differently. It may segment its customers based on if the customer is another bank or a corporation; the volume of transactions per day; the method of sending transfer instructions, whether by phone, fax, or PC; or any other relevant criteria.

After analysing the total industry (playing field) a firm should pick which industry segments to target, and in what order.

In practice, it is useful to think of 100 poker chips representing 100% of the total budget (or 100% of the total number of employees). Objectively place the 100 poker chips in the industry segments to reflect current resource allocations. Next, strategically (subjectively) place your bets through future allocations.

Share Capital and Authorised Capital

When a company is formed, it must be decided whether its members' liability will be limited by shares. The memorandum of association will state:

- The amount of share capital the company will have, and;
- The division of the share capital into shares of a fixed amount.

The members must agree to take some, or all, of the shares. The memorandum of association must show the names of the people (subscribers) who have agreed to take shares and the number of shares each will take.

Authorised capital is the amount of share capital stated in the memorandum of association.

Is There a Maximum and Minimum Share Capital?

For private limited companies, no. However, a public limited company must have an authorised share capital of at least £50,000 (and, if it is trading, issued capital of £50,000).

Can a Company Alter its Authorised Share Capital?

A company can increase its authorised share capital by passing an ordinary resolution (unless its articles of association require a special or extraordinary resolution). A copy of the resolution-and notice of the increase on Form 123-must reach Companies House within 15 days of being passed. No fee is payable to Companies House. If you want to increase share capital, Net Lawman supplies the required documents, forms and explanatory notes to guide you. Links are at the right of this article.

A company can decrease its authorised share capital by passing an ordinary resolution to cancel shares which have not been taken or agreed to be taken by any person. Notice of the cancellation, on Form 122, must reach Companies House within one month. No fee is payable to Companies House.

What is Issued Capital?

Issued capital is the value of the shares issued to shareholders. This means the nominal value of the shares rather than their actual worth. The amount of issued capital cannot exceed the amount of the authorised capital.

A private company need not issue all its capital at once, but a public limited company must have at least £50,000 of allotted share capital.

A company may increase its issued capital by allotting more shares but only up to the maximum allowed by its authorised capital. Allotments must only be done using the appropriate forms and documents.

Reducing Issued Capital

A company cannot normally reduce its issued capital because the shares are the personal property of the shareholder. However, there are exceptions, for example:

- If a court order confirms a 'minute of reduction' following a special resolution of the company;
- If shares are bought back in accordance with a redemption contract;
- If the company's articles allow it to buy its own shares and the purchase is authorised by a special resolution.

Allotment of Shares

Allotment' is the process by which people become members of a company.

More people may be admitted as members of the company and are allotted shares. However, the directors must not allot shares without the authority of the existing shareholders. The authority will either be stated in the company's articles of association or given to the directors by resolution passed at a general meeting of the company.

Types of Resolution Required to Give Authority to Allot Shares

Any public or private company with share capital may give authority for allotment of shares to its board of directors by ordinary resolution. Subject to an exception for private companies (noted in the following paragraph) authority must be for a fixed period which must not exceed five years and must set a limit on the amount of shares that the directors can allot under it.

The company must deliver a copy of a resolution giving, varying, revoking or renewing an authority to allot shares to Companies House within 15 days of passing it.

A private company with share capital may pass an elective resolution, authorising the directors to allot shares for an indefinite period or for a fixed period longer than five years, though such a resolution must still set a limit on the amount of shares which the directors may allot. The company must deliver a copy of any elective resolution to Companies House within 15 days of passing it. A public company cannot pass an elective resolution.

Notifying Companies House

You must notify Companies House within one month of an allotment of shares using Form 88(2).

Nominal Value and Share Premium

A company's authorised share capital is divided into shares of a nominal value. The real value of the shares may change over time, as the market fluctuates. However, their nominal value remains the same. When the company sells shares for more than their nominal value, the actual sum paid will be in two parts-the nominal value and a share premium. The share premium must be recorded separately in the company's financial records in a 'share premium account'.

Must Shares be Fully paid-up at the time of Allotment?

No. Payment may be deferred until later. However, shares allotted in a public company must be paid-up to at least a quarter of their nominal value and the whole of any premium (except that this does not apply to shares allotted under an employees' share scheme, that is, a scheme for encouraging share ownership by employees, former employees and their families).

Bonus Shares

If authorised by its articles, a company may use any undistributed profits, or any sum credited to the company's 'share premium account' or 'capital redemption reserve' in order to finance an issue of wholly or partly paid up 'bonus' shares to the members in proportion to their existing holdings. The shareholders to whom the shares are issued pay nothing.

A company can also use a capitalisation of profits to credit partly paid shares with further amounts to make them paid up.

The allotment of bonus shares must be notified to Companies House on Form 88(2).

Pre-emption Rights

Pre emption rights are the rights of existing members to be offered new shares by the company before the shares are offered elsewhere, for example, to a new member.

The memorandum or articles of a private company may exclude pre-emption rights; however, a public company's cannot.

What is paid-up capital, uncalled capital, reserve capital and share premium?

- These terms are used to describe the make-up of a company's share capital;
- Paid-up capital is the issued capital which has been fully or partly paid-up by the shareholders;
- Uncalled capital is that part of the issued capital on which the company has not requested payment;
- Reserve capital is that part of the share capital that the company has decided will only be called up if the company is being wound up;
- Share premium is the excess paid above a share's nominal value.

4

Source of Finance

Finance-money-is a scarce resource. To obtain it, a business has to compete for it. Individuals, the government and other businesses all seek money to finance their needs. Those with money to lend will lend it provided the rate of return (interest), the risk and flexibility (how quickly the money can be repossessed) are consistent with their expectations.

Note: The word 'lend' often implies short-term; the word 'invest' implies long-term. Individuals or organisations that lend money, expect to get their money back, with a fixed annual return in a comparatively short time. Those who invest in a company become part-owners-share holders. They expect regular payment of cash dividends (whose size varies with the company's success) plus an increase in the value of their shares.

A major source of finance for many businesses is the retained profit from sales to customers. A business just starting up or one expanding rapidly has to raise its finance from other sources.

When sourcing finance, management should consider the following questions:

- duration: for how long is the finance required?
- cost: which source of finance is the least expensive?
- repayment: what level is acceptable?

Usually companies will obtain finance from a variety of sources, including:

- Internal: Owners' capital and retained profits.

- External: Overdraft, leasing, hire purchase, loans, and mortgages.

Duration

Duration depends on the reason the money is needed. No-one would take out a 25 year mortgage to finance the purchase of a personal HiFi. Few people would buy a house with a bank overdraft. Businesses apply the same principles of matching the purpose of finance with the source of finance. This makes sense all round. For the business it ensures that finance is guaranteed as long as it is needed.

For the investor it ensures that adequate security is available for the duration of the loan-as in the case of a 20 year loan secured against a property that will continue to have value for all the 20 years.

Cost

In general, businesses look for the cheapest source of finance. The easiest way to compare the cost of finance is to express the annual payment to lenders/investors as a percentage of the amount of finance provided. Interest on a loan can be expressed in percentage terms. So can the rate of return to shareholders.

Return on investment in shares = Dividend per share, price change since the start of year The rate of return expected by shareholders becomes the cost to the business of using this form of finance.

Repayment

A business should not get into a position where all of its profits are being swallowed up in interest payments. There is a real danger of borrowing too much. The same applies to individuals.

Long term finance may be needed to fund expansion projects-maybe a firm is considering setting up new offices in a European capital, maybe they want to buy new premises in another part of the UK, maybe they have a new product that they want to develop and maybe they want to buy another company. The methods of financing these types of projects will generally be quite complex and can involve billions of pounds. It is important to remember that in most cases, a firm will not use just one source of finance but a number of sources. There might be a dominant source of funds but when you are raising hundreds of millions of pounds it is unlikely to come from just one source.

Shares

A share is a part ownership of a company. Shares relate to companies set up as private limited companies or public limited companies (plcs). There are many small firms who decide to set themselves up as private limited companies; there are advantages and disadvantages of doing so. It is possible, therefore, that a small business might start up and have just two shareholders in the business.

If the business wants to expand, they can issue more shares but there are limitations on who they can sell shares to-any share issue has to have the full backing of the existing shareholders. PLCs are different. They sell shares to the general public. This means that anyone could buy the shares in the business.

Some firms might have started out as a private limited company and have expanded over time. There might come a time when they cannot issue any more shares to friends or family and need more funds to continue expanding. They might then decide to become a public limited company. This is called 'floating the business'. It means that the business will have to go through a number of administrative and legal procedures to allow it to be able to offer shares to the general public.

It might be that a business wants to raise £300 million to finance its expansion plans. It might issue 300 million £1 shares in the company. The offering of these shares has to be accompanied by a prospectus which lays out details of the business-what it is involved in, how it is structured, how it will be managed and so on. This is so that prospective investors, people or institutions who might want to buy the shares, can get information about the company before committing to buying shares.

Often a business will employ the services of a merchant bank to help with a share issue. These institutions specialise in arranging large financial deals of this sort. Examples of such institutions are Morgan Stanley, Merrill Lynch, Rothschilds and Goldman Sachs. These institutions may agree to underwrite the share issue. What this means is that if all the shares are not sold, the institution will still provide all the money to the firm issuing the shares.

Once the shares are sold, share owners can buy and sell their shares through the stock exchange. Such buying and selling does not affect the business concerned directly and is one of the main advantages of the stock exchange. You can get more details of how the stock exchange works through our resource on the London Stock Exchange.

There may be times in the development of a plc when it needs to raise more funds. In this case it can issue more shares. Many firms will do this through what is called a 'rights issue'. This occurs where new shares are issued but existing shareholders get the right to purchase new additional shares at a reduced price. If the business is doing well and the new finance is needed for expansion, this can be an attractive proposition for existing shareholders. For the business it is a relatively quick and cheap way of raising new funds.

Venture Capital

Venture capital is becoming an increasingly important source of finance for growing companies. Venture capitalists are groups of (generally very wealthy) individuals or companies specifically set up to invest in developing companies. Venture capitalists are on the look out for companies with potential. They are prepared to offer capital (money) to help the business grow. In return the venture capitalist gets some say in the running of the company as well as a share in the profits made.

Venture capitalists are often prepared to take on projects that might be seen as high risk which some banks might not want to get involved in. The advantages of this might be outweighed by the possibility of the business losing some of its independence in decision making.

Examples of venture capitalists (who are also called private equity firms) are Advantage Capital Limited, Braveheart Ventures, Permira and Hermes Private Equity.

Government Grant

Some firms might be eligible to get funds from the government. This could be the local authority, the national government or the European Union. These grants are often linked to incentives to firms to set up in areas that are in need of economic development. In Cornwall, for example, there have been a number of initiatives to encourage new businesses to locate there.

Cornwall has the lowest gross domestic product (GDP) per head of the population in the UK. The average wage in Cornwall is 28% below the UK average. As a result, the area attracts funding from the

EU and the government. Firms looking to set up in Cornwall might be able to apply for some help in starting or moving a business to the area. One of the disadvantages of this type of funding is that it involves large amounts of paperwork and administration. This can add to costs and in some cases might not make the project worthwhile.

One famous example of how a business project can be developed using European Union funding was the Eden Project. The EU was not the only source of finance to help set up the project but was an important partner in helping to realise this important tourist destination for a deprived part of Cornwall.

Bank Loans

As with short term finance, banks are an important source of longer term finance. Banks may lend sums over long periods of time-possibly up to 25 years or even more in some cases. The loans have a rate of interest attached to them. This can vary according to the way in which the Bank of England sets interest rates. For businesses, using bank loans might be relatively easy but the cost of servicing the loan (paying the money and interest back) can be high. If interest rates rise then it can add to a businesses costs and this has to be taken into account in the planning stage before the loan is taken out.

Mortgage

A mortgage is a loan specifically for the purchase of property. Some businesses might buy property through a mortgage. In many cases, mortgages are used as a security for a loan. This tends to occur with smaller businesses. A sole trader, for example, running a florists shop might want to move to larger premises. They find a new shop with a price of £200,000. To raise this sort of money, the bank will want some sort of security-a guarantee that if the borrower cannot pay the money back the bank will be able to get their money back somehow.

The borrower can use their own property as security for the loan-it is often called taking out a second mortgage. If the business does not work out and the borrower could not pay the bank the loan then the bank has the right to take the home of the borrower and sell it to recover their money. Using a mortgage in this way is a very popular way of raising finance for small businesses but as you can see carries with it a big risk.

Owner's Capital

Some people are in a fortunate position of having some money which they can use to help set up their business.

The money may be the result of savings, money left to them by a relative in a will or money received as the result of a redundancy payment. This has the advantage that it does not carry with it any interest. It might not, however, be a large enough sum to finance the business fully but will be one of the contributions to the overall finance of the business.

Retained Profit

This is a source of finance that would only be available to a business that was already in existence.

Profits from a business can be used by the owners for their own personal use (shareholders in plcs receive a share of the company profits in the form of a dividend-usually expressed as Xp per share) or can be used to put back into the business. This is often called 'ploughing back the profits'.

The owners of a business will have to decide what the best option for their particular business is. In the early stages of business growth, it may be necessary to put back a lot of the profits into the business. This finance can be used to buy new equipment and machinery as well as more stock or raw materials and hopefully make the business more efficient and profitable in the future.

Selling Assets

As firms grow they build up assets. These assets could be in the form of property, machinery, equipment, other companies or even logos. In some cases it may be appropriate for a business to sell off some of these assets to finance other projects.

Lottery Funding

In the UK the National Lottery might be a possible source of funds for some types of business. These businesses will mostly be charities or charitable trusts. The Eden Project, referred to earlier, received some funding from the Lottery. The company that run the Eden Project are a not for profit business so any surplus they make is put back into the business to help develop and improve it.

Other Institutions Providing Finance

Sources of Finance

We require finance to carry out various production activities. For this, we-have to borrow funds. Now the question is-from where do we obtain this finance. We can take loans from friends, moneylenders, mahajans, relatives or from specialised agencies like banks, cooperative societies, finance corporations, Unit Trust of India (UTI), Life Insurance Corporation (LIC), etc. All these sources of finance can be classified into two :

(a) Non-institutional sources, and

(b) Institutional sources

(a) Non-institutional Sources of Finance : Loans from individuals, for example, loans taken from moneylenders, mahajans, friends, relatives, etc. are called non-institutional sources of finance.

(b) Institutional Sources of Finance : Institutional sources of finance include organisations or establishments which are set up to provide finance. They have a specialised objective and that is provision of finance. Such institutions or organisations are also called financial institutions. Examples of institutional sources of finance are banks, cooperative societies, insurance companies, UTI, State Finance Corporations, Development Banks, etc.

Arrangements for the Supply of Credit to Rural Areas

It provides short term, medium term and long term credit to State Cooperative Banks, Regional Rural Banks, and other financial institutions approved by the Reserve Bank of India.

It not only provides loans for agricultural activities but also for activities related to agriculture and also promotes research in agriculture and rural development.

Points to Remember

- In the agricultural sector, initially noninstitutional sources were the most important sources of finance.
- Due to the exploitative nature of the noninstitutional sources government and the Reserve Bank of India have helped set

up various agencies in the rural areas which provide institutional finance.

- Some of these agencies are Commercial Banks, Regional Rural Banks, Land Development Banks, Cooperative Credit Societies and the NABARD.
- NABARD is the apex bank in the provision of institutional finance in the rural areas.

Sources of Industrial Finance

(a) Need: Industries need two types of finance. First, to buy fixed capital goods tike land, building, machines, equipment etc. Second, to meet working capital requirements to buy raw materials, to pay wages and salaries, and to meet other day to day expenses. To meet fixed capital lang terra finance and to meet working capital need short term finance are required.

The main sources of industrial finance within the country are :

1. Public issues (of shares and debentures)
2. Public deposits
3. Loans from commercial banks
4. Industrial banks

Public Issues (Shares and Debentures)

By public issue is meant an open invitation to general public by an industrial unit to invest money in that unit. This invitation is designed according to law and is subject to certain rules and regulations. The invitation is given after obtaining permission from the relevant government department. The industrial unit extending the invitation has to follow certain rules.

Finance through public issues is obtained by issuing shares and debentures. Their price is fixed in advance. Any individual or institution buying shares is treated as one of the owners of share issuing company. In this way there can be thousands and lakhs of shareholders of a company. Debenture holders have no concern with ownership or management of the company. They get only interest at some predetermined rate of interest.

The major portion of the long term finance requirements of an industrial unit is met by issuing shares and debentures. Anybody can buy these shares and debentures, whether an individual, a firm, a bank or any other institution. That is why these issues are called public issues.

How much money people like to invest in a public issue depends on the business environment and the confidence of people on capital market If the environment is not favourable and the confidence in capital market shakes, the common man fights shy of making investment in public issues. During the recent years industrial concerns are finding it difficult to raise money through public issues due to uncertainties in the capital market.

Public Deposits is a method of taking loans from the general public. The companies invite fixed deposits from the general public. Companies pay a fixed rate of interest on these deposits. These deposits are usually for a period of one to five years. These deposits are guided by certain rules and regulations. The sales are framed by the Reserve Bank of India and the companies compulsorily adopt these rules. How much money a company can raise from this source depends on the confidence the people have in that company. Generally, the reputed companies are in a position to raise finance at reasonable rate of interest because the people have confidence in them. When the confidence is shaken people fight shy of making deposits.

Industrial units in general are not able to raise money from this source. Only a few well known companies are able to raise money from this source. Commercial Banks-Commercial banks give loans to industrial units. But these are generally short-term loans which meet only working capital requirement. Banks normally do not give long term loans.

They also do not subscribe to share and debentures because they find it risky. There is a fear of loss of investment. Banks need money continuously. Therefore, commercial banks do not show much interest in long term financial needs of the industries. Industrial Banks-We have observed that commercial banks do not show interest in long term financial needs of industries because they do not want to lock their money for a long period. This requirement is fulfilled by industrial banks. These banks were established after Independence.

Industrial banks are specialised financial institutions established by government to meet long term finance requirements of industries. Thus industrial banks are complementary to the commercial banks because commercial banks meet only the short term requirements. Some Examples of such Specialised Financial Institutions are:

1. Industrial Development Bank of India (IDBI)
2. Industrial Finance Corporation of India (IFCI)
3. Industrial Credit and Investment Corporation of India (ICICI)
4. Industrial Reconstruction Corporation of India (IRCI)
5. Unit Trust of India (UTI)
6. National Small Industries Corporation (NSIC)
7. State Financial Corporations (SFCs)
8. State Industrial Development Corporations (SIDCs)
9. State Industrial Investment Corporations (SIICs)
10. Export-Import Bank of India (EXIM Bank).

These are only some examples. There are other institutions also. These institutions do not only finance but encourage industries by giving them technical advice, market information and evaluating projects.

(c) Industrial banks vs. Commercial Banks: These banks are different from commercial banks in these respects :

   (i) People cannot deposit money in industrial banks while they can do so in commercial banks.

   (ii) These banks give medium term and long term loans while commercial banks give short term loans,

   (iii) These banks, in addition to finance, help in the development of industries by offering technical advice and market information. Commercial banks confine to giving loans only.

Some Specialised Financial Institutions

We have given a list of some specialised financial institutions. Now we discuss some of these specialised financial institutions in detail.

Industrial Finance Corporation of India (IFCI)

IFCI was the first to be set up m the existing chain of development banks in 1948 by the Government of India. It provides medium and long term credit to industry.

The Corporation performs three important functions:

(i) It grants loans and advances to industrial concerns and subscribes to the debentures floated by them,

(ii) It guarantees loans raised by the industrial concerns in the capital market,

(iii) It underwrites the issue of stock, shares, bonds and debentures of industrial concerns. IFCI provides long and medium term finance only to companies engaged in manufacturing, mining, shipping and generation and distribution of electricity.

The limit of assistance to any single concern is now Rs. 1 croie and the period of loans is not to exceed 25 years.

Industrial Development Bank of India (IDBI)

The IDBI came into existence in 1964 and is now the apex institution providing term finance.The main function of IDBI is to finance industrial enterprises such as manufacturing, mining, processing, shipping and other transport industries and hotel industry.

It provides direct assistance by way of project loans, underwriting of and direct subscription to industrial securities.

It also refinances term loans given. By other financial institutions.

Industrial Credit and Investment Corporation of India (ICIO)

ICIO was set up in January, 195 5 for the purpose of developing small and medium industries in the private sector.

The aim of ICICI is to stimulate the promotion of new industries, to assist the expansion and modernisation of existing industries and to furnish technical and managerial guidance.

The Corporation grants:

(i) long term or medium term loans

(ii) guarantees loans from other private sources

(iii) participates in equity capital and underwrites new issues of shares and debentures.

ICICI has so rar assisted industries manufacturing paper, chemicals and pharmaceuticals, electrical equipment, textiles, sugar, metal ore, lime and cement works, glass manufacture etc. ICICI assists all sectors, mat is, the private sector, the joint sector, the public sector and the cooperative sector but the major beneficiary is the private sector

Small Industries Development Bank of India (SIDBI)

SIDBI was set up in 1990 as a wholly owneo Vsubsidiary of IDBI. It is the principal financial institution for financing and development of small scale industries in the country. It extends financial assistance to the small units scattered all over the country.

Export-Impart Bank of India (EXIM Bank)

The EXIM Bank of India was set up in 1982 to provide finance for the development of exports. Its mam objective is to solve the problems of exporters, provide special attention to capital goods exports and export of technical services. It provides financial assistance to the exporters and importers and acts as the principal financial institution for coordinating the working of other institutions engaged in financing exports and imports.

Unit Trust of India (UTI)

The UTI was setup in 1964 at the initiative of the RBI. It is a 50 per cent subsidiary of the LIC, the State Bank of Ind.a. other scheduled banks, and the ICICI. The main source of funds of the UTI is the sale of units to the public under various schemes. By selling these units they collect and mobilise savings from the general public and lends them to the investors. It also participates in the underwriting of the new issues of debentures and shares.

Points to Remember

The main sources of industrial finance are-Shares and Debentures, Loans from Commercial Banks, Deposits from the public. Industrial banks are specialised institutions which in addition to giving loans help in the development of industrial units. Some of the important industrial banks are IDBI, IFCI, ICICI, SIDBI, EXIM Bank etc.

International Management

Environmental Management

Environmental management refers to the management of modern human society with, and its impact on, the environment. Because natural resources are finite and limited, they can only support a certain population within any species. Environmental management works on the principle of conservation of the environment in order sustain human development.

Factors

Because of the complexity of the environment and its interconnected nature with all species, environmental management incorporates both living and nonliving components of the environment. In other words, both biological and physical aspects of the environment are considered. Relationships within the human environment, like social, cultural or economic issues, are also factored. Environmental managers are affected by politics, programs and "unnatural" resources (like money or facilities) in their attempt to manage natural resources.

Standards

In order for environmental management to remain effective, standards and systems have been implemented. These standards attempt to measure the success of management, as measured by some objective criteria. ISO 4001 is a common standard for environmental management put forth by the International Organization for Standardization. Environmental Management Systems (EMS) are usually based on the ISO 4001 standard.

One Approach

Environmental Management System (EMS) is a structured, documented approach to respond to environmental challenges by focusing on environmental regulations and standards, and customer requirements. Environmental management involves conducting a life-cycle assessment of the process at hand, seeking ways to lessen environmental burdens discovered, and then optimizing the use of limited natural resources utilized.

Considerations

The goal of environmental management is to find effective ways to use limited resources. When businesses are involved, products and services are to be produced in an environmentally conscious way. EMS attempts to create, reinforce and improve a sound environmental policy through a cycle of planning, implementation, checking (involves monitoring and taking correcting action), and review. The cycle of "plan—do—check—act" moves towards continual improvement.

Planning

Within EMS, planning is considered an essential counterpart of environmental management. Any good policy needs to start with a solid plan that would consider all potential factors and offer a way to optimize resources. Effective planning anticipates future environmental changes or alternative scenarios, and leads to preventive measures. After implementation of the plan, checking and reviewing the results always lead back to more planning for a better policy.

Environmental management refers to the management of modern human society with, and its impact on, the environment. Because natural resources are finite and limited, they can only support a certain population within any species. Environmental management works on the principle of conservation of the environment in order sustain human development.

The mid 1990s and was followed by other major paint manufacturers such as Benjamin Moore and Sherman-Williams. Homeowners have responded very well to this development. Today, all major paint manufacturers market zero-VOC paint and offer lower-VOC coatings for a variety of substrates. Some manufacturers such as Rodda Paint of Portland, OR; have gained Green Seal on their paint products and that has given it a competitive edge. It joins the likes of big players like Benjamin Moore.

The energy industry has also reacted to *green power* which has been defined by the National Association of Attorney Generals [NAAG] as the use of replenishable or sustainable fuel sources in the generation and transmission of electricity and the disposal of spent fuels. These releases into the environment would not create harmful substances and would pose no significant concern to the ecosystem and to land use. The focus is on renewable energy supply. Studies have shown that homeowners are willing to pay more to use green power. This program is similar to the waste recycling program in many communities that are paid for by consumers.

The trend toward green is on the rise in every sector of the economy. According to a study by Yanklovich Clancy Schulman, 78% of people are "influenced greatly" to buy products that make environmental claims. The Organic Trading Association notes that products with the word "organic" have 34% sell-through rate compared to conventional products. Furthermore, the rate of growth of natural or organic food has been steady at 18-25% while conventional foods remain flat at 3-4%3. The demand for organic products has also affected the clothing industry where the current trend calls for the use of organic cotton.

The growth of "*conspicuous conservation*" is also on the rise as the demand for hybrid vehicles skyrocket. Companies like Toyota and Honda that were among the first to manufacture hybrid cars that combine gas engines with battery-powered electric motors have witnessed surge in demand. These products are not only environmentally friendly but are also economical. Aside from the fact that these hybrid cars ut emissions, owners in the US can write off a one-time deduction of $2,000 of the purchase price for these vehicles since the Internal Revenue Services (IRS) has recognized them as eligible for the clean-burning fuel tax deduction. This law also applies to other vehicles that operate on natural gas, liquefied natural gas, liquefied petroleum gas, hydrogen, or any other fuel that is at least 85% alcohol. Owners of completely electric vehicles would even get tax credit of up to $4,000. Customers who patronize these products want to be seen as saving energy and believe that their consumption behaviour reflect who they are. The trend towards environmental conservation is further reflected in the emergence of energy saving products such as energy star appliances, compact fluorescent lights, photovoltaic solar cells, "high performance" homes and others.

The green trend is on the rise and green products offer a new market niche to global companies. According to The LOHAS journal, about 63 million consumers or about 30% of US adults purchase goods and services that are classified as healthy, environmentally friendly, socially conscious and sustainable. The LOHAS index constitutes of five major areas that comprise sustainable economy, healthy living, alternative health care, personal development and ecological life style. While there are more to this index, however, environmental issues are prominent.

The discussions above highlight the growing importance of environmental management systems and the need to effectively plan and manage in order to harness the values that would accrue to companies that adopt environmental strategies. We shall next look at how to assess the cost of environmental quality. It is very important that managers understand the cost side of environmental quality. Knowledge of the costs would obviously, hit home the need to be proactive and prevent environmental errors from occurring.

Environmental Management Systems (EMS)

The focus of this book is on Environmental Management and Planning. Naturally, Environmental Management System (EMS) forms the core of any environmental management and planning program. EMS has become increasingly popular in the past few years mainly due to ISO 14000 series which is labelled EMS. EMS is a well structured and documented approach to respond to environmental challenges by focusing on environmental regulations and standards, and customer requirements.

It is based on the need to respond proactively to the management of natural environment by conducting life cycle assessment to lessen environmental burden and optimize the use of limited natural resources. Firms that adopt the EMS approach focus on effective ways to use such limited resources to produce environmentally conscious products and services. One of the popular approaches to achieve this is to adopt a plan-do-check (study)-act (PDCA) which was popularized by the father of Total Quality Management (TQM) Dr. Edward Deming.

Using PDCA requires that the firm focuses on how to develop environmental policies by recognizing corporate, industry, local, national and international environmental policies and standards. The consideration of these policies and standards constitutes a major factor in designing a product or service for the environment.

Planning is important to any successful EMS program. Effective planning leads to successful consideration of factors that may support or hamper EMS efforts. Planning offers a way to optimization of resources and stops the firm from "*fighting fires.*" Planning leads to preventive measures and anticipation of future environmental changes. It positions the firm to take competitive advantage rather than responding only to challenges as they occur.

Effective planning also smoothens out implementation and minimizes environmental burden since many of the sources of environmental burden would be anticipated and addressed. It also helps address "*what if*" or sensitivity analysis questions. Thus, different scenarios and alternatives will be anticipated, investigated, and prototypes looked at to identify at least a *satisficing* solution that may not necessarily be optimal but give a very good resolution to the environmental problem. When products and services are designed for the environment, they are properly planned and fully tested before introduction into the marketplace. However, pushing these products and services to the market does not end the responsibility of the firm.

Environmental scanning is an ongoing process that would lead to continuous review of the products and services to achieve continuous improvement. Our approach in this book is to focus on management issues as key to the success of environmental planning program. The traditional focus of environmental systems has been on the natural sciences. While natural sciences continue to play a major role in understanding the natural environment, the problem of environmental burden or optimization of natural resources would not be achieved without a focus on how such burden or resources can be effectively managed.

This book therefore focuses on the strategic context of environmental management. It focuses on corporate strategies to develop a new vision of environmental management systems. Some of the areas that are looked into are:

- *Top Management Commitment:* Since the era of TQM, it has become apparent that most problems organizations face can be blamed on top management. Top management wields a lot of power and authority. It provides the mission and vision of the organization. It lays down organizational strategies and it provides the resources to achieve organizational goals. If top management is not committed to a cause, it would not devote the needed resources to it. Top management must take EMS to heart for it to be successfully implemented. Employees respond to the call from their leaders. Corporate leaders have the responsibility to educate their employees and make them buy into the corporate mission. When top management views environmental management as strategic, integrate it in corporate mission and devote resources and commit time to it, others will follow. These resources would enable to provide proper training, education, and technology to address environmental burden.

- *Cross-Functional Team:* There is a need to develop crossfunctional teams that would work concurrently to address environmental issues. The use of cross-functional teams is vogue in managing successful organization. It is important that members of the teams have a single view of the organization.

Functional units within organizations are interdependent and should not be treated as independent silos. Members of the manufacturing unit should be able to work together with marketing and express and share views at the same time. The concurrency at the design stage helps to reduce the cycle time to introduce new products and makes the organization more competitive. The different backgrounds of team members also expose different worldviews that could be captured and used to develop an acceptable plan to all the departments.

- *Stakeholder Teams:* In conjunction with the cross-functional teams that may comprise mostly of organizational employees, it is important to also work with stakeholder teams. Stakeholders constitute those whose actions and reactions affect or are affected by organizational actions. As cited in the book, many organizations are today working with various interest groups to develop environmental strategies. The involvement of different stakeholder teams also helps win acceptance of final decisions that are reached.
- *Responsibility for the Environment:* Who is responsible for environmental management in the organization? Our response to this question is that everyone is responsible. The approach adopted in this book is known as Total Environmental Quality Management (TEQM). Environmental management is not relegated to a particular department or to particular individuals in the organization. Instead, every member of the organization takes full responsibility for his or her own action and works hard to make sure that EMS is fully implemented. Each member of the organization seeks out ways to contribute, and identifies ways to limit pollution and minimize waste in whatever function or activity he or she is involved in.
- *The Bottom Line:* Businesses operate to maximize stockholders wealth and must pay attention to the bottom line. If an activity is not value-adding, then there is no need to continue with such

an activity. In the past, many corporate leaders complained about the *high cost* of environmental management to justify inaction or disinterest. Today, things have changed. Businesses are observing that the *external cost* for environmental quality has been underestimated and that such costs significantly affect the survival of the business. In addition, they are acknowledging that being environmentally conscious is being competitive. In this book, we illustrate several case studies of companies who regained market shares because they developed successful environmental management programs. The recognition of the importance of environmental management as a competitive weapon could also explain the growing interest of companies to get environmental certifications such as ISO 14000 and the other environmental seals. Companies flout such recognition in advertisement campaigns because they understand that social consciousness influences purchasing decisions. Therefore, it pays to be green.

The Road to EMS

While there is a need to develop EMS, this road is not always smooth sailing. Companies are often bewildered by the avalanche of materials and guidelines on environmental laws. There is a need for universal standards that would overcome some of the national laws.

These standards need to be simplified and designed with implementation in mind. ISO focuses on such issues. However, its guidelines still need to be trimmed to make it easier to implement.

Unfortunately many countries such as the United States are too litigious. This poses a risk to companies who would actually want to identify and rectify problems with their products and processes. There is need to protect such corporate activities as environmental auditing.

With the free access to information coupled with "cradle-to-grave" responsibilities for organizational products and services, environmental auditing that detects serious environmental flaws may actually present serious problems to a firm. The government may need to wade in to encourage and protect firms that do environmental auditing to improve environmental quality.

Environmental management should be required for all businesses irrespective of size. Small and medium-sized firms may have more problems due to limited resources and may also lack the knowledge to effectively manage the environment. Government initiatives and incentives may be necessary to encourage such businesses. Adoption of EMS does not replace sound business strategies.

While it would complement the efforts, however, sound business strategies that focus on the organization's core competencies would still be needed to survive in today's highly competitive environment.

Thus, the goal should be to include environmental management system as part of the strategic framework. Such consideration would help to ensure that:

- Products and services are designed for the environment. In other words, such products and services will create minimal environmental burdens, optimize limited natural resources, and satisfy the growing needs of stakeholders for sustainable or environmentally conscious products and services.
- The firm is competitive and able to survive in its market environment. As mentioned above, auto manufacturers that produced hybrid vehicles have reaped tremendous profits while producing green products; Kodak repositioned itself with the single-use camera; and Xerox regained market share with its remanufacturing program.
- External cost which also affects customer goodwill is diminished. Companies today have to take a "cradle-to-grave" approach of their products. Their actions today may haunt them in later years. In addition to punitive damages, top management may still be held personally liable. It is important to be socially responsible and adopt the correct course of action now, rather than *fight fires* later. Furthermore, these costs could be further diminished by working well with stakeholder teams. This would allow several options or alternatives to be considered in the product design and development stages, reduce cost, and quicken introduction into the market. Designing for the environment becomes a competitive weapon the firm can enjoy.
- The strategic importance of EMS decisions is very high. When poor environmental decisions are made, they are irreversible and the consequences are very high. The Union Carbide plant

explosion in Bhopal, India in 1984 is still a glimpse reminder of the problems of poor environmental judgment. Apart from the so many deaths, irreversible blindness, long-lasting pollution, the ensuing public condemnation and labelling of the company has for long, dented its image and made it very difficult for the firm to operate. Poor environmental decisions lead to high production costs, poor public perception, poor quality, and would ultimately starve the firm of needed cash to conduct research and development or finance new projects.

Environmental Action Box

Hybrid Cars

The history of hybrid vehicles dates back to 1665. Flemish astronomer and Jesuit priest Ferdinand Verbiest developed plans for a miniature four-wheel unmanned steam "car" for Chinese Emperor Khang Hsi. Since then, there have been several efforts to develop efficient hybrid cars. The most successful commercial effort to this effect could be traced to 1992 when Toyota Motor Corporation outlined in its document titled "Earth Charter," plans to develop and market vehicles that will yield the lowest emission possible. By 1997, Toyota began marketing Pirus in Japan and sold nearly 18,000 cars in its first year. By 1997-1999, other big auto manufacturers including Honda, GM and Ford introduced all-electric cars and those cars were sold mostly in California where environmental protection laws are stricter due to its poor quality air.

Honda released its two-door Insight in 1999 and it is considered the first hybrid car to be offered to mass market in the United States. Insight was very successful winning several awards and was rated by EPA to receive 61 miles per gallon (mpg) in city driving and 70 mpg on highway. Toyota followed suit by releasing Toyota Pirus in the year 2000. Unlike the 2-door Insight, Pirus was the first 4-door sedan sold to mass market in the United States. By 2002, Honda introduced Honda Civic Hybrid and in 2004, Toyota Pirus II won Car of the Year Awards from Motor Trend Magazine and North American Auto Show. The demand for Pirus has skyrocketed in the US with Toyota's production of this vehicle rising from 36,000 to 47,000 in the US market. There was also a six month wait to purchase the vehicle in 2004. These hybrid cars are gradually making it into the mainstream market and other car makers have joined Honda and Toyota. The US auto manufacturer Ford introduced Escape Hybrid in September 2004 as both the first American hybrid and the first SUV hybrid.

The use of hybrid cars has enormous potential to minimize the burden on the environment. We shall summarize some of the implications on the environment that could be minimized through this effort. There has been a drastic increase in the demand for motor vehicles since the 1970s. It is estimated that there are over 700 million vehicles worldwide and if the present trend continues, this number could exceed 1 billion by 2025. There are more cars than adults in the US alone, vehicles are driven more than two trillion miles annually.

Motor vehicles contribute to all kinds of environmental and health hazards. While they are necessity for transportation purposes, however, the demand and use of vehicles need to be tamed to improve environmental quality. There are alternatives that could be pursued to limit the environmental impacts of vehicles.

Global Warming – About 5.5 million tons of carbon is released annually by the burning of gas, coal, and oil. The consequence is that heat is trapped in the atmosphere and causes the warming of the planet, thus producing greenhouse effect. Burning of gasoline contributes to greenhouse effect. When a gallon of gasoline weighing about 6 pounds is burned, it combines with oxygen to produce about 20 pounds of carbon dioxide (CO2). With the increasing demand for motor vehicles, it is estimated that over 300 metric tons of carbon are produced by cars and light trucks every year in the US. The carbon dioxide emission from transportation constitutes more than a third of all other sources of emission. It is therefore prudent that efforts be spent on developing fuel efficient vehicles that would burn less fossil fuel or use alternative technologies to limit environmental burdens.

The focus on hybrid vehicles could help achieve reduction in the volume of carbon that is generated. The ensuing temperature fluctuations caused by Global warming could affect wildlife survival and the entire ecosystem. In addition, carbon dioxide is the main greenhouse gas and minimizing its production could help to build a cleaner environment. The burning of fossil fuels by motor vehicles lead to the generation of several gases and pollutants which are environmentally unfriendly and unsafe to human health. We shall adapt and present some of the statistical information from *hybridcars.com* to show the significant gain of hybrid cars over conventional gas-powered vehicles.

In addition to gases and pollutants associated with motor vehicles, there are also the production of sulphur oxides and lead. Sulphur oxides contribute in the formation of acid rain and are potentially dangerous to children and elderly people. The production of lead is also of concern although some countries have banned the use of leaded gasoline. Lead poisoning is known to damage organs and other tissues in the body.

This table did show that a shift to hybrid vehicles could help to minimize environmental burden by improving fuel efficiency and thereby reducing the amount of pollutants that are produced. Some countries now give tax incentives to encourage the shift to hybrid vehicles. Even with this shift, motor vehicles in general pose major environmental hazard.

There are still the issues of water pollution from runoff oil or fluids or chemicals that manage to sip into the waterways; with the increasing number of vehicles on the road, noise pollution is still a major concern; and there is concern about solid waste disposal. All these problems continue to affect both ecological and health risks. Motor vehicles need to be designed more efficiently, made lighter, and resort to alternative energy sources to reduce environmental burden. Hybrid vehicles are contributing in improving environmental quality but human conscious effort to use mass transit systems and change driving habits could even help further. Countries like the United States also offer tax incentives to commuters who use mass transit systems to commute to work.

External Environment of Organization

Modern day decision-makers tend to deal with rather complicated problems that highly influence the operations of their respective organisations. This requires them to make decisions promptly and at the same time make sure that it directly deals with the issues that they are facing. They have to make sure that they make things right the first-time. One definite way of dealing with this is by consulting the general environment of the organisation. This paper intends to analyse the how the information that organisations acquire from the environment help them in keeping their operations on track. Specifically, the study will look into the use of the external environment. Close consideration will look on the situation regarding the company's competitors, economic system, general society, business environment, and the legal situation that may or may not have an effect on their industry. Moreover, specific companies will also be taken into consideration to show how theories are implemented in real world settings. The companies that will be observed will be those involved in the IT and computer industry. The arguments and observations that will be provided in this paper are going to be based on academic and scholarly journals directly related to management and operational administration of organisations.

Organization and its Environment

Understanding the environment of the organisation offers the key to possibly uncovering the needed developmental changes that the organisation requires. The following discussions will provide a brief description on the internal and external environment and their importance for the modern organisation.

Internal Environment

The internal environment encompasses the company's "physical and cultural aspects" that have major implications to the processes and executive development of the organisation., 2001, 801) With this in mind, the internal environment tends to tread the trails but not limited to human resource management concepts. In the study of (2003, 491), she indicated that the internal environment is rather important in the context of strategic planning for the organisation. She noted that in using the information relating to the internal environment, allows the decision makers of the organisation to become conscious of the qualities of work on how it is structured and carried out. In this respect, the said study has manifested the very elements that make up the internal environment of the organisation. These include the skill-level of the employees as well as the tacit and explicit knowledge displayed within the organisation. Another element included is the attributes of "the objects to which the work is performed," as well as the implications of the relationships held within the organisation.

Based on this definition, one could surmise that the general elements held in the internal environment of the organisation include the knowledge management practiced which also complements the general culture held by the personnel. In following this line of logic, this does have some significant implications on the decision making of the company.

External Environment

Among with the internal environment of the firm, the external environment has similarly been marked as one of the major elements that influence the firm's operations. As seen in the article of (2001, 38) the external environment is seen to be marred with uncertainty. This highlights the need for understanding this environment not only for the reason of having the needed data as a security blanket but to minimise the risk offered by uncertainty posed by the external environment. The following study will provide a set of observations based on existing literature relating to the external environment of the organisation.

Competitors

The modern setting where businesses conduct their operations tends to be marked with a level of viciousness where competing organisations tends to drive each other to the brink of leaving the market or even filing a claim of bankruptcy. As indicated in the seminal organisational theory of Porter, merely identifying the competitors of a particular company is not enough. (2000, 103) To a certain extent, knowing the other players in the industry is merely a part of the process. A more important factor in this endeavour is to distinguish the level of rivalry present in the marker.

The intensity of the rivalries among the players in the industry tends to provide certain indications on the kind of organisations a particular firm is against. For instance, if an organisation finds out that the level of rivalry is considerably intense, then the firm may be battling against competitors with resource capabilities equal or greater from their own. This is especially true in instances where the number of player similarly increases. r, 2000, 104) The number of competitors tends to diminish the felt demand on the product or services offered by the organisation. However, if the firm finds out that the intensity of rivalry is rather unstable and unpredictable, then it could be an indicator of diversity in the competitors present in the industry.

Specifically, difference in the strategies held by each organisation and the drive for far greater modes of differentiation tends to be present in the players in the industry.

In looking at the discussions above, the importance of knowing the competitors and the level of rivalry is manifested in the market and the consequent industry of the firm. The bottom-line is that modern day competition among modern-day organisations tends to seek better value for their resources. Companies will find ways to establish strong differentiation for the main service or product that they offer along with other means of getting a fair (or otherwise) advantage over the other players in the industry.

Economics

The context of economics in an organisation tends to emulate the classical economic concept defined as the production, distribution, and consumption of resourcesic, 2006, 575) There has been a considerable number studies that has indicated the effects of the changes in the economic systems in the business sector. For instance, there is the study of (2002, 953) indicates that the economic systems of certain locales tend to provide the business sector one of the most indispensable elements of trade: coordination. Specifically, this phenomenon issues the necessary requirement of coordination among the different social institutions that directly and indirectly affect the organisation. The said author also indicated that a rather stable economic system provides the business sector the protection they need from the adverse implications of a considerably variable one.

Other studies also indicated that the economic system may inadvertently influence the internal environment of the organisation. An earlier study provided by (1994, 1) indicated that the market economy of China has provided certain implications to the state-based companies' human resource management Practices. Specific changes include those from the centralised planning to a more strategic one as the shift towards global trade ensues. Moreover, the reforms made in the said country have created a "dramatic growth" on the processes of the state-owned and private companies in the country. Seeing the points of these discussions, it appears that a thriving economic system provides more opportunities for businesses to flourish and eventually prosper.

Society (Social System)

In considering the issue of social systems, the context of culture prevails over the existing organisational studies. Specifically, the influential theory of Hofstede highlights the need to know of the culture of a particular location to create situation that will complement it with the goals of the organisation. The study of (1996, 753) indicated that the businesses in a particular country tends to manifest a high level of economic efficiency if the management processes implemented in each organisations emulate and goes together with the national culture.

In looking at the discussions above, it appears that companies have another important factor to consider especially if they intend to expand their operations in an international level. To this extent, the company could opt to seek markets where they could operate effectively without incurring major changes in the core business processes or they could display flexibility and adapt their system to the culture of the market. At any rate, if improvements in the operations of the organisation are fervently sought by a particular firm, they must ensure that their principles, policies and goals complement the national culture.

Business Exchange

The issue of business exchange covers the financial element of the external environment. Specifically, the monetary system is taken into consideration. Some organisational studies have connected the monetary system of a particular state to have a major effect on the accumulation of capital of the organisations. To illustrate, the study of Beuving (2006, 324) indicated that the presence of opportunities in accumulating capital in the Lebanese setting has triggered an increase in the effectiveness in the second-hand car trade. In the same manner, the rather rich set of opportunities has created a business pattern unique on this market niche.

Moreover, an earlier study made bon (1982, 48) noted that the issue of capital accumulation does not only affect a particular organisation. The social structure, in the same way, has also been influenced in the context of Indonesia. As the said study claimed, it has contributed greatly for the transformation of Indonesia in the later part of the 1980s and the earlier part of the 1990s. The creation of opportunities at this juncture eventually made the state dominantly capitalist in nature.

Looking at the cited studies in this section, the presence of opportunities for capital accumulation allows the organisation to improve eventually. Nevertheless, this assumption also requires organisations to actually 'take advantage of the opportunity provided for by business exchange that complement their operations.

Political Situation

The political situation of an external environment tends to similarly have some implications in the business subjected to it. One such implication is highlighted in the studyeiga (2006, 1379) which stated that political instability makes it more likely for the external environment to incur a rather high rate of inflation. This means that prices of the products and services of the businesses tends to be higher than they can actually spend. Thus, this means that whenever businesses acquire the raw materials that they need, they automatically incur loss. Though they could pass this loss to the end-users of their product or service, the increased price of the major commodities that they are selling tends to diminish the demands and possibly limit the actual consumption of the public given the issue of high price as deterrence.

In specific studies, (2000, 43) noted that the political instability in Turkey was the main factor that triggered a crisis in the business sector of the country. This also took place in the (2000, 93) indicating that Indonesia's SME sector have acquired considerable damage as the volatility of the political situation in the country has emerged in the later part of 1997.

Seeing the discussions above, it appears that the state have similarly been deemed as an important part of the external environment of any organization. The policies made and ratified by the government that the business sector may find either unfavourable or otherwise share this effect on specific organisations. Moreover, assuming that the policies ratified by the government are highly favourable to organisations, then the issue of stability tends to cancel it out. The changeability of the leadership or type of government tends to manifest some level of doubt on the part of the investor or owner may have doubts as to whether the operations of the business are safe in the said environment.

The Computer Industry

The computer industry has become one of the most flourishing industries in the world. The study has chosen this industry for the reason that the companies have the propensity to change market as they want and not to mention play at the international level. This reflects that any changes from the external environment will essentially have a effect on their operations.

The Case of IBM

IBM is one of the pioneers in the IT industry, particularly in terms of manufacturing hardware. In the early part of the 1990s, they have experienced considerable losses in business opportunities from their German counterparts 2006, 389) As it turned out, the German government have made attempts to create a policy that will collect information in their own markets. IBM has not foreseen the possibility that these ratified policies have allowed German agencies to inadvertently eavesdrop on the communication lines of the company. Thus, this set of sensitive information is leaked to their competitors in the German market. As a result, significant loses has been incurred in terms of the business opportunities of the company.

Circumstances in Microsoft

The issue relating to Microsoft is that its operations in the United States have gone against the Anti-trust law of the country. (2002, 65) provided a detailed discussion on the case. The said article noted that Microsoft was pursued by the American government because of their supposed monopolistic hold on the operating system industry. Specifically, the Windows operating system was held in question. The company contended that the said actions it took were a product of competition not of any other intentions held in bad faith.

The problem, according too (2002, 66) is that the actions manifested by the government is slightly tantamount to harassment. It was closely held that the company was merely holding on and controlling a large market and not actually holding a monopoly over the industry.

In this sense, it is seen that Microsoft has considerably been affected by the laws protecting thew land. The context on this issue is that companies tend to vie for supremacy of the market. However, with the governments seemingly proctoring the principles of fair competition and fair trade will inevitably find fault whenever a firm succeeds over its competitors. The case of Microsoft highlights the issue on how the government should draw the line on these types of situations. To a certain extent, the Microsoft case may have become a deterrent for successful companies in holding on and controlling large markets.

Conclusion

In order for real development to take place, change must also ensue. The discussions above have highlighted the need of organizations to monitor changes in the external environment given that these elements provide the greatest implications. Changes in the economy, society, legal, and political environments essentially falls under the changes of the external environment. The practitioner-based research cited above has manifested the need to recognise the changes required of the external environment such that they are able to adapt flexibly and meet its demands. A perceptive limitation of this study is the use of rather large corporations like Microsoft and IBM, which indicate that they have the capability to rebound on the possible adverse implications provided by the fluctuations in the external environment. This also means that the discussions presented above may less likely to be applicable for smaller companies in the industry. At any rate, the bottom-line of the discussions above is to espouse vigilance on the part of the organisation regarding their general environment. On the whole, one must recognise that the operations of the organisation require a balance of consideration on the overall environment, both internal and external. A clear understanding of the external environment will allow the organisation to manipulate the internal environment to deal with the changes brought upon them. At this point, established theories could help but one must realise that at some point, they don't complement the respective situations where companies find themselves. Theories only provide some sort of guidelines as opposed to offering a panacea to the issues relating to the external environment.

Social Responsibilities of Management

The term social responsibilities can be defined as the obligation of management towards the society and others concerned.

Reason for Social Responsibilities: Business enterprises are creatures of society and should respond to the demands of society. If the management does not react to changes in social demands, the society will either force them to do so through laws or will not permit the enterprise to survive. Therefore the longterm interests of business are best served when management assume social responsibilities. The image of business organization liked with the quality of its products and customer service and the extent to which it fulfils the expectations of owners, employees, consumers, government and the community at large. For longterm success it matters a great deal if the firm has a favourable image in the public mind. Every business enterprise is a organ of society and its activities have impact on the social scene. Therefore, it is important for management to consider whether their policies and actions are likely to promote the public good, advances the basic values of society, and constitute to its stability, strength and harmony.

Increasing concern for the social responsibility of management, it is now recognized that besides taking care of the financial interest of owners, managers of business firms must also take into account the interest of various other groups such as employees, consumers, the government and the community as a whole. These interested groups are directly or indirectly affected by the pursuit of business activities and they are the stake-holders of the business enterprise.

Responsibility towards owners: The primary responsibilities of management is to assure a fair and reasonable rate of return on capital and fair return on investment can be determined on the basis of difference in the risks of business in different fields of activity. With the growth of business the shareholders can also expect appreciation in the value of their capital.

Responsibility towards employees: Management responsibility towards employees relate to the fair wages and salaries, satisfactory work environment, labour management relations and employee welfare. Fair wages should be fixed in the light of labour productivity, the prevailing wage rates in the same or neighbouring areas and relative importance of jobs. Managers salaries and allowances are expected to be linked with their responsibility, initiative and skill. But the spread between minimum wages and highest salaries should be reasonable. Employees are expected to build up and maintain harmonious relationships between superior and subordinates. Another aspect of responsibility towards employees is the provision of welfare amenities like safety and security of working conditions, medical facilities, housing, canteen, leave and retirement benefits.

Responsibility towards consumers: In a competitive market, serving consumers is supposed to be a prime concern of management. But in reality perfect competition does not prevail in all product markets. In the event of shortage of supply there is no automatic correction. Besides consumers are often victims of unfair trade practices and unethical conduct of business. Consumer interests are thus protected to some extent with laws and pressure of organized consumer groups. Management should anticipate these developments, satisfy consumer needs and protect consumer interests. Goods must be of appropriate standard and quality and be available in adequate quantities at reasonable prices. Management should avoid resorting to hoarding or creating artificial scarcity as well as false and misleading advertisements.

Responsibility towards the Governments: As a part of their social responsibility, management must conduct business affair in lawful manner, honestly pay all the taxes and dues, and should not corrupt public officials for selfish ends. Business activities must also confirm to the economic and social policies of the government.

Responsibility towards the community and society: The socially responsible role of management in relation to the community are expected to be revealed by its policies with respect to the employment of handicapped persons, and weaker sections of the community, environmental protection, pollution control, setting up industries in backward areas, and providing relief to the victims of natural calamities etc.

Corporate Social Responsibility

Corporate social responsibility (CSR), also known as corporate responsibility, corporate citizenship, responsible business, sustainable responsible business (SRB), or corporate social performance, is a form of corporate self-regulation integrated into a business model. Ideally, CSR policy would function as a built-in, self-regulating mechanism whereby business would monitor and ensure its adherence to law, ethical standards, and international norms. Business would embrace responsibility for the impact of their activities on the environment, consumers, employees, communities, stakeholders and all other members of the public sphere. Furthermore, business would proactively promote the public interest by encouraging community growth and development, and voluntarily eliminating practices that harm the public sphere, regardless of legality. Essentially, CSR is the deliberate inclusion of public interest into corporate decision-making, and the honoring of a triple bottom line: People, Planet, Profit.

The practice of CSR is subject to much debate and criticism. Proponents argue that there is a strong business case for CSR, in that corporations benefit in multiple ways by operating with a perspective broader and longer than their own immediate, short-term profits. Critics argue that CSR distracts from the fundamental economic role of businesses; others argue that it is nothing more than superficial window-dressing; others yet argue that it is an attempt to pre-empt the role of governments as a watchdog over powerful multinational corporations.

Development

Business ethics is one of the forms of applied ethics that examines ethical principles and moral or ethical problems that can arise in a business environment.

In the increasingly conscience-focused marketplaces of the 21st century, the demand for more ethical business processes and actions (known as ethicism) is increasing. Simultaneously, pressure is applied on industry to improve business ethics through new public initiatives and laws (e.g. higher UK road tax for higher-emission vehicles).

Business ethics can be both a normative and a descriptive discipline. As a corporate practice and a career specialization, the field is primarily normative. In academia, descriptive approaches are also taken. The range and quantity of business ethical issues reflects the degree to which business is perceived to be at odds with non-economic social values. Historically, interest in business ethics accelerated dramatically during the 1980s and 1990s, both within major corporations and within academia. For example, today most major corporate websites lay emphasis on commitment to promoting non-economic social values under a variety of headings (e.g. ethics codes, social responsibility charters). In some cases, corporations have re-branded their core values in the light of business ethical considerations (e.g. BP's "beyond petroleum" environmental tilt).

The term CSR came in to common use in the early 1970s although it was seldom abbreviated. The term stakeholder, meaning those impacted by an organization's activities, was used to describe corporate owners beyond shareholders as a result of an influential book by R Freeman in 1984.

Whilst there is no recognized standard for CSR, public sector organizations (the United Nations for example) adhere to the Triple Bottom Line (TBL). It is widely accepted that CSR adheres to similar principles but with no formal act of legislation. The UN has developed the Principles for Responsible Investment as guidelines for investing entities.

Approaches

Some commentators have identified a difference between the Continental European and the Anglo-Saxon approaches to CSR. And even within Europe the discussion about CSR is very heterogeneous.

An approach for CSR that is becoming more widely accepted is community-based development projects, such as the Shell Foundation's involvement in the Flower Valley, South Africa. Here they have set up an Early Learning Centre to help educate the community's children, as well as develop new skills for the adults. Marks and Spencer is also active in this community through the building of a trade network with the community-guaranteeing regular fair trade purchases. Often alternative approaches to this is the establishment of education facilities for adults, as well as HIV/AIDS education programmes. The majority of these CSR projects are established in Africa. A more common approach of CSR is through the giving of aid to local organizations and impoverished communities in developing countries. Some organizations do not like this approach as it does not help build on the skills of the local people, whereas community-based development generally leads to more sustainable development.

Procurement of Fair Trade tea and coffee has been adopted by various businesses: KPMG CSR manager commented, "Fairtrade fits very strongly into our commitment to our communities."

Social Accounting, Auditing, and Reporting

Taking responsibility for its impact on society means in the first instance that a company accounts for its actions. Social accounting, a concept describing the communication of social and environmental effects of a company's economic actions to particular interest groups within society and to society at large, is thus an important element of CSR.

A number of reporting guidelines or standards have been developed to serve as frameworks for social accounting, auditing and reporting:

- Account Ability's AA1000 standard, based on John Elkington's triple bottom line (3BL) reporting
- Accounting for Sustainability's Connected Reporting Framework.
- Global Reporting Initiative's Sustainability Reporting Guidelines
- Good Corporation's Standard developed in association with the Institute of Business Ethics
- Green Globe Certification/Standard
- Social Accountability International's SA8000 standard
- The ISO 14000 environmental management standard
- The United Nations Global Compact promotes companies reporting in the format of a Communication on Progress (COP). A COP report describes the company's implementation of the Compact's ten universal principles.
- The United Nations Intergovernmental Working Group of Experts on International Standards of Accounting and Reporting (ISAR) provides voluntary technical guidance on eco-efficiency indicators, corporate responsibility reporting and corporate governance disclosure.
- Verite's Monitoring Guidelines: The FTSE Group publishes the FTSE4Good Index, an evaluation of CSR performance of companies.

In some nations legal requirements for social accounting, auditing and reporting exist (e.g. in the French bilan social), though agreement on meaningful measurements of social and environmental performance is difficult. Many companies now produce externally audited annual reports that cover Sustainable Development and CSR issues ("Triple Bottom Line Reports"), but the reports vary widely in format, style, and evaluation methodology (even within the same industry). Critics dismiss these reports as lip service, citing examples such as Enron's yearly "Corporate Responsibility Annual Report" and tobacco corporations' social reports.

Potential Business Benefits

The scale and nature of the benefits of CSR for an organization can vary depending on the nature of the enterprise, and are difficult to quantify, though there is a large body of literature exhorting business to adopt measures beyond financial ones (e.g., Deming's Fourteen Points, balanced scorecards). Orlitzky, Schmidt, and Rynes found a correlation between social/environmental performance and financial performance. However, businesses may not be looking at short-run financial returns when developing their CSR strategy.

The definition of CSR used within an organization can vary from the strict "stakeholder impacts" definition used by many CSR advocates and will often include charitable efforts and volunteering. CSR may be based within the human resources, business development or public relations departments of an organisation, or may be given a separate unit reporting to the CEO or in some cases directly to the board. Some companies may implement CSR-type values without a clearly defined team or programme. The business case for CSR within a company will likely rest on one or more of these arguments:

Human Resources

A CSR programme can be an aid to recruitment and retention, particularly within the competitive graduate student market. Potential recruits often ask about a firm's CSR policy during an interview, and having a comprehensive policy can give an advantage. CSR can also help improve the perception of a company among its staff, particularly when staff can become involved through payroll giving, fundraising activities or community volunteering.

Risk Management

Managing risk is a central part of many corporate strategies. Reputations that take decades to build up can be ruined in hours through incidents such as corruption scandals or environmental accidents. These can also draw unwanted attention from regulators, courts, governments and media. Building a genuine culture of 'doing the right thing' within a corporation can offset these risks.

Brand Differentiation

In crowded marketplaces, companies strive for a unique selling proposition that can separate them from the competition in the minds of consumers. CSR can play a role in building customer loyalty based on distinctive ethical values. Several major brands, such as The Cooperative Group, The Body Shop and American Apparel are built on ethical values. Business service organizations can benefit too from building a reputation for integrity and best practice.

License to Operate

Corporations are keen to avoid interference in their business through taxation or regulations. By taking substantive voluntary steps, they can persuade governments and the wider public that they are taking issues such as health and safety, diversity, or the environment seriously as good corporate citizens with respect to labour standards and impacts on the environment.

Criticisms and Concerns

Critics of CSR as well as proponents debate a number of concerns related to it. These include CSR's relationship to the fundamental purpose and nature of business and questionable motives for engaging in CSR, including concerns about insincerity and hypocrisy.

CSR and the Nature of Business

Milton Friedman and others have argued that a corporation's purpose is to maximize returns to its shareholders, and that since (in their view), only people can have social responsibilities, corporations are only responsible to their shareholders and not to society as a whole. Although they accept that corporations should obey the laws of the countries within which they work, they assert that corporations have no other obligation to society. Some people perceive CSR as incongruent with the very nature and purpose of business, and indeed a hindrance to free trade. Those who assert that CSR is incongruent with capitalism and are in favour of neoliberalism argue that improvements in health, longevity and/or infant mortality have been created by economic growth attributed to free enterprise.

Critics of this argument perceive neoliberalism as opposed to the well-being of society and a hindrance to human freedom. They claim that the type of capitalism practiced in many developing countries is a form of economic and cultural imperialism, noting that these countries usually have fewer labour protections, and thus their citizens are at a higher risk of exploitation by multinational corporations.

A wide variety of individuals and organizations operate in between these poles. For example, the REALeadership Alliance asserts that the business of leadership (be it corporate or otherwise) is to change the world for the better. Many religious and cultural traditions hold that the economy exists to serve human beings, so all economic entities have an obligation to society (e.g., cf. Economic Justice for All). Moreover, many CSR proponents point out that CSR can significantly improve long-term corporate profitability because it reduces risks and inefficiencies while offering a host of potential benefits such as enhanced brand reputation and employee engagement.

CSR and Questionable Motives

Some critics believe that CSR programs are undertaken by companies such as British American Tobacco (BAT), the petroleum giant BP (well-known for its high-profile advertising campaigns on environmental aspects of its operations), and McDonald's to distract the public from ethical questions posed by their core operations.

They argue that some corporations start CSR programs for the commercial benefit they enjoy through raising their reputation with the public or with government. They suggest that corporations which exist solely to maximize profits are unable to advance the interests of society as a whole.

Another concern is when companies claim to promote CSR and be committed to Sustainable Development whilst simultaneously engaging in harmful business practices. For example, since the 1970s, the McDonald's Corporation's association with Ronald McDonald House has been viewed as CSR and relationship marketing. More recently, as CSR has become mainstream, the company has beefed up its CSR programs related to its labour, environmental and other practices All the same, in McDonald's Restaurants v Morris & Steel, Lord Justices Pill, May and Keane ruled that it was fair comment to say that McDonald's employees worldwide 'do badly in terms of pay and conditions' and true that 'if one eats enough McDonald's food, one's diet may well become high in fat etc., with the very real risk of heart disease.'

Shell has a much-publicised CSR policy and was a pioneer in triple bottom line reporting, but this did not prevent the 2004 scandal concerning its misreporting of oil reserves, which seriously damaged its reputation and led to charges of hypocrisy. Since then, the Shell Foundation has become involved in many projects across the world, including a partnership with Marks and Spencer (UK) in three flower and fruit growing communities across Africa.

Critics concerned with corporate hypocrisy and insincerity generally suggest that better governmental and international regulation and enforcement, rather than voluntary measures, are necessary to ensure that companies behave in a socially responsible manner.

Motivations

Corporations are motivated to adopt CSR practices by several different factors.

Ethical Consumerism

The rise in popularity of ethical consumerism over the last two decades can be linked to the rise of CSR. As global population increases, so does the pressure on limited natural resources required to meet rising consumer demand (Grace and Cohen 2005, 147). Industrialization in many developing countries is booming as a result of technology and globalization. Consumers are becoming more aware of the environmental and social implications of their day-to-day consumer decisions and are beginning to make purchasing decisions related to their environmental and ethical concerns. However, this practice is far from consistent or universal.

Globalization and Market Forces

As corporations pursue growth through globalization, they have encountered new challenges that impose limits to their growth and potential profits. Government regulations, tariffs, environmental restrictions and varying standards of what constitutes labour exploitation are problems that can cost organizations millions of dollars. Some view ethical issues as simply a costly hindrance. Some companies use CSR methodologies as a strategic tactic to gain public support for their presence in global markets, helping them sustain a competitive advantage by using their social contributions to provide a subconscious level of advertising. (Fry, Keim, Meiners 1986, 105) Global competition places particular pressure on multinational corporations to examine not only their own labour practices, but those of their entire supply chain, from a CSR perspective.

Social Awareness and Education

The role among corporate stakeholders to work collectively to pressure corporations is changing. Shareholders and investors themselves, through socially responsible investing are exerting pressure on corporations to behave responsibly. Non-governmental organizations are also taking an increasing role, leveraging the power of the media and the Internet to increase their scrutiny and collective activism around corporate behaviour. Through education and dialogue, the development of community in holding businesses responsible for their actions is growing (Roux 2007).

Ethics Training

The rise of ethics training inside corporations, some of it required by government regulation, is another driver credited with changing the behaviour and culture of corporations. The aim of such training is to help employees make ethical decisions when the answers are unclear. Tullberg believes that humans are built with the capacity to cheat and manipulate, a view taken from (Trivers 1971, 1985), hence the need for learning normative values and rules in human behaviour (Tullberg 1996). The most direct benefit is reducing the likelihood of "dirty hands" (Grace and Cohen 2005), fines and damaged reputations for breaching laws or moral norms. Organizations also see secondary benefit in increasing employee loyalty and pride in the organization. Caterpillar and Best Buy are examples of organizations that have taken such steps (Thilmany 2007).

Increasingly, companies are becoming interested in processes that can add visibility to their CSR policies and activities. One method that is gaining increasing popularity is the use of well-grounded training programs, where CSR is a major issue, and business simulations can play a part in this.

Laws and Regulation

Another driver of CSR is the role of independent mediators, particularly the government, in ensuring that corporations are prevented from harming the broader social good, including people and the environment. CSR critics such as Robert Reich argue that governments should set the agenda for social responsibility by the way of laws and regulation that will allow a business to conduct themselves responsibly.

The issues surrounding government regulation pose several problems. Regulation in itself is unable to cover every aspect in detail of a corporation's operations. This leads to burdensome legal processes bogged down in interpretations of the law and debatable grey areas (Sacconi 2004). General Electric is an example of a corporation that has failed to clean up the Hudson River after contaminating it with organic pollutants.

The company continues to argue via the legal process on assignment of liability, while the cleanup remains stagnant. (Sullivan & Schiafo 2005). The second issue is the financial burden that regulation can place on a nation's economy. This view shared by Bulkeley, who cites the Australian federal government's actions to avoid compliance with the Kyoto Protocol in 1997, on the concerns of economic loss and national interest.

The Australian government took the position that signing the Kyoto Pact would have caused more significant economic losses for Australia than for any other OECD nation. Critics of CSR also point out that organisations pay taxes to government to ensure that society and the environment are not adversely affected by business activities.

Denmark made a law on CSR. 16 December 2008, the Danish parliament adopted a bill making it mandatory for the largest Danish companies, investors and state owned companies to include information on corporate social responsibility (CSR) in their annual financial reports. The reporting requirements became effective on 1 January 2009.

The information shall include:

- information on the companies' policies for CSR or socially responsible investments (SRI)
- information on how such policies are implemented in practice and

- information on what results have been obtained so far and managements expectations for the future with regard to CSR/SRI.

CSR/SRI is still voluntary in Denmark, but if a company has no policy on this they must state information to that effect explicitly in their annual financial report.

Crises and their Consequences

Often it takes a crisis to precipitate attention to CSR. One of the most active stands against environmental management is the CERES Principles that resulted after the Exxon Valdez incident in Alaska in 1989 (Grace and Cohen 2006). Other examples include the lead poisoning paint used by toy giant Mattel, which required a recall of millions of toys globally and caused the company to initiate new risk management and quality control processes. In another example, Magellan Metals in the West Australian town of Esperance was responsible for lead contamination killing thousands of birds in the area. The company had to cease business immediately and work with independent regulatory bodies to execute a cleanup.

Stakeholder Priorities

Increasingly, corporations are motivated to become more socially responsible because their most important stakeholders expect them to understand and address the social and community issues that are relevant to them. Understanding what causes are important to employees is usually the first priority because of the many interrelated business benefits that can be derived from increased employee engagement (i.e. more loyalty, improved recruitment, increased retention, higher productivity, and so on). Key external stakeholders include customers, consumers, investors (particularly institutional investors, regulators, academics, and the media).

Overview of Issues in Business Ethics

General Business Ethics:

- This part of business ethics overlaps with the philosophy of business, one of the aims of which is to determine the fundamental purposes of a company. If a company's main purpose is to maximize the returns to its shareholders, then it should be seen as unethical for a company to consider the interests and rights of anyone else.

- Corporate social responsibility or CSR: an umbrella term under which the ethical rights and duties existing between companies and society is debated.
- Issues regarding the moral rights and duties between a company and its shareholders: fiduciary responsibility, stakeholder concept v. shareholder concept.
- Ethical issues concerning relations between different companies: e.g. hostile take-overs, industrial espionage.
- Leadership issues: corporate governance.
- Political contributions made by corporations.
- Law reform, such as the ethical debate over introducing a crime of corporate manslaughter.
- The misuse of corporate ethics policies as marketing instruments.

Ethics of Accounting Information

- Creative accounting, earnings management, misleading financial analysis.
- Insider trading, securities fraud, bucket shops, forex scams: concerns (criminal) manipulation of the financial markets.
- Executive compensation: concerns excessive payments made to corporate CEO's and top management.
- Bribery, kickbacks, facilitation payments: while these may be in the (short-term) interests of the company and its shareholders, these practices may be anti-competitive or offend against the values of society.

Ethics of Human Resource Management

The ethics of human resource management (HRM) covers those ethical issues arising around the employer-employee relationship, such as the rights and duties owed between employer and employee.

- Discrimination issues include discrimination on the bases of age (ageism), gender, race, religion, disabilities, weight and attractiveness.

- Issues arising from the traditional view of relationships between employers and employees, also known as At-will employment.
- Issues surrounding the representation of employees and the democratization of the workplace: union busting, strike breaking.
- Issues affecting the privacy of the employee: workplace surveillance, drug testing.
- Issues affecting the privacy of the *employer*: whistle-blowing.
- Issues relating to the fairness of the employment contract and the balance of power between employer and employee: slavery, indentured servitude, employment law.
- Occupational safety and health.

All of the above are also related to the hiring and firing of employees. An employee or future employee can not be hired or fired based on race, age, gender, religion, or any other disciminatory act.

Ethics of Sales and Marketing

Marketing, which goes beyond the mere provision of information about (and access to) a product, may seek to manipulate our values and behaviour.

To some extent society regards this as acceptable, but where is the ethical line to be drawn? Marketing ethics overlaps strongly with media ethics, because marketing makes heavy use of media. However, media ethics is a much larger topic and extends outside business ethics.

- Pricing: price fixing, price discrimination, price skimming.
- Anti-competitive practices: these include but go beyond pricing tactics to cover issues such as manipulation of loyalty and supply chains.
- Specific marketing strategies: greenwash, bait and switch, shill, viral marketing, spam (electronic), pyramid scheme, planned obsolescence.
- Content of advertisements: attack ads, subliminal messages, sex in advertising, products regarded as immoral or harmful
- Children and marketing: marketing in schools.
- Black markets, grey markets.

Ethics of Production

This area of business ethics usually deals with the duties of a company to ensure that products and production processes do not cause harm. Some of the more acute dilemmas in this area arise out of the fact that there is usually a degree of danger in any product or production process and it is difficult to define a degree of permissibility, or the degree of permissibility may depend on the changing state of preventative technologies or changing social perceptions of acceptable risk.

- Defective, addictive and inherently dangerous products and services (e.g. tobacco, alcohol, weapons, motor vehicles, chemical manufacturing, bungee jumping).
- Ethical relations between the company and the environment: pollution, environmental ethics, carbon emissions trading
- Ethical problems arising out of new technologies: genetically modified food, mobile phone radiation and health.
- Product testing ethics: animal rights and animal testing, use of economically disadvantaged groups (such as students) as test objects.

Ethics of Intellectual Property, Knowledge and Skills

Knowledge and skills are valuable but not easily "ownable" as objects. Nor is it obvious who has the greater rights to an idea: the company who trained the employee, or the employee themselves? The country in which the plant grew, or the company which discovered and developed the plant's medicinal potential? As a result, attempts to assert ownership and ethical disputes over ownership arise.

- Patent infringement, copyright infringement, trademark infringement.
- Misuse of the intellectual property systems to stifle competition: patent misuse, copyright misuse, patent troll, submarine patent.
- Even the notion of intellectual property itself has been criticised on ethical grounds.
- Employee raiding: the practice of attracting key employees away from a competitor to take unfair advantage of the knowledge or skills they may possess.

- The practice of employing all the most talented people in a specific field, regardless of need, in order to prevent any competitors employing them.
- Bioprospecting and biopiracy.
- Business intelligence and industrial espionage.

Ethics and Technology The computer and the World Wide Web are two of the most significant inventions of the twentieth century. There are many ethical issues that arise from this technology. It is easy to gain access to information. This leads to data mining, workplace monitoring, and privacy invasion. Medical technology has improved as well. Pharmaceutical companies have the technology to produce life saving drugs. These drugs are protected by patents and there are no generic drugs available. This raises many ethical questions.

International Business Ethics and Ethics of Economic Systems

The issues here are grouped together because they involve a much wider, global view on business ethical matters.

International Business Ethics

While business ethics emerged as a field in the 1970s, international business ethics did not emerge until the late 1990s, looking back on the international developments of that decade. Many new practical issues arose out of the international context of business. Theoretical issues such as cultural relativity of ethical values receive more emphasis in this field. Other, older issues can be grouped here as well. Issues and subfields include:

- The search for universal values as a basis for international commercial behaviour.
- Comparison of business ethical traditions in different countries. Also on the basis of their respective GDP and [Corruption rankings].
- Comparison of business ethical traditions from various religious perspectives.
- Ethical issues arising out of international business transactions; e.g. bioprospecting and biopiracy in the pharmaceutical industry; the fair trade movement; transfer pricing.
- Issues such as globalization and cultural imperialism.

- Varying global standards-e.g. the use of child labour.
- The way in which multinationals take advantage of international differences, such as outsourcing production (e.g. clothes) and services (e.g. call centres) to low-wage countries.
- The permissibility of international commerce with pariah states.

Foreign countries often use dumping as a competitive threat, selling products at prices lower than their normal value. This can lead to problems in domestic markets. It becomes difficult for these markets to compete with the pricing set by foreign markets. In 2009, the International Trade Commission has been researching anti-dumping laws. Dumping is often seen as an ethical issue, as larger companies are taking advantage of other less economically advanced companies.

Ethics of Economic Systems

This vaguely defined area, perhaps not part of but only related to business ethics, is where business ethicists venture into the fields of political economy and political philosophy, focusing on the rights and wrongs of various systems for the distribution of economic benefits. John Rawls and Robert Nozick are both notable contributors.

Theoretical Issues in Business Ethics

Conflicting Interests

Business ethics can be examined from various new perspectives, including the perspective of the employee, the commercial enterprise, and society as a whole. Very often, situations arise in which there is conflict between one or more of the parties, such that serving the interest of one party is a detriment to the other(s). For example, a particular outcome might be good for the employee, whereas, it would be bad for the company, society, or vice versa. Some ethicists (e.g., Henry Sidgwick) see the principal role of ethics as the harmonization and reconciliation of conflicting interests.

Ethical Issues and Approaches

Philosophers and others disagree about the purpose of a business ethic in society. For example, some suggest that the principal purpose of a business is to maximize returns to its owners, or in the case of a publicly-traded concern, its shareholders. Thus, under this view, only those activities that increase profitability and shareholder value should be encouraged, because any others function as a tax on profits. Some believe that the only companies that are likely to survive in a competitive marketplace are those that place profit maximization above everything else. However, some point out that self-interest would still require a business to obey the law and adhere to basic moral rules, because the consequences of failing to do so could be very costly in fines, loss of licensure, or company reputation. The noted economist Milton Friedman was a leading proponent of this view.

Some take the position that organizations are not capable of moral agency. Under this, ethical behaviour is required of individual human beings, but not of the business or corporation.

Other theorists contend that a business has moral duties that extend well beyond serving the interests of its owners or stockholders, and that these duties consist of more than simply obeying the law. They believe a business has moral responsibilities to so-called stakeholders, people who have an interest in the conduct of the business, which might include employees, customers, vendors, the local community, or even society as a whole. Stakeholders can also be broken down into primary and secondary stakeholders. Primary stakeholders are people that are affected directly such as stockholders, where secondary stakeholders are people who are not affected directly such as the government. They would say that stakeholders have certain rights with regard to how the business operates, and some would suggest that this includes even rights of governance.

Some theorists have adapted social contract theory to business, whereby companies become quasi-democratic associations, and employees and other stakeholders are given voice over a company's operations. This approach has become especially popular subsequent to the revival of contract theory in political philosophy, which is largely due to John Rawls' *A Theory of Justice*, and the advent of the consensus-oriented approach to solving business problems, an aspect of the "quality movement" that emerged in the 1980s. Professors Thomas Donaldson and Thomas Dunfee proposed a version of contract theory for business, which they call Integrative Social Contracts Theory. They posit that conflicting interests are best resolved by formulating a "fair agreement" between the parties, using a combination of i) macro-principles that all rational people would agree upon as universal principles, and, ii) micro-principles formulated by actual agreements among the interested parties. Critics say the proponents of contract theories miss a central point, namely, that a business is someone's property and not a mini-state or a means of distributing social justice.

Ethical issues can arise when companies must comply with multiple and sometimes conflicting legal or cultural standards, as in the case of multinational companies that operate in countries with varying practices. The question arises, for example, ought a company to obey the laws of its home country, or should it follow the less stringent laws of the developing country in which it does business? To illustrate, United States law forbids companies from paying bribes either domestically or overseas; however, in other parts of the world, bribery is a customary, accepted way of doing business. Similar problems can occur with regard to child labour, employee safety, work hours, wages, discrimination, and environmental protection laws.

It is sometimes claimed that a Gresham's law of ethics applies in which bad ethical practices drive out good ethical practices. It is claimed that in a competitive business environment, those companies that survive are the ones that recognize that their only role is to maximize profits.

Business Ethics in the Field

Corporate Ethics Policies

As part of more comprehensive compliance and ethics programs, many companies have formulated internal policies pertaining to the ethical conduct of employees. These policies can be simple exhortations in broad, highly-generalized language (typically called a corporate ethics statement), or they can be more detailed policies, containing specific behavioural requirements (typically called corporate ethics codes). They are generally meant to identify the company's expectations of workers and to offer guidance on handling some of the more common ethical problems that might arise in the course of doing business. It is hoped that having such a policy will lead to greater ethical awareness, consistency in application, and the avoidance of ethical disasters.

An increasing number of companies also requires employees to attend seminars regarding business conduct, which often include discussion of the company's policies, specific case studies, and legal requirements. Some companies even require their employees to sign agreements stating that they will abide by the company's rules of conduct.

Many companies are assessing the environmental factors that can lead employees to engage in unethical conduct. A competitive business environment may call for unethical behaviour. Lying has become expected in fields such as trading. An example of this are the issues surrounding the unethical actions of the Saloman Brothers.

Not everyone supports corporate policies that govern ethical conduct. Some claim that ethical problems are better dealt with by depending upon employees to use their own judgment.

Others believe that corporate ethics policies are primarily rooted in utilitarian concerns, and that they are mainly to limit the company's legal liability, or to curry public favour by giving the appearance of being a good corporate citizen.

Ideally, the company will avoid a lawsuit because its employees will follow the rules. Should a lawsuit occur, the company can claim that the problem would not have arisen if the employee had only followed the code properly.

Sometimes there is disconnection between the company's code of ethics and the company's actual practices. Thus, whether or not such conduct is explicitly sanctioned by management, at worst, this makes the policy duplicitous, and, at best, it is merely a marketing tool.

To be successful, most ethicists would suggest that an ethics policy should be:

- Given the unequivocal support of top management, by both word and example.
- Explained in writing and orally, with periodic reinforcement.
- Doable....something employees can both understand and perform.
- Monitored by top management, with routine inspections for compliance and improvement.
- Backed up by clearly stated consequences in the case of disobedience.
- Remain neutral and nonsexist.

Ethics Officers

Ethics officers (sometimes called "compliance" or "business conduct officers") have been appointed formally by organizations since the mid-1980s. One of the catalysts for the creation of this new role was a series of fraud, corruption and abuse scandals that afflicted the U.S. defence industry at that time. This led to the creation of the Defence Industry Initiative (DII), a pan-industry initiative to promote and ensure ethical business practices. The DII set an early benchmark for ethics management in corporations. In 1991, the Ethics & Compliance Officer Association (ECOA) — originally the Ethics Officer Association (EOA)— was founded at the Centre for Business Ethics (at Bentley College, Waltham, MA) as a professional association for those responsible for managing organizations' efforts to achieve ethical best practices. The membership grew rapidly (the ECOA now has over 1,100 members) and was soon established as an independent organization.

Another critical factor in the decisions of companies to appoint ethics/compliance officers was the passing of the Federal Sentencing Guidelines for Organizations in 1991, which set standards that organizations (large or small, commercial and non-commercial) had to follow to obtain a reduction in sentence if they should be convicted of a federal offence. Although intended to assist judges with sentencing, the influence in helping to establish best practices has been far-reaching.

In the wake of numerous corporate scandals between 2001-04 (affecting large corporations like Enron, WorldCom and Tyco), even small and medium-sized companies have begun to appoint ethics officers. They often report to the Chief Executive Officer and are responsible for assessing the ethical implications of the company's activities, making recommendations regarding the company's ethical policies, and disseminating information to employees. They are particularly interested in uncovering or preventing unethical and illegal actions. This trend is partly due to the Sarbanes-Oxley Act in the United States, which was enacted in reaction to the above scandals. A related trend is the introduction of risk assessment officers that monitor how shareholders' investments might be affected by the company's decisions.

The effectiveness of ethics officers in the marketplace is not clear. If the appointment is made primarily as a reaction to legislative requirements, one might expect the efficacy to be minimal, at least, over the short term. In part, this is because ethical business practices result from a corporate culture that consistently places value on ethical behaviour, a culture and climate that usually emanates from the top of the organization.

The mere establishment of a position to oversee ethics will most likely be insufficient to inculcate ethical behaviour: a more systemic programme with consistent support from general management will be necessary.

The foundation for ethical behaviour goes well beyond corporate culture and the policies of any given company, for it also depends greatly upon an individual's early moral training, the other institutions that affect an individual, the competitive business environment the company is in and, indeed, society as a whole.

Business Ethics as an Academic Discipline

As an academic discipline, business ethics emerged in the 1970s. Since no academic business ethics journals or conferences existed, researchers published their papers in general management outlets, and attended general conferences, such as the Academy of Management. Over time, several peer-reviewed journals appeared, and more researchers entered the field. Especially, higher interest in business topics among academics was observed after several corporate scandals in the earlier 2000s. As of 2009, sixteen academic journals devoted to various business ethics issues existed, with Journal of Business Ethics and Business Ethics Quarterly being considered the leading A+ outlets.

Religious Views on Business Ethics

The historical and global importance of religious views on business ethics is sometimes underestimated in standard introductions to business ethics. Particularly in Asia and the Middle East, religious and cultural perspectives have a strong influence on the conduct of business and the creation of business values.

Examples include:

- Islamic banking, associated with the avoidance of charging interest on loans.
- Traditional Confucian disapproval of the profit-seeking motive.
- Quaker testimony on fair dealing.

Related Disciplines

Business ethics should be distinguished from the philosophy of business, the branch of philosophy that deals with the philosophical, political, and ethical underpinnings of business and economics. Business ethics operates on the premise, for example, that the ethical operation of a private business is possible — those who dispute that premise, such as libertarian socialists, (who contend that "business ethics" is an oxymoron) do so by definition outside of the domain of business ethics proper.

The philosophy of business also deals with questions such as what, if any, are the social responsibilities of a business; management theory; theories of individualism vs. collectivism; free will among participants in the marketplace; the role of self interest; invisible hand theories; the requirements of social justice; and natural rights, especially property rights, in relation to the business enterprise.

Business ethics is also related to political economy, which is economic analysis from political and historical perspectives. Political economy deals with the distributive consequences of economic actions. It asks who gains and who loses from economic activity, and is the resultant distribution fair or just, which are central ethical issues.

Multinational Corporation

A multinational corporation (MNC) or transnational corporation (TNC), also called multinational enterprise (MNE), is a corporation or enterprise that manages production or delivers services in more than one country. It can also be referred to as an *international corporation.*

The first modern MNC is generally thought to be the Poor Knights of Christ and the Temple of Solomon, first endorsed by the pope in 1129. The key element of transnational corporations was present even back then: the British East India Company and Dutch East India Company were operating in different countries than the ones where they had their headquarters.

Nowadays many corporations have offices, branches or manufacturing plants in different countries than where their original and main headquarter is located. This is the very definition of a transnational corporation. Having multiple operation points that all respond to one headquarter.

This often results in very powerful corporations that have budgets that exceed some national GDPs. Multinational corporations can have a powerful influence in local economies as well as the world economy and play an important role in international relations and globalization. The presence of such powerful players in the world economy is reason for much controversy.

Market Imperfections

It may seem strange that a corporation can decide to do business in a different country, where it doesn't know the laws, local customs or business practices. Why is it not more efficient to combine assets of value overseas with local factors of production at lower costs by renting or selling them to local investors?

One reason is that the use of the market for coordinating the behaviour of agents located in different countries is less efficient than coordinating them by a multinational enterprise as an institution The additional costs caused by the entrance in foreign markets are of less interest for the local enterprise. According to Hymer, Kindleberger and Caves, the existence of MNEs is reasoned by structural market imperfections for final products. In Hymer's example, there are considered two firms as monopolists in their own market and isolated from competition by transportation costs and other tariff and non-tariff barriers. If these costs decrease, both are forced to competition; which will reduce their profits. The firms can maximize their joint income by a merger or acquisition which will lower the competition in the shared market. Due to the transformation of two separated companies into one MNE the pecuniary externalities are going to be internalized. However, this doesn't mean that there is an improvement for the society.

This could also be the case if there are few substitutes or limited licenses in a foreign market. The consolidation is often established by acquisition, merger or the vertical integration of the potential licensee into overseas manufacturing. This makes it easy for the MNE to enforce price discrimination schemes in various countries. Therefore Humyer considered the emergence of multinational firms as "an (negative) instrument for restraining competition between firms of different nations".

Market imperfections had been considered by Hymer as structural and caused by the deviations from perfect competition in the final product markets. Further reasons are originated from the control of proprietary technology and distribution systems, scale economies, privileged access to inputs and product differentiation. In the absence of these factors, market are fully efficient. The transaction costs theories of MNEs had been developed simultaneously and independently by McManus (1972), Buckley & Casson (1976) Brown (1976) and Hennart (1977, 1982). All these authors claimed that market imperfections are inherent conditions in markets and MNEs are institutions which try to bypass these imperfections. The imperfections in markets are natural as the neoclassical assumptions like full knowledge and enforcement don't exist in real markets.

International Power

Tax Competition

Multinational corporations have played an important role in globalization. Countries and sometimes subnational regions must compete against one another for the establishment of MNC facilities, and the subsequent tax revenue, employment, and economic activity. To compete, countries and regional political districts sometimes offer incentives to MNCs such as tax breaks, pledges of governmental assistance or improved infrastructure, or lax environmental and labour standards enforcement. This process of becoming more attractive to foreign investment can be characterized as a race to the bottom, a push towards greater autonomy for corporate bodies, or both.

However, some scholars for instance the Columbia economist Jagdish Bhagwati, have argued that multinationals are engaged in a 'race to the top.' While multinationals certainly regard a low tax burden or low labour costs as an element of comparative advantage, there is no evidence to suggest that MNCs deliberately avail themselves of lax environmental regulation or poor labour standards. As Bhagwati has pointed out, MNC profits are tied to operational efficiency, which includes a high degree of standardisation. Thus, MNCs are likely to tailor production processes in all of their operations in conformity to those jurisdictions where they operate (which will almost always include one or more of the US, Japan or EU) which has the most rigorous standards. As for labour costs, while MNCs clearly pay workers in, e.g.

Vietnam, much less than they would in the US (though it is worth noting that higher American productivity—linked to technology—means that any comparison is tricky, since in America the same company would probably hire far fewer people and automate whatever process they performed in Vietnam with manual labour), it is also the case that they tend to pay a premium of between 10% and 100% on local labour rates. Finally, depending on the nature of the MNC, investment in any country reflects a desire for a long-term return. Costs associated with establishing plant, training workers, etc., can be very high; once established in a jurisdiction, therefore, many MNCs are quite vulnerable to predatory practices such as, e.g., expropriation, sudden contract renegotiation, the arbitrary withdrawal or compulsory purchase of unnecessary 'licenses,' etc. Thus, both the negotiating power of MNCs and the supposed 'race to the bottom' may be overstated, while the substantial benefits which MNCs bring (tax revenues aside) are often understated.

Market Withdrawal

Because of their size, multinationals can have a significant impact on government policy, primarily through the threat of market withdrawal. For example, in an effort to reduce health care costs, some countries have tried to force pharmaceutical companies to license their patented drugs to local competitors for a very low fee, thereby artificially lowering the price. When faced with that threat, multinational pharmaceutical firms have simply withdrawn from the market, which often leads to limited availability of advanced drugs. In these cases, governments have been forced to back down from their efforts. Similar corporate and government confrontations have occurred when governments tried to force MNCs to make their intellectual property public in an effort to gain technology for local entrepreneurs. When companies are faced with the option of losing a core competitive technological advantage or withdrawing from a national market, they may choose the latter. This withdrawal often causes governments to change policy. Countries that have been the most successful in this type of confrontation with multinational corporations are large countries such as United States and Brazil, which have viable indigenous market competitors.

Lobbying

Multinational corporate lobbying is directed at a range of business concerns, from tariff structures to environmental regulations. There is no unified multinational perspective on any of these issues. Companies that have invested heavily in pollution control mechanisms may lobby for very tough environmental standards in an effort to force non-compliant competitors into a weaker position. Corporations lobby tariffs to restrict competition of foreign industries. For every tariff category that one multinational wants to have reduced, there is another multinational that wants the tariff raised. Even within the U.S. auto industry, the fraction of a company's imported components will vary, so some firms favour tighter import restrictions, while others favour looser ones. Says Ely Oliveira, Manager Director of the MCT/IR: This is very serious and is very hard and takes a lot of work for the owner.

Multinational corporations such as Wal-mart and McDonald's benefit from government zoning laws, to create barriers to entry. Many industries such as General Electric and Boeing lobby the government to receive subsidies to preserve their monopoly.

Patents

Many multinational corporations hold patents to prevent competitors from arising. For example, Adidas holds patents on shoe designs, Siemens A.G. holds many patents on equipment and infrastructure and Microsoft benefits from software patents. The pharmaceutical companies lobby international agreements to enforce patent laws on others.

Government Power

In addition to efforts by multinational corporations to affect governments, there is much government action intended to affect corporate behaviour. The threat of nationalization (forcing a company to sell its local assets to the government or to other local nationals) or changes in local business laws and regulations can limit a multinational's power. These issues become of increasing importance because of the emergence of MNCs in developing countries.

Micro-Multinationals

Enabled by Internet based communication tools, a new breed of multinational companies is growing in numbers." How startups go global".

These multinationals start operating in different countries from the very early stages. These companies are being called micro-multinationals.

What differentiates micro-multinationals from the large MNCs is the fact that they are small businesses. Some of these micro-multinationals, particularly software development companies, have been hiring employees in multiple countries from the beginning of the Internet era. But more and more micro-multinationals are actively starting to market their products and services in various countries. Internet tools like Google, Yahoo, MSN, Ebay and Amazon make it easier for the micro-multinationals to reach potential customers in other countries.

Service sector micro-multinationals, like Indigo Design & Engineering Associates Pvt. Ltd., Facebook, Alibaba etc. started as dispersed virtual businesses with employees, clients and resources located in various countries. Their rapid growth is a direct result of being able to use the internet, cheaper telephony and lower travelling costs to create unique business opportunities

Criticism of Multinationals

The rapid rise of multinational corporations has been a topic of concern among intellectuals, activists and laypersons who have seen it as a threat of such basic civil rights as privacy. They have pointed out that multinationals create false needs in consumers and have had a long history of interference in the policies of sovereign nation states. Evidence supporting this belief includes invasive advertising (such as billboards, television ads, adware, spam, telemarketing, child-targeted advertising, guerilla marketing), massive corporate campaign contributions in democratic elections, and endless global news stories about corporate corruption (Martha Stewart and Enron, for example). Anti-corporate protesters suggest that corporations answer only to shareholders, giving human rights and other issues almost no consideration. Films and books critical of multinationals include *Surplus: Terrorized into Being Consumers*, *The Corporation*, *The Shock Doctrine*, *Downsize This* and others.

Small Business Management

Small Business

A small business is a business that is privately owned and operated, with a small number of employees and relatively low volume of sales. Small businesses are normally privately owned corporations, partnerships, or sole proprietorships. The legal definition of "small" varies historically, by country and by industry, but generally has fewer than 100 employees in the United States and under 50 employees in the European Union. However, in Australia, a small business is defined by the *Fair Work Act 2009* as one with fewer than 15 employees. By comparison, a medium sized business or mid-sized business has under 500 employees in the US, 250 in the European Union and fewer than 200 in Australia.

In addition to number of employees, other methods used to classify small companies include annual sales (turnover), value of assets and net profit (balance sheet), alone or in a mixed definition. These criteria are followed by the European Union, for instance (headcount, turnover and balance sheet totals). Small businesses are usually not dominant in their field of operation.

Small businesses are common in many countries, depending on the economic system in operation. Typical examples include: convenience stores, other small shops (such as a bakery or delicatessen), hairdressers, tradesmen, lawyers, accountants, restaurants, guest houses, photographers, small-scale manufacturing etc.

The smallest businesses, often located in private homes, are called microbusinesses (term used by international organizations such as the World Bank and the International Finance Corporation) or SoHos. The term "mom and pop business" is a common colloquial expression for a single-family operated business with few (or no) employees other than the owners. When judged by the number of employees, the American and the European definitions are the same: under 10 employees.

Advantages of Small Business

A small business can be started at a very low cost and on a part-time basis. Small business is also well suited to internet marketing because it can easily serve specialized niches, something that would have been more difficult prior to the internet revolution which began in the late 1990s. Adapting to change is crucial in business and particularly small business; not being tied to any bureaucratic inertia, it is typically easier to respond to the marketplace quickly. Small business proprietors tend to be intimate with their customers and clients which results in greater accountability and maturity.

Independence is another advantage of owning a small business. One survey of small business owners showed that 38% of those who left their jobs at other companies said their main reason for leaving was that they wanted to be their own bosses. Freedom to operate independently is a reward for small business owners. In addition, many people desire to make their own decisions, take their own risks, and reap the rewards of their efforts. Small business owners have the satisfaction of making their own decisions within the constraints imposed by economic and other environmental factors. However, entrepreneurs have to work very long hours and understand that ultimately their customers are their bosses.

Several organizations also provide help for the small business sector, such as the Internal Revenue Service's Small Business and Self-Employed One-Stop Resource.

Problems Faced by Small Businesses

Small businesses often face a variety of problems related to their size. A frequent cause of bankruptcy is undercapitalization. This is often a result of poor planning rather than economic conditions-it is common rule of thumb that the entrepreneur should have access to a sum of money at least equal to the projected revenue for the first year of business in addition to his anticipated expenses. For example, if the prospective owner thinks that he will generate $100,000 in revenues in the first year with $150,000 in start-up expenses, then he should have no less than $250,000 available. Failure to provide this level of funding for the company could leave the owner liable for all of the company's debt should he end up in bankruptcy court, under the theory of undercapitalization.

In addition to ensuring that the business has enough capital, the small business owner must also be mindful of contribution margin (sales minus variable costs). To break even, the business must be able to reach a level of sales where the contribution margin equals fixed costs. When they first start out, many small business owners underprice their products to a point where even at their maximum capacity, it would be impossible to break even. Cost controls or price increases often resolve this problem. In the United States, some of the largest concerns of small business owners are insurance costs (such as liability and health), rising energy costs and taxes. In the United Kingdom and Australia, small business owners tend to be more concerned with excessive governmental red tape.

Another problem for many small businesses is termed the 'Entrepreneurial Myth' or E-Myth. The mythic assumption is that an expert in a given technical field will also be expert at running that kind of business. Additional business management skills are needed to keep a business running smoothly.

Marketing the Small Business

Common marketing techniques for small business include networking, word of mouth, customer referrals, yellow pages directories, television, radio, outdoor (roadside billboards), print, email marketing, and internet. Electronic media like TV can be quite expensive and is normally intended to create awareness of a product or service.

Many small business owners find internet marketing more affordable. Google AdWords and Yahoo! Search Marketing are two popular options of getting small business products or services in front of motivated Web searchers. Advertising on niche sites can also be effective, but with the long tail of the internet, it can be time intensive to advertise on enough sites to garner an effective reach.

Franchise Businesses

Franchising is a way for small business owners to benefit from the economies of scale of the big corporation (franchisor). McDonald's restaurants, TrueValue hardware stores, and NAPA Auto Parts stores are examples of a franchise. The small business owner can leverage a strong brand name and purchasing power of the larger company while keeping their own investment affordable. However, some franchisees conclude that they suffer the "worst of both worlds" feeling they are too restricted by corporate mandates and lack true independence. However, in some chains, such as the aforementioned True Value and NAPA, franchises may have their own name alongside the franchise's name.

Small Business Bankruptcy

When small business fails, the owner may file bankruptcy. In most cases this can be handled through a personal bankruptcy filing. Corporations can file bankruptcy, but if it is out of business and valuable corporate assets are likely to be repossessed by secured creditors there is little advantage to going to the expense of a corporate bankruptcy.

Many states offer exemptions for small business assets so they can continue to operate during and after personal bankruptcy. However, corporate assets are normally not exempt, hence it may be more difficult to continue operating an incorporated business if the owner files bankruptcy.

Certification and Trust

Building trust with new customers can be a difficult task for a new and establishing business. Some organizations like the Better Business Bureau and the International Charter now offer Small Business Certification, which certifies the quality of the services and goods produced and can encourage new and larger customers. These services may require a few hours of work, but a certification may reassure potential customers. However, the most effective way to earn trust is through customer referrals.

Contribution to the Economy

In the US, small business (less than 500 employees) accounts for around half the GDP and more than half the employment. Regarding small business, the top job provider is those with less than 10 employees, and those with 10 or more but less than 20 employees comes in as the second, and those with 20 or more but less than 100 employees comes in as the third (interpolation of data from the following references). The most recent data shows firms with less than 20 employees account for slightly more than 18% of the employment.

Of the 5,369,068 employer firms in 1995, 78.8 percent had fewer than 10 employees, and 99.7 percent had fewer than 500 employees.

5

Corporate Strategy and Planning

Definition

Systematic process of determining goals to be achieved in the foreseeable future. It consists of: (1) Management's fundamental assumptions about the future economic, technological, and competitive environments. (2) Setting of goals to be achieved within a specified time frame. (3) Performance of SWOT analysis. (4) Selecting main and alternative strategies to achieve the goals. (5) Formulating, implementing, and monitoring the operational or tactical plans to achieve interim objectives.

Strategic planning is the management task concerned with growth and future of a business enterprise. It ensures that the organization keeps moving in the right direction. It was fast changes in environment since 1950s that compelled organizations to approach the management task with strategic perspective, as the future was no more a measured extension of the past or the present. Instead of making extrapolated estimates about future, it was essential to endow the enterprise with certain fundamental competencies/distinctive strengths which could take care of eventualities resulting from unexpected environmental changes.

Environmental Changes which Forced the firms to adopt a Strategic Perspective:

- Fast changing technologies
- Proliferation of new products
- Faster commercialization of new product ideas and patents
- Socio political changes

- Emergence of global markets.

Consequent to the Changes in Environment an Enterprise had:

- To be strategically alert
- To be future oriented
- To develop the competence for assimilating changes faster
- To grow big by generating sufficient resources and
- To gain expertise in technology, marketing and decision support systems.

Business firms took up the challenge all over the world, each working it out in its own way. Management schools, consultancy organizations and management authors added their contributions to the experiment. These cumulative attempts gave rise to the body of knowledge that we now call strategic planning. The subject is now known by different names as business policy, strategic management, corporate strategy, strategic business planning etc.

Igor Ansoff a top expert in strategic planning explains nicely the process of strategy formulation in his book Corporate strategy as, "The interest in strategy grew out of the realization that the firm needed a well defined scope and growth direction; objectives alone do not serve the purpose, additional rules are required for an orderly and profitable growth. Such decision rules and guidelines have been broadly defined as strategy. Thus the objectives and strategy together describe the concept of a firms' business. It specifies the amount of growth, the area of growth, the directions for growth, the leading strengths and the profitability target."

Peter Drucker, discussing the importance of business policy and strategic planning in his book The practice of management says "we cannot be content with plans for a future that we can foresee. We must prepare for all possible and a good many impossible contingencies. We must have a workable solution for anything that may come up."

Thelevitt, the doyen of Harvard says, "it is wrong to say that the most important and creatively challenging act of corporate decision making is about choices regarding what is to be done. The most important and challenging work involves thinking up the possibilities from among which choices may have to be made i.e. a possibility has to be created before it can be chosen".

Alfred Chandler feels that business planning is concerned with the determination of basic long-term goals and objectives and the adoption of courses of action and allocation of resources necessary for carrying out these goals.

The Strategic Planning is Concerned with Certain Fundamental Issues such as :

- Purpose and mission/vision
- Corporate objectives
- Choice of businesses
- Courses of action for achieving the objectives.

Strategic planning provides the root map for the firm. It makes it possible for the firm to take decisions concerning the future with a greater awareness of their implications. It lends a frame work which can ensure that decisions concerning the future are taken in a systematic and purposeful way. Strategic planning offers a methodology by which, firm could anticipate and project the future, and be internally equipped to face it.

Nature and Scope of Strategic Planning :

- Serves as a route map for the corporation
- Lends a frame work for systematic handling of corporate decisions
- Lays down growth objectives of the firm and also provides methodology needed for achieving them
- Ensures that opportunities are chosen widely
- Ensure best utilization of resources
- Serves as a hedge against uncertainty as it enables to understand trends in advance and provides the benefit of a lead time for taking crucial decisions
- Helps build competitive advantages and core competencies.

Strategic Planning is Basically Concerned with:

- Future (long term dynamics not day to day tasks)
- Growth (direction, extent, pace and timing)
- Environment (fit between business and environment)
- Portfolios of business (product-market scope and postures) .

Strategic decisions differ from other functions of management as strategic decisions deal with growth of an organization (long range focus). Whereas, operational decisions are routine ones pertaining to day to day activities and administrative decisions are by and large patterned after existing practices in the corporation. In short, strategic planning provides the company with an easily discernible, clear cut, objective-strategy design which in turn takes the company in the required direction.

Strategic planning is however not a single task, it is an integrated package of several tasks that are distinct, yet inter-related :

- Clarifying vision/mission
- Defining the business
- Surveying the environment
- Internal appraisal of the firm
- Setting the corporate objectives
- Formulating the corporate/business strategy
- Monitoring the strategy.

Clarifying the vision of the corporation is the first task in strategic planning process. In fact, strategic planning originates at the point of articulation of its vision/mission. It is the expression of corporate intent.

Defining the business correctly is a pre-requisite for selecting the right opportunities and steering the firm on correct path. Very genesis of strategic planning can be traced to environmental turbulence, so it is only obligatory for an organization to survey the environment to compile an opportunities threat profile (OTP). Internal appraisal is a process of assessing corporation's capabilities and resources, strengths and weaknesses, core competencies and competitive advantages. The firms compare themselves against competitors and develop competitive advantage profile (CAP) and ward off threats to zero on the environmental opportunities.

Objectives are a statement of results the corporation seeks in given area, in a specific time frame. Clarity in objectives is of utmost importance, it facilitates the corporate to march along the direction of vision with minimum errors and diffusion of efforts with maximum utilization of resources. In addition to growth, objectives are set towards profitability, productivity, technology, competitive position, human resources, social responsibility and corporate image. Objectives emphasize where the organization wants to go, and strategies provide the design for getting there. Objectives and strategies together describe an organizations' concept of business. Time to time, strategies are monitored for compatibility with external environment and re-worked based on internal realities. In fact it is not a one shot affair – it is a continuous process.

The task of formulating a vision and defining the business is carried out with utmost clarity for the strategic planning exercise to be effective. Without a clear idea of firms' core purpose, values and arena it prefers to play in, the firm can not size up the multifarious developments taking place in the environment; its' choice of opportunities and strategies is impaired.

A vision statement does not represent a specific target. At the same time it is not all euphoria either, nor is it a PR statement. Zeal and ambition are the main constituents. It also contains the statement on values the organization cherishes and what it will give to and expect from its people and society.

The purpose of the firm is also spelt out clearly. It is a grand design of organizations' future. It is a tool to build and sustain commitment of people to corporate policies and provide motivation and is a guiding philosophy for the enterprise. Firms must ensure that vision remains relevant over time. At times, changes in environment/accomplishment of mission may develop a need for a firm to pursue in a different direction in order to keep serving its purpose and values – a time for re-visioning.

AT&T in its initial years had a mission to "give a telephone to every American" and this set pace of AT&T's growth. Later when AT&T realized that its mission was almost accomplished it refined its mission as of connecting people "any time anywhere". And AT&T moved forward in the direction by taking over several instrumentation/telecom firms all over the world to have a global telecom network so that it could accomplish its new mission.

Formulation of vision requires a zealous and passionate approach, in contrast with strategy formulation which needs a totally cool headed approach. These tasks are taken up with the direct intervention of chief executive. Also help from reputed consultants can be sought.

Business definition may follow then; it is an elaboration of the arena the firm will play in. It prescribes the boundaries of the firm's business/businesses. Vision/mission statements generally provide a clue of the businesses that the organization would be in, and the business definition makes the business clear from the point of product–market choice. A better understanding emerges when we consider that the mission of Unilever was "to make cleanliness commonplace, to lessen work for women ... " and the business definition makes it clear, that they would be in the business of detergents, soaps and scouring powders among other things. A firm can not be myopic in defining its mission and business. Definition should not be from a narrow product oriented perspective, instead it should be from need oriented or function oriented perspective, because substitute products serving the same need or function are always in the offing. Often the case of American Railroad industries is sited as a classic example, if they had defined their business as 'transportation' rather than 'railroads', they would have strategized accordingly with the changing times and stayed in business.

Next step towards strategic planning is formulating the objectives for the corporate, which basically represent the quantum of growth the corporate seeks to achieve in a given time frame. Corporate objectives do not get fixed abruptly, but they emanate from vision of the chief executive, opportunities in the environment and capability of the firm.

To identify the opportunities in the external environment, a thorough environmental survey is carried out, which places before the firm a list of carefully picked opportunities and threats. Since a business firm functions as a part of environment and seeks to benefit the environment on the way to its profitability, careful survey of environment is considered central to strategic planning. Here a firm studies the environmental factors at macro level and those related to the specific industry – this is truly a diagnosis of changes in environment in all respects.

Some of the Macro Environmental Factors Covered in the Survey:

- Demographic environment – covers size of population, growth rate of population, age distribution, literacy levels, composition of work force, population shifts etc. in the areas of interest.
- Socio-cultural environment – for getting a meaningful insight into lifestyles, traditions, behaviour etc.

- Economic environment – factors to be considered are general economic conditions, rate of growth of economy, behaviour of capital markets, interest rates, labour scene etc.
- Political environment – political stability
- Natural environment – covers ecology, natural resources etc.
- Technological environment – assessment of technology options available for specific industry, relative merits and cost-effectiveness of alternative technologies etc.
- Legal environment – aspects covered are control on trade practices, protection of society as a whole, legislations, enactments and legal provisions relating to conduct of specific business etc.

Environment Survey Specific to the Industry Concerned May Include:

- Demand related factors – decisions regarding entry into businesses and expansion are based on this factor which surveys natures of demand, potential, demand patterns, analysis of customer value etc.
- Industry and competition – a fundamental input for developing strategy-building competitive advantage.
- Government policies – have significant affect on strategy choice of the firms based on subsidies, being a large potential buyer etc.
- Supplier related factors – influence availability and cost of raw materials. Tradeoff between integrating and outsourcing of supplies is a crucial consideration.

Environmental survey is generally carried out using many of the available forecasting techniques, with the purpose of forecasting the status of various factors at a future point of time.

Environment survey is a means to analyze industry and competition, which is of special relevance to the firm in formulating strategy, in other words it brings to the fore the firms' competitive position with in the industry. Hence the subject is being dealt with in some more detail.

Growth potential and profitability are two major determinants of industrial attractiveness. A company with excellent competitive capabilities may not be profitable because it might be operating in an unattractive (e.g. low growth, small size etc.) industry. A firm has to assess industry attractiveness correctly, as strategy must grow out of it.

Industry attractiveness is a product of several factors such as industry potential, current size of industry, rate of growth of industry, structure and profitability of the industry, like wise company's business strength is also product of several factors such as company's current market share, growth rate, differential strength, brand image, corporate image etc. Each company will have to identify the factors specific to its industry and its competitive position before moving on with the job of setting objectives and strategies.

Industry structure has to be thoroughly analysed for number of players, nature of competition, differentiation practiced by the various players etc. in the industry.

Knowing ones' competitor and one's own position relative to the competition is critical to effective strategy. Developing successful strategy basically means designing products and services that would enable the firm to score over competition. By analysing competition a firm can identify areas of advantage and disadvantage and build competitive advantage, so that it can launch more precise attack on competitors and also prepare stronger defences against other competitors. Both industry attractiveness and competitive position, especially the later can be shaped through strategy. Strategy and competitive advantage are inter-related. It is competitive advantage around which strategies are woven and also competitive advantages are developed through carefully articulated strategies. Technology as a strategy plays an important role too. Companies, which bring in technological innovations and expand their distribution reach, considerably grow faster and have an edge over others.

Michael Porter's thesis says that there are five Forces that shape Competition

- Threat of new entrants
- Bargaining power of customers – powerful customers usually bargain for better services which involve cost and investment
- Bargaining power of suppliers – may determine the cost of raw materials and other inputs effecting profitability

- Rivalry among competitors – competition influences the pricing and other costs like advertising etc.
- Threats from substitutes – where-ever substantial investments in R&D is taking place, the threat of substitutes is large. It also affects profitability.

"Value chain" concept proposed by Michael Porter can also be applied to competitor analysis. Value chain is a tool for identifying ways in which value can be created/enhanced by a company and this can be used for comparing with the value chain of the competitor.

Value creation depends not only on how well each department of the company performs its activities but also on how well the various departmental activities are coordinated. The business process is basically a value creating and value delivering process. Customers patronize the company that offers the highest delivered value. Hence, the name of the game is to locate the activities in which value could be created and create maximum possible value in each of them.

In analysing the value chain of the competitor, the company actually identifies the strengths and weaknesses of the competitor; it also gets insights into the strategy followed by the competitor. These revelations help the company improve its assumptions about the competitors while formulating its own strategy.

Basic Approach to Competitor Analysis

- Identify competitor's objectives
- Identify their strategy
- Identify their strengths and weaknesses
- Predict their future actions.

Once the environmental survey is completed, the information thus gathered is integrated in a meaningful pattern. Opportunities – threats profile (OTP) is made by the company to understand where they stand with respect to environment and competitors. The summary of environmental survey is of core importance to the strategic planning process.

The fact, that industry structure, competition, customer etc. are constantly in a flux, compels a company to be vigilant towards environment and have a dynamic analysis of the environmental factors.

Main purpose of the constant vigil towards environmental factors is to facilitate appropriate strategic response at the right time.

Once the opportunities present in the environment are identified next step is to have an understanding of its own strengths and weaknesses through methodical internal appraisal. The firm should get rid of some untested assumptions, which it might have developed over time. Only properly assessed facts can be of help.

Internal Appraisal Helps in:

- Assessing its position in terms of capabilities, strengths and weaknesses.
- Selecting opportunities to be tapped in line with its capabilities.
- Assessing capability gap and take steps for elevating the same in line with growth opportunities.

Assessment of strengths and weaknesses should cover all functional areas in the company e.g.

- Marketing
- Product wise positioning
- Finance
- Manufacturing
- R&D
- Human resources
- Corporate factors (corporate image, organizational culture, organizational structure, use of IT, adequacy of policy deployment, assessment and review mechanism etc.)

Analysis of strengths and weaknesses portfolio brings out the competitive advantage the company has over its competitors and the core competencies of the company.

Competitive advantage is a position of superiority on the part of the company in some function/factor/activity in relation to its competitors and it is through this superiority that the company attempts to carve out a comfortable position for itself in the industry. For example some companies may be strong in production and some others may be strong in marketing. The strength in production may mean that a particular company may be an efficient producer when compared to its competitor, or it may have more flexible production system, or else it may have strength of variety. As a general rule big firms have strength of size and smaller ones have the strength of flexibility. But here is an example contrary to the rule just mentioned

Toshiba of Japan is huge company operating in electronic goods. Through a flexible manufacturing system it manufactures different products/ varieties of some products on the same assembly lines. At Ohme it assembles nine varieties of computers on the same line and on the adjacent line it assembles 20 varieties of lap top computers. It is able to switch from one product/ variety to another instantly at low cost and makes profits on low volume runs too. This flexibility of Toshiba to respond quickly and easily to the fast changing market demand is definitely one of its competitive advantages. Where as its competitors make profits only through long volume runs of a particular model.

The phenomenal winners in any industry usually possess competitive advantage in several functions/areas. It actually serves as a back up for strategy as a company not having a competitive advantage may struggle to place a worthwhile strategy. It is not strategy alone but the acquisition of competitive advantage and its utilization through strategy that takes a company to its objectives. Scoring over competition and defending against competition requires a solid and sustainable base of competitive advantage.

In short competitive advantage is the heart of strategy and for strategy to succeed the firm should have relevant competitive advantage.

All strengths identified in internal assessment do not amount to competitive advantage. Strength is a necessity but not sufficient condition for a competitive advantage. For strength to become competitive advantage, whether from production factors or marketing factors or some other factor, it must lead to a cost or differential advantage to the company. A cost or differential advantage may accrue through lower cost of capital, unique production facilities, efficient distribution, latest technology or innovative raw material handling. General rule is that a factor could be counted a competitive advantage if could influence in company's favour, one or more of the forces shaping the competition.

HLL has distribution as its distinctive competitive advantage with a network to reach the remotest rural areas of the country. Well managed firms are aware of competitive advantage they enjoy and factors that contributed to that, but with so many changes taking place in the environment and so many new forces of competition coming up all the time, a firm can maintain the competitive edge it enjoys only through a process of continuous monitoring.

The companies should correctly spot their competitive advantage factors and draw up their competitive advantage profile (CAP). Competitive advantages are spotted only after internal appraisal as well as industry and competition analysis as competitive advantage is always relative to the competition.

Corporate creates a built in mechanism in their corporate strategy to take care of the task of competitive advantage building. In fact corporate level decisions on acquisitions, mergers, alliances, fresh investments etc. are all steps that would result in competitive advantage building. Corporate may use benchmarking as a practice to ensure excellence instead of mere improvement, and in the process build some competitive advantages. Ford has used this tool effectively in their "Taurus" project and built competitive advantage in that segment of cars. Value chain approach is also used to develop competitive advantage through customer value created by the company by creating/enhancing value in each of its activities.

Developing and nurturing durable competitive advantages involves a conscious choice and medium/long term efforts. Right share of resources should always go to factors that constitute the source of competitive advantage.

A durable and higher order competitive advantage rests on some fundamental and enduring strength of the firm that is unique to the firm. This unique strength of the company can not be easily imitated by the competitors and from which newer and stronger competitive advantages can keep emerging. Companies which enjoy such unique and fundamental strength keep winning in an enduring manner. Such strength is referred as core competency of the firm.

In other words companies acquire lasting and higher competitive advantages only by building core competencies.

Competency can be in technology, process or any other field of expertise but it should be an exclusive preserve of the company or the company should possess it in substantially large measure when compared to the competitors. Such a preserve of competency is core competency.

C.K. Prahlad and Gary Hamel, after an examination of globally successful corporations and their reputed products, in an HBR article say that the battle for global market leadership is waged on the strength of core competence of the competing companies and not on some products/brands put out by them. Behind the visible battle of products and brands, lies the substantive war of core competence of the companies.

- *Sony has a core competence in miniaturization.*
- *Philips has a core competence in optical media expertise.*
- *Honda has core competence in engines.*
- *3M have a core competence in making substrates, coatings and adhesives and in combining them in multiple ways.*

Acquiring core competence is much more difficult than acquiring competitive advantage. Technological excellence, especially competence at the root of technologies, capacity to integrate multiple streams of technologies and expertise to harness diverse production skills are some of the requirements for acquiring core competencies. Critical components required for the business should not be outsourced, because those who do perhaps are denying themselves an opportunity to build core competencies in their chosen business, to enjoy a short term cost benefit.

A comparison of Chrysler and Honda will make the point clearer. Chrysler an American auto giant outsourced as crucial a component as engines from Mitsubishi and Hyundai and Honda on the other hand designed and manufactured its engines well supported by centralized R&D centre. No wonder, in the long run Honda built up core competence in engines and based on this competence has gained competitive advantage in several of its product categories, besides cars.

Focus is yet another requirement for developing core competence. A company needs to identify and concentrate on one or two core skills which it should develop as core competencies through well planned and sustained efforts.

After an extensive environmental survey a company gets a list of possibilities, indicating what it might do, and after an in-depth internal appraisal of the business, it narrows down to what it could do, and when it takes core values, purpose and vision into account, the corporate can prune the list to what it would do – setting the stage for corporate objectives. Put differently, through the tasks of vision clarification, environmental survey, appraisal of internal realities, scrutiny of its competitive advantages and core competencies the company finishes the groundwork, getting on with the crucial task of formulating corporate objectives and strategy.

The process does not stop with fixing of growth target. The conditions necessary for realizing the growth are also covered in the process. The objectives provide the basis for all major decisions of the firm and also set the organizational performance to be realized at each level.

Arriving at objectives-an organization breaks its overall growth ambition, which flows from the vision, into suitable blocks with a time frame.

The vision/growth ambition of Federal Express, a major air freight carrier is to be No.1 air craft carrier in the world. The company however can not achieve it at one go as it faces tough global competition from DHL, UPS, TNT etc. and in U.S. its market share is 45%, so it put the objectives for next five years (1995-2000) as

- 50 % growth in its turnover globally
- Market share growth of 10% from 45% to 55% in U.S.
- Market share growth of 20% increase out side U.S.

Through such time bound blocks of growth ambition, Federal Express sought to ultimately achieve its growth ambition.

While setting the objectives a company takes cognizance of various performance levels. First being currently achieved level next is currently achievable level which the company may achieve with current framework of resources, just by sharpening the efforts and improving efficiencies. But the company may like to achieve much higher growth in assets, revenue and profits.

This is aspiration level of performance. It is obvious that the company may not be able to achieve aspiration level of performance at one go so for the period of planning, the company sets a target, which is below the aspiration level but higher than currently achievable levels of performance. That becomes the growth objective for the planning period. The gap between the currently achievable level of performance and the growth objective set is to be filled through strategic planning.

Along with specifying the objectives in terms of growth target, the exercise also covers the conditions/factors/attributes essential for achieving the targeted growth. All subsequent decisions from finance to manufacturing to marketing, human resources etc. will be aligned with the objectives.

These overall objectives are split into functional targets with clear demarcation of responsibility for achievement. Finally objectives reach shop floor/sales men in the form of performance targets. So objectives should be well formulated, specific, unambiguous (with out leaving any room for wrong interpretation), quantified, challenging yet attainable, controllable and time bound. Objectives indicate the destination where as strategy constitutes the game plan to reach there. Corporate objectives and strategy are not separate entities, only together do they gain meaning and significance.

Growth constitutes the chief objective of a firm, and since growth is multi dimensional in character, objectives are to be set in all factors governing growth

- Growth (assets, revenue, profits, market share, competitive position etc.)
- Profitability (return on investment, earning per share etc.)
- Productivity (resource utilization, cost reduction, efficiency etc.)
- Technology (adoption of new technology and being a leader, modernization etc.)
- R&D innovation
- Human resources
- Corporate image
- Social responsibility (community welfare, civic roles, environment protection).

A point to remember here is though most companies get carried away by objectives concerning to growth (profits, revenue, market share etc.), by specifying specific objective with regard to profitability and monitoring it carefully, the company continuously monitors the profit potential of investment.

In the process of finalizing objectives, intuitions and logic play equally important roles.

Corporate strategy is basically growth design of the firm. Apart from providing a means to fill the gap between currently achievable performance and the target specified in the objectives, creating sustainable competitive advantage is a major concern of strategy. Strategy spells out the program of action for achieving the results and together with objectives clarifies the future plan. Objectives, product-market scope, growth vector, competitive advantage and synergy are all constituents of corporate growth.

The broad corporate strategy that a company may adopt has been classified into four generic categories, stability, expansion, divestment and combination.

Growth objective of firms employing stability strategy will be quite modest. It merely tries to bring about incremental improvements in operation of the business. Focus is on improving functional efficiencies in an incremental way. Here the company has the benefit of concentrating its resources and attention on the existing business/products and markets. It is fairly frequently employed strategy with no additional investments and risks.

When a firm seeks sizeable growth, it turns to expansion strategy. It tries to grow by exploiting the opportunities in the environment, which may lie either with in existing business or outside them. Two broad possibilities under expansion strategy are intensification strategy and diversification strategy.

Intensifying means the firm is strengthening its involvement and position in existing business. Intensification strategy encompasses three alternative routes – market penetration strategy, market development strategy and product development strategy.

Through market penetration strategy a company achieves growth through existing products in existing markets by increasing its market share.

Core parentrals, a leader in IV fluid business, during 1990s, implemented a series of expansion supported by capacity increases. Its objective was to raise its market share from 20% o 60% in Indian markets. So it put up additional capacity required for desired growth and shaped a pricing strategy to match its market penetration strategy, offered prices almost 25% less than the competitors. Core's strategy had been one of intensification – fighting in the same market, with same products, achieving higher market share and income through greater penetration.

Market development strategy tries to achieve growth through existing products in new markets. There are two ways of implementing the strategy. One, a company expands the marketing territory by capturing new markets in terms of customers and, two, it finds new uses for its products and finds new customers.

Foray into Asian markets by so many auto-mobile manufactures from Europe and America is a good example of intensification through market development – expansion of market by entering newly opened up parts of the global market.

Product development strategy tries to achieve growth through new products in existing markets. New products means improved products serving the same need of the customers.

Singer India in 1990s went in for expansion through intensification by product development route. It introduced improved products in the range of sewing machines.

It launched Fashion maker – a decorative sewing machine and followed that up with the introduction of an improved version of Fashion Maker that offered 158 varieties of decorative designs. It kept on improving the product to meet its long term objective of expansion of sales through value added products.

Companies also adopt intensification strategy by any combination of three sub-strategies available. Generally intensification is the first and natural choice of firms in pursuit of expansion.

Diversification strategy has three broad variants, vertically integrated diversification, concentric diversification and conglomerate diversification.

Intensification limits the growth path to existing businesses of the firm, where as diversification takes the growth to new products and new markets. Firms eager to achieve rapid and big growth opt for diversification. There are many reasons for adopting this path, like need to provide flexibility to portfolio, growth ambition, fresh opportunities, environmental uncertainty, higher profitability, availability of surplus resources etc. are some of the inducements to venture on this path. The characteristic feature of vertically integrated diversification is that the firm does not jump outside the vertically linked product – process chain.

For captive consumption too, firms may resort to vertical integration. Reliance had adopted this strategy effectively through 1980s to improve their business portfolio and also for their captive consumption.

Concentric diversification also amounts to related diversification. Here the new product is a spin off from the existing facilities/ processes. The new product is only connected in a loop like manner at one or more points in the firm's existing process/technology/product chain.

Conglomerate diversification has no such linkages, the new businesses/products are disjointed from existing businesses/products in every way. It is totally an unrelated diversification. Conglomerate diversification has no common thread at all with a firm's present position. Strategies are executed through mergers, acquisitions, alliances etc.

Normally the risk is less with related diversification due to greater scope of sharing of skills and competencies and greater synergy among the businesses. IBM, for example, always prefers such diversification. It operates in more than 20 fields all related to each other, each business deriving synergy of one kind or other from the rest.

With unrelated diversification the scope of opportunities to be pursued and rewards accrued is higher.

Divestment strategy involves dropping some of the activities in a given business of the firm through sale or liquidation. There is nothing negative about it and is as positive and useful as any other strategy. Under certain circumstances it becomes the right strategy choice for the firm.

For example, when GE was in troubles it laid down a policy that it should be either No.1 or No.2 in the businesses/markets in which it is present, or else get out of the concerned business. Also Tatas divested Excel Industries, a profit-making company, because it fell out side the Tatas' definition of core business.

Combination Strategy is any Combination of Generic Strategies.

The choice of strategy that company makes depend on the results of grinding exercise carried out by it though survey, internal appraisal and setting of objectives. Finding from all the preparatory exercises may be handled compositely. Analysis flows and decision flows criss cross. Past data, current data and forecasted data are sifted and studied using qualitative and quantitative information and strategies are evolved employing logic and intuition.

The process of strategy choice is intrinsically linked with the marketing planning process. That is, the opportunities are translated into strategy options/product – market propositions and the ones most suited to the firm are chosen.

Strategy choice must take into account firm's ability to execute the plan; also elements like people, skills, processes and culture of the organization are to be taken into account. Strategic organizations lay emphasis on execution ability and develop it through conscious efforts. Strategy choice, relative priorities and resources are organically linked issues. With strategy choice, scope and priority is made clear, resources in terms of money, people, facilities etc. are to be allotted next, to move on.

The corporate strategies are finally executed at business level through one or both of the two routes

- Price route
- Differentiation route.

Cost advantage can emanate from different factors like efficient scale of economies, benefit of early entry, a larger market share built over a period of time, locational advantage etc. Whole strategy revolves around building such cost advantage – always looking for opportunities for cost reduction through experience, dropping unprofitable customers/ segments etc. Developing such a cost leadership is the main task of firms that adopt this strategy at business level.

Differentiation route revolves basically around the principle of making its offer distinctive from all competing offers and win through distinctiveness. Differentiation route is more dynamic and powerful route in competitive strategy. Most business battles are fought on the strength of differentiation rather than price. Differentiation route gives a company the strength of uniqueness and specialty to its products. Brand image, channel clout, competent structure, unique process, integrated production facilities, advanced (expensive) R&D setup and product innovations are all avenues for differentiation. The success of differentiation strategy depends on firm's capacity to develop such avenues. Michael Porter adds a third route, focus, to concentrate on serving special needs of niche market. Even under focus the firm has to resort to price route or differentiation route for successfully serving the market, with only the difference being a narrow market segment, a niche, forms the target.

To summarize, in giving a final shape to the strategy, the firm has to size up the forces shaping competition in the industry. Build defences against these competitive forces, build relevant competitive advantages and also identify, utilize and nurture its synergies.

6

Analysis of Risk and Sensitivity

Introduction

The financial and economic benefit-cost analysis of water supply projects (WSPs) is based on forecasts of quantifiable variables such as demand, costs, water availability and benefits. The values of these variables are estimated based on the most probable forecasts, which cover a long period of time. The values of these variables for the most probable outcome scenario are influenced by a great number of factors, and the actual values may differ considerably from the forecasted values, depending on future developments. It is therefore useful to consider the effects of likely changes in the key variables on the viability (EIRR and FIRR) of a project. Performing sensitivity and risk analysis does this.

Management in a Non-Profit-Making Organization

Non-profit Organization

A nonprofit organization (abbreviated NPO, also not-for-profit) is an organization that does not distribute its surplus funds to owners or shareholders, but instead uses them to help pursue its goals. Examples of NPOs include charities (i.e. charitable organizations), trade unions, and public arts organizations. Most governments and government agencies meet this definition, but in most countries they are considered a separate type of organization and not counted as NPOs.

Non-profit Distinction

Whereas for-profit corporations exist to earn and distribute taxable business earnings to shareholders, the nonprofit corporation exists solely to provide programs and services that are of public benefit. Often these programs and services are not otherwise provided by local, state, or federal entities. While they are able to earn a profit, more accurately called a surplus, such earnings must be retained by the organization for its future provision of programs and services.

Earnings may not benefit individuals or stake-holders. Nonprofit organizations may put substantial funds into hiring leadership and management personnel. In the past, many nonprofits considered this to be unreasonably businesslike and money-focused, but since the late 1980s there has been a growing consensus that nonprofits can achieve their missions more effectively by using some of the same methods developed in for-profit enterprises. These include effective internal management, ensuring accountability for results, and monitoring the performance of different divisions or projects in order to make the best use of their funds and people. Those require management and that, in turn, begins with the organization's mission.

Nature and Goals

NPOs are often charities or service organizations; they may be organized as a not-for-profit corporation or as a trust, a cooperative, or they may be purely informal.

Sometimes they are also called foundations, or endowments that have large stock funds. A very similar organization called the supporting organization operates like a foundation, but they are more complicated to administer, they are more tax favoured, and the public charities that receive grants from them must have a specially determined relationship.

Foundations give out grants to other NPOs, or fellowships and direct grants to participants. However, the name *foundations* may be used by any not-for-profit corporation — even volunteer organizations or grass roots groups.

Applying Germanic or Nordic law (e.g., Germany, Sweden, Finland), NPOs typically are voluntary associations, although some have a corporate structure (e.g. housing cooperatives). Usually a voluntary association is founded upon the principle of one-person-one-vote.

Legal Aspects

There is a wide diversity of structures and purposes in the NPO landscape. For legal classification and eventual scrutiny, there are, nevertheless, some structural elements of prime legal importance:

- Economic activity
- Supervision and management provisions
- Representation
- Accountability and Auditing provisions
- Provisions for the amendment of the statutes or articles of incorporation
- Provisions for the dissolution of the entity
- Tax status of corporate and private donors
- Tax status of the foundation.

Some of the above must be, in most jurisdictions, expressed in the document of establishment. Others may be provided by the supervising authority at each particular jurisdiction. While affiliations will not affect a legal status, they may be taken into consideration in legal proceedings as an indication of purpose.

Most countries have laws which regulate the establishment and management of NPOs, and which require compliance with corporate governance regimes. Most larger organizations are required to publish their financial reports detailing their income and expenditure for the public. In many aspects they are similar to business entities though there are often significant differences. Both non-profit and for-profit entities must have board members, steering committee members, or trustees who owe the organization a fiduciary duty of loyalty and trust. A notable exception to this involves churches, which are often not required to disclose finances to anyone, including church members, though most churches remain fiscally transparent with their members.

Formation and Structure

In the United States, nonprofit organizations are formed by incorporating in the state in which they expect to do business. The act of incorporating creates a legal entity enabling the organization to be treated as a corporation under law and to enter into business dealings, form contracts, and own property as any other individual or for-profit corporation may do.

Nonprofits can have members but many do not. The nonprofit

may also be a trust or association of members. The organization may be controlled by its members who elect the Board of Directors, Board of Governors or Board of Trustees. Nonprofits may have a delegate structure to allow for the representation of groups or corporations as members. Alternately, it may be a non-membership organization and the board of directors may elect its own successors.

A primary difference between a nonprofit and a for-profit corporation is that a nonprofit does not issue stock or pay dividends, (for example, The Code of the Commonwealth of Virginia includes the Non-Stock Corporation Act that is used to incorporate nonprofit entities) and may not enrich its directors. However, like for-profit corporations, nonprofits may still have employees and can compensate their directors within reasonable bounds.

The two major types of nonprofit organization structure are membership and board-only. A membership organization elects the board and has regular meetings and power to amend the bylaws. A board-only organization typically has a self-selected board, and a membership whose powers are limited to those delegated to it by the board. A board-only organization's bylaws may even state the organization has no membership, although the organization's literature may refer to its donors as "members"; examples of such structures are Fairvote and the National Organization for the Reform of Marijuana Laws. The Model Nonprofit Corporation Act imposes many complexities and requirements on membership decision-making.

Accordingly, many organizations, such as the American Society of Association Executives and Wikimedia, have formed board-only structures. The National Association of Parliamentarians has raised concerns about the implications of this trend for the future of openness, accountability, and understanding of grassroots concerns in nonprofit organizations. Specifically, they note that nonprofit organizations, unlike business corporations, are not subject to market discipline for products and shareholder discipline over their capital; therefore, without membership control of major decisions such as election of the board, there are few inherent safeguards against abuse. A rebuttal to this might be that as nonprofit organizations grow and seek larger donations, the level of scrutiny rises, including expectations of audited financial statements.

Tax Exemption

In many countries, nonprofits may apply for tax exempt status, so that the organization itself may be exempt from income tax and other taxes. In the United States, to be exempt from federal income taxes the organization must meet the requirements set forth by the Internal Revenue Service.

United States

After a recognized type of legal entity has been formed at the state level, it is customary for the nonprofit organization to seek tax exempt status with respect to its income tax obligations. That is typically done by applying to the Internal Revenue Service (IRS), although statutory exemptions exist for limited types of nonprofit organizations. The IRS, after reviewing the application to ensure the organization meets the conditions to be recognized as a tax exempt organization (such as the purpose, limitations on spending, and internal safeguards for a charity), may issue an authorization letter to the nonprofit granting it tax exempt status for income tax payment, filing, and deductibility purposes. The exemption does not apply to other Federal taxes such as employment taxes. Additionally, a tax-exempt organization must pay federal tax on income that is unrelated to their exempt purpose. Failure to maintain operations in conformity to the laws may result in an organization losing its tax exempt status.

Individual states and localities offer nonprofits exemptions from other taxes such as sales tax or property tax. Federal tax-exempt status does not guarantee exemption from state and local taxes. These exemptions generally have separate application processes and their requirements may differ from the IRS requirements. Furthermore, even a tax exempt organization may be required to file annual financial reports (IRS Form 990) at the state and federal level.

Canada

In Canada, NPOs may be formed at either the federal or provincial levels. Charities must generally be registered with the Canada Revenue Agency and may issue tax receipts for donations.

India

In India, NPOs are commonly known as Non-Governmental

Organizations (NGOs). They can be registered in four ways, viz. 1. Trust 2. Society 3. Section-25 Company 4. Special Licensing.

Registration can be done with the Registrar of Companies(RoC).

The following laws or Constitutional Articles of the Republic of India are relevant to the NGOs:

- Articles 19(1)(c) and 30 of the Constitution of India
- Income Tax Act, 1961
- Public Trusts Acts of various states
- Societies Registration Act, 1860
- Section 25 of the Indian Companies Act, 1956
- Foreign Contribution (Regulation) Act, 1976.

South Africa

In South Africa, charities issue a tax certificate when requested by donors which can be used as a tax deduction by the donor.

United Kingdom

In the UK, many non-profit companies are incorporated as a company limited by guarantee. This means that the company doesn't have shares or shareholders, but it has the benefits of corporate status. This includes limited liability for its members and being able to enter into contracts and purchase property in its own name. The goals ("objects") of the company are defined in the Memorandum of Association when the company is formed. The profits of the company (also referred to as the trading surplus) must be invested in achieving these goals and not distributed to the company's members.

Alternatively, non-profit companies may be formed as a Community Interest Company. This is in many ways similar to a Limited Liability Company, but is intended specifically to ensure that the profits and assets of the company are used for public good.

A charity is a non-profit organisation that meets stricter criteria regarding its purpose and the way in which it makes decisions and reports its finances.. For example, a charity is generally not allowed to pay its Trustees. In England and Wales, charities may be registered with the Charity Commission. In Scotland, the Office of the Scottish Charity

Regulator serves the same function. Other organizations which are classified as non-profit organizations elsewhere, such as trade unions, are subject to separate regulations, and are not regarded as "charities" in the technical sense.

Issues Faced by NPOs

Capacity building is an ongoing problem faced by NPOs for a number of reasons. Most rely on external funding (government funds, grants from charitable foundations, direct donations) to maintain their operations and changes in these sources of revenue may influence the reliability or predictability with which the organization can hire and retain staff, sustain facilities, or create programs. In addition, unreliable funding, long hours and low pay can lead to employee burnout and high rates of turnover.

Founder's syndrome is an issue organizations face as they grow. Dynamic founders with a strong vision of how to operate the project try to retain control over the organization, even as new employees or volunteers want to expand the project's scope and try new things.

Examples

In the United States, two of the wealthiest non-profit organizations are the Bill and Melinda Gates Foundation, which has an endowment of $38 billion, and the Howard Hughes Medical Institute, which has an endowment of approximately $14.8 billion. Outside the United States, another large NPO is the British Wellcome Trust, which is a "charity" in British usage. Note that this assessment excludes universities, at least a few of which have assets in the tens of billions of dollars.

Measuring an NPO by its monetary size has obvious limitations, as the power and significance of NPOs are defined by more qualitative measurements such as effectiveness at carrying out charitable mission and goals.

Some NPOs which are particularly well known, often for the charitable or social nature of their activities conducted over a long period of time, include Amnesty International, the Better Business Bureau, Oxfam, Carnegie Corporation of New York, DEMIRA Deutsche Minenräumer (German Mine Clearers), Goodwill Industries, United Way, Habitat for Humanity, Teach For America, the Red Cross and Red

Crescent organizations, UNESCO, IEEE, World Wide Fund for Nature, Heifer International, and SOS Children's Villages.

However, there are also millions of smaller NPOs that provide social services and relief efforts on a more focused level (such as Crosswind — Community Outreach Ministry and Literacy Centre West) to people throughout the world. There are more than 1.6 million NPOs in the United States alone.

On the Internet

Many NPOs often use the .org or .us (or the CCTLD of their respective country) or .edu top-level domain (TLD) when selecting a domain name to differentiate themselves from more commercially focused entities which typically use the .com space.

In the traditional domain categories as noted in RFC 1591, .org is for "organizations that didn't fit anywhere else" in the naming system, which implies that it is the proper category for non-commercial organizations if they are not governmental, educational, or one of the other types with a specific TLD. It is not specifically designated for charitable organizations or any specific organizational or tax-law status, however; it encompasses anything that does not fall into another category.

Currently, no restrictions are enforced on registration of .com or .org, so you can find organizations of all sorts in either of these domains, as well as other top-level domains including newer, more-specific ones which may fit particular sorts of organizations such as .museum for museums or .coop for cooperatives. Organizations might also register under the appropriate country code top-level domain for their country.

Other Terminology for the Sector

There is a growing movement within the "non"-profit and "non"-government sector to define itself using more proactive wording. Instead of being defined by "non" words, organizations are suggesting new terminology to describe the sector. The term "civil society organization" (CSO) has been used by a growing number of organizations, such as the Centre for the Study of Global Governance. The term "citizen sector organization" (CSO) has also been advocated to describe the sector — as one of citizens, for citizens — by organizations such as

Ashoka: Innovators for the Public. This labels and positions the sector as its own entity, without relying on language used for the government or business sectors. However, use of terminology by a nonprofit of self-descriptive language such as "public service organization" or other term that is not legally compliant risks confusing the public about nonprofit abilities, capabilities and limitations.

Planning

Strategic Planning

Members of the Board and staff conduct strategic planning to determine the overall purpose (mission) and direction (vision and goals) for the nonprofit, as well as the methods (values, strategies and programs) for the nonprofit to work toward the purpose and direction. The strategic planning process provides input to all other major functions in the organization, especially program planning and resource planning. Thus, if strategic planning is not done well, the entire organization can be adversely effected.

Planning for Programs

Programs are designed or refined as means to implement the service-oriented strategies from the Strategic Plan. During program planning, the marketing research (or "inbound marketing") activities are conducted to identify, for example, specific community needs for the nonprofit to meet, what outcomes are needed to meet those needs, what specific groups of clients to serve, and how to serve them to achieve those outcomes. Program planning provides input to many other functions, such as resource planning (regarding staff, funds, people), financial management, advertising and promotions, and also fundraising. Many problems commonly associated with fundraising and promotions are really the result of poor program planning.

Resource Planning

Planners identify what resources are needed to implement the strategic and program plans.

Usually, resources include people, funding, facilities, equipment, supplies, and even certain polices and procedures. Budgets usually are developed that include listings of resources that are needed, along with the estimated costs to obtain and support the use of those resources.

Resource planning directly affects the quality of all operating activities because, without adequately identifying what resources are needed, major functions in the organization struggle to be effective.

Developing

Revenue/Fundraising Development

Planning for programs specifies how much money the programs might earn (expected revenues), how much money they might cost (expected expenses) and if there are any deficits (expenses exceeding revenue) for the programs. The deficits often are addressed by fundraising. The planning for fundraising is often carried out by developing and implementing a Fundraising Plan, which specifies the overall amounts of money that must be raised, where it might be raised, how it will be raised, by who and when. If the planning for fundraising is not done systematically and comprehensively, nonprofits miss opportunities for funding and, instead, focus their fundraising activities on a few methods, for example, continued fundraising events.

Board, staff and Volunteer Development (Leadership and Management)

Members of the Board and staff are developed by first identifying what expertise is needed to achieve the goals in the strategic and program plans. Development activities continue by obtaining, training and organizing members to better achieve the strategic and program goals. Note that many nonprofits recruit and develop personnel as an activity somewhat Adapted from "Field Guide to Consulting and Organizational Development With Nonprofits" – to obtain the entire book, select "Publications" at apart from their strategic and program planning activities.

That approach may result in the nonprofit being run more by personalities than by plans. The results of successful development of the Board and senior staff greatly influence the success of the nonprofit because Board and staff provide the leadership that drives the entire system with its phases of planning, developing, operating and evaluating. However, strategic planning and program planning must occur before development of the Board and staff to provide direction for how they should be successfully developed.

Development of Other Resources

There usually is a variety of types of resources (other than money and people) that needed to be obtained and developed, for example, facilities, equipment, policies and procedures.

Perhaps most important among these resources are policies and procedures. They form the "glue" that aligns and integrates the resources of money and people. If those policies and procedures are not integrated and up-to-date, they can cause inefficiencies in the operating activities. As a result, members of the organization experience increasing inefficiencies and conflicts. Successful leaders have learned to focus on developing a firm foundation of plans and policies from which their organizations can more reliably grow.

Operating

Supervision and Teamwork

A supervisor is someone who oversees the progress and productivity of people who report directly to the supervisor. Thus, a Board supervises the Chief Executive Officer, and a CEO supervises, for example, the Program Director.

Teamwork is about how people work together to coordinate goals, roles, leadership and communication. The activities of supervision and teamwork are critical to the success of a nonprofit because those activities ensure that goals are established in accordance with strategic and program goals, progress toward the goals is monitored, and adjustments are made among individuals to more effectively achieve the goals. Many times, recurring problems in other types of operating activities are really symptoms of poor teamwork.

Program Operations

This includes the ongoing activities that provide services directly to the clients. The nature of these activities depends on the types of needs met by the program.

For example, health services often require highly trained program staff and technologies. Food shelves require large facilities to store groceries. The success of programs depends a great deal on the effectiveness of strategic and program planning and of teamwork in the organization.

Advertising and Promotions

These "outbound" marketing activities are geared to inform stakeholders (clients, funders, community leaders) about new and current programs, and also to keep those programs in the minds of stakeholders. Many times, problems in advertising and promotions are the result of poor program planning, such as unclear identification of what specific groups of clients should be served, the needs of each group, and how the programs meet each need.

Facilities Management

This includes identifying what major facilities will be needed, such as buildings, equipment and computer systems. The need for major facilities is identified during resource planning.

Thus, problems caused by lack of facilities often are a result of poor resource planning.Problems caused by ineffective use of facilities often are a result of poor staff development.

Financial Management

Activities of financial management include documenting financial transactions (bookkeeping), generating and analysing financial statements, and making adjustments to budgets based on the various analyses. This is usually done to Board-approved fiscal policies and procedures. Many times, people report problems with finances when they really mean problems with inadequate funding.

Those problems are often caused by ineffective program planning, resource development and/or fundraising activities. Problems that are truly about financial management often can be addressed by training personnel about bookkeeping, and about generating and analysing financial statements.

Administrative Activities

This includes the extensive range of detailed activities that must be coordinated and conducted on a daily basis to ensure the efficient operations of the nonprofit.

Many people think of these activities as clerical, or "paperwork." Problems with administrative tasks often are the result of poor resource planning and staff development, or lack of appreciation for policies and procedures.

Evaluating

Board self-evaluation

Members of the Board of Directors should regularly evaluate the quality of their activities on a regular basis. Activities might include staffing the Board with new members, developing the members into well-trained and resourced members, discussing and debating topics to make wise decisions, and supervising the CEO. Probably the biggest problem with Board self-evaluation is that it does not occur frequently enough. As a result, Board members have no clear impression of how they are performing as members of a governing Board. Poor Board operations, when undetected, can adversely affect the entire organization.

Staff and Volunteer (individual) Performance Evaluation

Most of us are familiar with employee performance appraisals, which evaluate the quality of an individual's performance in their position in the organization. Ideally, those appraisals reference the individual's written job description and performance goals to assess the quality of the individual's progress toward achieving the desired results described in those documents. Continued problems in individual performance often are the results of poor strategic planning, program planning and staff development. If overall planning is not done effectively, individuals can experience continued frustration, stress and low morale, resulting in their poor overall performance. Experienced leaders have learned that continued problems in performance are not always the result of a poor work ethic – the recurring problems may be the result of larger, more systemic problems in the organizations.

Program Evaluation

Program evaluations have become much more common, particularly because donors demand them to ensure that their investments are making a difference in their communities. Program evaluations are typically focused on the quality of the program's process, goals or outcomes. An ineffective program evaluation process often is the result of poor program planning – programs should be designed so they can be evaluated. It can also be the result of improper training about evaluation. Sometimes, leaders do not realize that they have the responsibility to verify to the public that the nonprofit is indeed making a positive impact in the community. When program evaluations are not performed well, or at all, there is little feedback to the strategic and program planning activities. When strategic and program planning are done poorly, the entire organization is adversely effected.

Evaluation of cross-functional Processes

Cross-functional processes are those that span several systems, such as programs, functions and projects. Common examples of major processes include information technology systems and quality management of services. Because these cross-functional processes span so many areas of the organization, problems in these processes can be the result of any type of ineffective planning, development and operating activities.

Organizational Evaluation

Ongoing evaluation of the entire organization is a major responsibility of all leaders in the organization. Leaders sometimes do not recognize the ongoing activities of management to actually include organizational evaluations – but they do. The activities of organizational evaluation occur every day. However, those evaluations usually are not done systematically.

As a result, useful evaluation information is not provided to the strategic and program planning processes. Consequently, both processes can be ineffective because they do not focus on improving the quality of operations in the workplace.

Decision Making

Decision making can be regarded as an outcome of mental processes (cognitive process) leading to the selection of a course of action among several alternatives. Every decision making process produces a final choice. The output can be an action or an opinion of choice.

Overview

Human performance in decision making terms has been the subject of active research from several perspectives. From a psychological perspective, it is necessary to examine individual decisions in the context of a set of needs, preferences an individual has and values they seek. From a cognitive perspective, the decision making process must be regarded as a continuous process integrated in the interaction with the environment. From a normative perspective, the analysis of individual decisions is concerned with the logic of decision making and rationality and the invariant choice it leads to.

Yet, at another level, it might be regarded as a problem solving activity which is terminated when a satisfactory solution is found. Therefore, decision making is a reasoning or emotional process which can be rational or irrational, can be based on explicit assumptions or tacit assumptions.

Logical decision making is an important part of all science-based professions, where specialists apply their knowledge in a given area to making informed decisions. For example, medical decision making often involves making a diagnosis and selecting an appropriate treatment. Some research using naturalistic methods shows, however, that in situations with higher time pressure, higher stakes, or increased ambiguities, experts use intuitive decision making rather than structured approaches, following a recognition primed decision approach to fit a set of indicators into the expert's experience and immediately arrive at a satisfactory course of action without weighing alternatives. Recent robust decision efforts have formally integrated uncertainty into the decision making process. However, Decision Analysis, recognized and included uncertainties with a structured and rationally justifiable method of decision making since its conception in 1964.

Everyday Techniques

Some of the decision making techniques people use in everyday life include:

- Listing the advantages and disadvantages of each option, popularized by Plato and Benjamin Franklin
- Choosing the alternative with the highest probability-weighted utility for each alternative
- Accepting the first option that seems like it might achieve the desired result
- Acquiesce to a person in authority or an "expert"
- Flipping a coin, cutting a deck of playing cards, and other random or coincidence methods
- Prayer, tarot cards, astrology, augurs, revelation, or other forms of divination

Cognitive and Personal Biases

Biases can creep into our decision making processes. Many different people have made a decision about the same question (*e.g.* "Should I have a doctor look at this troubling breast cancer symptom I've discovered?" "Why did I ignore the evidence that the project was going over budget?") and then craft potential cognitive interventions aimed at improving decision making outcomes. Below is a list of some of the more commonly debated cognitive biases.

- Selective search for evidence (a.k.a. Confirmation bias in psychology) (Scott Plous, 1993) – We tend to be willing to gather facts that support certain conclusions but disregard other facts that support different conclusions. Individuals who are highly defensive in this manner show significantly greater left prefrontal cortex activity as measured by EEG than do less defensive individuals.
- Premature termination of search for evidence – We tend to accept the first alternative that looks like it might work.
- Inertia – Unwillingness to change thought patterns that we have used in the past in the face of new circumstances.
- Selective perception – We actively screen-out information that we do not think is important. In one demonstration of this effect, discounting of arguments with which one disagrees (by judging them as untrue or irrelevant) was decreased by selective activation of right prefrontal cortex.
- Wishful thinking or optimism bias – We tend to want to see things in a positive light and this can distort our perception and thinking.
- Choice-supportive bias occurs when we distort our memories of chosen and rejected options to make the chosen options seem relatively more attractive.
- Recency – We tend to place more attention on more recent information and either ignore or forget more distant information. The opposite effect in the first set of data or other information is termed Primacy effect (Plous, 1993).
- Repetition bias – A willingness to believe what we have been told most often and by the greatest number of different of sources.

- Anchoring and adjustment – Decisions are unduly influenced by initial information that shapes our view of subsequent information.
- Group think – Peer pressure to conform to the opinions held by the group.
- Source credibility bias – We reject something if we have a bias against the person, organization, or group to which the person belongs: We are inclined to accept a statement by someone we like.
- Incremental decision making and escalating commitment – We look at a decision as a small step in a process and this tends to perpetuate a series of similar decisions. This can be contrasted with zero-based decision making.
- Attribution asymmetry – We tend to attribute our success to our abilities and talents, but we attribute our failures to bad luck and external factors. We attribute other's success to good luck, and their failures to their mistakes.
- Role fulfilment (Self Fulfilling Prophecy) – We conform to the decision making expectations that others have of someone in our position.
- Underestimating uncertainty and the illusion of control – We tend to underestimate future uncertainty because we tend to believe we have more control over events than we really do. We believe we have control to minimize potential problems in our decisions.

Cognitive Styles

Influence of Briggs Myers Type

According to behaviourist Isabel Briggs Myers, a person's decision making process depends to a significant degree on their cognitive style. Myers developed a set of four bi-polar dimensions, called the Myers-Briggs Type Indicator (MBTI). The terminal points on these dimensions are: *thinking* and *feeling*; *extroversion* and *introversion*; *judgment* and *perception*; and *sensing* and *intuition*. She claimed that a person's decision making style correlates well with how they score on these four dimensions. For example, someone who scored near the thinking, extroversion, sensing, and judgment ends of the dimensions would tend to have a logical, analytical, objective, critical, and empirical decision making style. Other studies suggest that these national or cross-cultural differences exist across entire societies. For example, Maris Martinsons has found that American, Japanese and Chinese business leaders each exhibit a distinctive national style of decision making.

Optimizing vs. Satisficing

Herbert Simon coined the phrase "bounded rationality" to express the idea that human decision-making is limited by available information, available time, and the information-processing ability of the mind. Simon also defined two cognitive styles: *maximizers* try to make an optimal decision, whereas *satisficers* simply try to find a solution that is "good enough". Maximizers tend to take longer making decisions due to the need to maximize performance across all variables and make tradeoffs carefully; they also tend to more often regret their decisions.

Combinatoral vs. Positional

Styles and methods of decision making were elaborated by the founder of Predispositioning Theory, Aron Katsenelinboigen. In his analysis on styles and methods Katsenelinboigen referred to the game of chess, saying that "chess does disclose various methods of operation, notably the creation of predisposition—methods which may be applicable to other, more complex systems."

In his book Katsenelinboigen states that apart from the methods (reactive and selective) and sub-methods (randomization, predispositioning, programming), there are two major styles – positional and combinational. Both styles are utilized in the game of chess. According to Katsenelinboigen, the two styles reflect two basic approaches to the uncertainty: deterministic (combinational style) and indeterministic (positional style). Katsenelinboigen's definition of the two styles are the following. The combinational style is characterized by:

- a very narrow, clearly defined, primarily material goal, and
- a program that links the initial position with the final outcome.

In defining the combinational style in chess, Katsenelinboigen writes: The combinational style features a clearly formulated limited objective, namely the capture of material (the main constituent element of a chess position). The objective is implemented via a well defined and in some cases in a unique sequence of moves aimed at reaching the set goal. As a rule, this sequence leaves no options for the opponent. Finding a combinational objective allows the player to focus all his energies on efficient execution, that is, the player's analysis may be limited to the pieces directly partaking in the combination. This approach is the crux of the combination and the combinational style of play.

The positional style is distinguished by

- a positional goal and
- a formation of semi-complete linkages between the initial step and final outcome.

"Unlike the combinational player, the positional player is occupied, first and foremost, with the elaboration of the position that will allow him to develop in the unknown future. In playing the positional style, the player must evaluate relational and material parameters as independent variables. (...) The positional style gives the player the opportunity to develop a position until it becomes pregnant with a combination. However, the combination is not the final goal of the positional player—it helps him to achieve the desirable, keeping in mind a predisposition for the future development. The Pyrrhic victory is the best example of one's inability to think positionally." The positional style serves to:

a) create a predisposition to the future development of the position;
b) induce the environment in a certain way;
c) absorb an unexpected outcome in one's favour;
d) avoid the negative aspects of unexpected outcomes.

The positional style gives the player the opportunity to develop a position until it becomes pregnant with a combination. Katsenelinboigen writes:

> *"As the game progressed and defence became more sophisticated the combinational style of play declined. ... The positional style of chess does not eliminate the combinational one with its attempt to see the entire program of action in advance. The positional style merely prepares the transformation to a combination when the latter becomes feasible."*

Neuroscience Perspective

The anterior cingulate cortex (ACC), orbitofrontal cortex (and the overlapping ventromedial prefrontal cortex) are brain regions involved in decision making processes. A recent neuroimaging study, found distinctive patterns of neural activation in these regions depending on whether decisions were made on the basis of personal volition or following directions from someone else. Patients with damage to the ventromedial prefrontal cortex have difficulty making advantageous decisions.

A recent study involving Rhesus monkeys found that neurons in the parietal cortex not only represent the formation of a decision but also signal the degree of certainty (or "confidence") associated with the decision. Another recent study found that lesions to the ACC in the macaque resulted in impaired decision making in the long run of reinforcement guided tasks suggesting that the ACC is responsible for evaluating past reinforcement information and guiding future action.

Emotion appears to aid the decision making process: Decision making often occurs in the face of uncertainty about whether one's choices will lead to benefit or harm. The somatic-marker hypothesis is a neurobiological theory of how decisions are made in the face of uncertain outcome. This theory holds that such decisions are aided by emotions, in the form of bodily states, that are elicited during the deliberation of future consequences and that mark different options for behaviour as being advantageous or disadvantageous. This process involves an interplay between neural systems that elicit emotional/ bodily states and neural systems that map these emotional/bodily states.

Simple Processes for Problem-Solving and Decision-Making

Problem solving and decision-making are important skills for business and life. Problem-solving often involves decision-making, and decision-making is especially important for management and leadership. There are processes and techniques to improve decision-making and the quality of decisions. Decision-making is more natural to certain personalities, so these people should focus more on improving the quality of their decisions. People that are less natural decision-makers are often able to make quality assessments, but then need to be more decisive in acting upon the assessments made. Problem-solving and decision-making are closely linked, and each requires creativity in identifying and developing options, for which the brainstorming technique is particularly useful. SWOT analysis helps assess the strength of a company, a business proposition or idea; PEST analysis helps to assess the potential and suitability of a market. Good decision-making requires a mixture of skills: creative development and identification of options, clarity of judgement, firmness of decision, and effective implementation. For group problem-solving and decision-making, or when a consensus is required, workshops help, within which you can incorporate these tools and process as appropriate. Here are some useful methods for effective decision-making and problem-solving: First a simple step-by-step process for effective decision-making and problem-solving.

Decision-Making Process

1. Define and clarify the issue-does it warrant action? If so, now? Is the matter urgent, important or both.
2. Gather all the facts and understand their causes.
3. Think about or brainstorm possible options and solutions.
4. Consider and compare the pros and cons of each option-consult if necessary-it probably will be.
5. Select the best option-avoid vagueness or 'foot in both camps' compromise.
6. Explain your decision to those involved and affected, and follow up to ensure proper and effective implementation.

Decision-making maxims will help to reinforce the above decision-making process whether related to problem-solving or not, for example:

"We know what happens to people who stay in the middle of the road. They get run down." (Aneurin Bevan)

"In any moment of decision the best thing you can do is the right thing, the next best thing is the wrong thing, and the worst thing you can do is nothing." (attributed to Theodore Roosevelt-more maxims on the quotes page)

JFDI-Just Frigging Do it (polite version). The decision-maker's motto. There are usually several right answers when you are faced with a complex decision. When you've found the best solution you can find, get on with it, make it work, and it most probably will. (More useful rules, acronyms and training ideas on the acronyms page) pros and cons decision-making method

Another simple process for decision-making is the pros and cons list. Pro means 'for', and con means 'against'. In other words, advantages and disadvantages. This method also applies to all sorts of problem-solving where issues and implications need to be understood and a decision has to be made.

Some decisions are a simple matter of whether to make a change or not, such as moving, taking a new job, or buying something, selling something, replacing something, etc. Other decisions involve number of options, and are concerned more with how to do something, involving a number of choices. Use the brainstorming process to identify and develop options for decision-making and problem-solving.

1. First you will need a separate sheet for each identified option.
2. On each sheet write clearly the option concerned, and then beneath it the headings 'pros' and 'cons' (or 'advantages' and disadvantages', or simply 'for' and 'against'). Many decisions simply involve the choice of whether to go ahead or not, to change or not; in these cases you need only one sheet.
3. Then write down as many effects and implications of the particular option that you (and others if appropriate) can think of, placing each in the relevant column.
4. If helpful 'weight' each factor, by giving it a score out of three or five points (e.g., 5 being extremely significant, and 1 being of minor significance).
5. When you have listed all the points you can think of for the option concerned compare the number or total score of the items/effects/factors between the two columns.
6. This will provide a reflection and indication as to the overall attractiveness and benefit of the option concerned. If you have scored each item you will actually be able to arrive at a total score, being the difference between the pros and cons column totals. The bigger the difference between the total pros and total cons then the more attractive the option is.
7. If you have a number of options and have complete a pros and cons sheet for each option, compare the attractiveness-points difference between pros and cons-for each option. The biggest positive difference between pros and cons is the most attractive option.

8. N.B. If you don't like the answer that the decision-making sheet(s) reflect back to you, it means you haven't included all the cons-especially the emotional ones, or you haven't scored the factors consistently, so re-visit the sheet(s) concerned.

You will find that writing things down in this way will help you to see things more clearly, become more objective and detached, which will help you to make clearer decisions.

Pros and cons Weighted Decision-Making Template-Example

This example weighs the pros and cons of buying a new car to replace an old car.

The weighted pros and cons are purely examples-they are not in any way suggestions of how you should make such a decision. Our decision-making criteria depend on our own personal situations and preferences. And your criteria and weighting will change according to time, situation, and probably your mood too.

Use whatever scoring method you want to. The example shows low scores but you can score each item up to 10, or 20 or 100-whatever makes sense to you personally. Or you can use an 'A/B/C' or three-star scoring method, whatever works for you.

Should I replace my old car with a new one?

pros (for-advantages)	*score*	*cons (against-disadvantages)*	*score*
better comfort	3	cost outlay will mean making sacrifices	5
lower fuel costs	3	higher insurance	3
lower servicing costs	4	time and hassle to choose and buy it	2
better for family use	3	disposal or sale of old car	2
better reliability	5	big decisions like this scare and upset me	4
it'll be a load	2		
off my mind	2		
total 6 pros	20	total 5 cons	16

In the above example, on the basis of the pros and cons and the weighting applied, there seems to be a a clear overall (and quantifiable) advantage in the decision to go ahead and buy a new car.

Notice that with this decision-making method it's even possible to include 'intangible' emotional issues in the pros and cons comparison, for example 'it'll be a load off my mind', and 'decisions scare and upset me'.

A decision-making pros and cons list like this helps remove the emotion which blocks clear thinking and decision-making. It enables objectivity and measurement, rather than reacting from instinct, or avoiding the issue altogether. Objective measurement helps in making a confident decision.

The total weighted scores are the main deciding factor rather than the total number of pros and cons, although there is not a scientific 'right' or 'wrong' way to consider the total number of pros and cons compared with the total weighted scores.

If the weighted scores are indicating a decision which makes you feel uncomfortable, then check your weightings, and also check that you've not missed out any factors on either side of the table.

If the decision makes you feel uncomfortable and this is not reflected in the table, then add it as a factor and give it a score.

Seeking feedback or input from a trusted neutral friend can be helpful in confirming your factors and their scores.

Blank Pros and Cons Decision-Making Template

You should be able to cut and paste this template into a text editor or spreadsheet. Add more rows as required.

Complex Problems and Decisions

For more complex decisions and problems involving more than two possible options you can use several pros and cons tables in conjunction, to compare the overall weight of each option.

In such cases the wording of the options is important, for example, if considering the best path for one's own career and work development the options might be:

- be employed, working for a big company

- be self-employed, working as a consultant or freelancer from home
- start a business, with premises and staff.

A situation like this can be approached by completing three separate pros and cons tables and then comparing the net effects (difference between weighted pros and cons) of each one.

While this won't necessarily evaluate and compare all possible interrelated aspects of the whole situation, it will help to give great clarity and detached objectivity (detached as in unemotional), which can be very difficult to find when confronted with a complicated and big challenge offering several options.

Also consider that some decisions and challenges are difficult because you don't have the necessary knowledge or experience, in which case you need first to decide if the decision or challenge is actually appropriate and necessary for you at this stage.

Some decisions have to be made whether you are ready or not. Others might not be as pressing as you imagine. Do not be forced into a change-based decision if having considered the implications carefully you decide that it's not the best thing to do.

The decision to do nothing different, in the right way for the right reasons, is often a perfectly good option. Whatever you do-try to be as objective as you can be. Well prepared decisions are easier to make and to implement, and generally produce the best results.

What's a "Decision"?

The word *decide* gets a great deal of mileage in English, being critical in the definitions of dozens of other concepts, including *arbitrate*, *conclude*; *convict*, *declare*, *define*, *disagree*, *intervene*, and *judge*. Another use is adverbial: the idea of acting "decisively," achieving a final determination with clear and definitive intent. "Decide" also works as a transitive verb, meaning to influence or determine: for example, "This new development finally decided me," or "The vote in New Hampshire often decides the outcome of the presidential election."

The modern English word "decision" comes from the Sanskrit "/ khidati/"—meaning to tear and then to Latin "caedare," meaning to kill or cut down (as in battle), and then to "de +caedere" meaning to cut off from or to cut thoroughly. We see here a notion that the decision is a point, and a final point or action separating one thing from another (historically, a human head or limb from its body). All dictionary definitions preserve this sense of bringing a series of events, including a mental sequence, to a final, point-like conclusion. For example, WordNet as "To make up one's mind, to reach, make, or come to a decision about something." While the circularity is obvious and troublesome, this essay starts with the idea that decisions are things that are "made."

You can't help but be struck by the irony that many scholarly books on judgment and decision making typically forego an attempt at defining this thing called "decision." Only in one textbook and one edited volume do we find the word "decision" even as an entry in the subject index. Only in a few sources do we find an explicit discussion of the difference between "decision" and "judgment." (A "judgment" is an assessment or opinion as to what was, is, or will be the state of some decision-relevant aspect of the world—for example, whether a defendant committed a crime, whether a patient has a particular disease, or whether product sales will exceed the break-even point.

The Final-Point Notion

A decision can be defined as a commitment to a course of action having the intention of serving the interests and values of particular people. A decision is generally understood as a mental event that occurs at a singular point in time—a psychological moment of choice—that leads immediately or directly to action (for example, push the button, or wait 30 seconds and then push the button). Most views of decision making in the literatures of psychology and of judgment and decision making locate the notion of decision in the final stage of a stage-theoretic framework.

7

Management Information System

Introduction

A management information system (MIS) is a subset of the overall internal controls of a business covering the application of people, documents, technologies, and procedures by management accountants to solve business problems such as costing a product, service or a business-wide strategy. Management information systems are distinct from regular information systems in that they are used to analyze other information systems applied in operational activities in the organization. Academically, the term is commonly used to refer to the group of information management methods tied to the automation or support of human decision making, e.g. Decision Support Systems, Expert systems, and Executive information systems.

It has been described as, "MIS 'lives' in the space that intersects technology and business. MIS combines tech with business to get people the information they need to do their jobs better/faster/smarter. Information is the lifeblood of all organizations-now more than ever. MIS professionals work as systems analysts, project managers, systems administrators, etc., communicating directly with staff and management across the organization."

Overview

At the start, in businesses and other organizations, internal reporting was made manually and only periodically, as a by-product of the accounting system and with some additional statistic(s), and gave limited and delayed information on management performance. Previously, data had to be separated individually by the people as per the requirement and necessity of the organization. Later, data and information was distinguished and instead of the collection of mass of data, important and to the point data that is needed by the organization and was stored.

In their infancy, business computers were used for the practical business of computing the payroll and keeping track of accounts payable and accounts receivable As applications were developed that provided managers with information about sales, inventories, and other data that would help in managing the enterprise, the term "MIS" arose to describe these kinds of applications. Today, the term is used broadly in a number of contexts and includes (but is not limited to): decision support systems, resource and people management applications, project management and database retrieval application.

Definition

An 'MIS' is a planned system of the collecting, processing, storing and disseminating data in the form of information needed to carry out the functions of management. In a way it is a documented report of the activities those were planned and executed. According to Philip Kotler "A marketing information system consists of people, equipment, and procedures to gather, sort, analyze, evaluate, and distribute needed, timely, and accurate information to marketing decision makers."

The terms *MIS* and *information system* are often confused. Information systems include systems that are not intended for decision making. The area of study called MIS is sometimes referred to, in a restrictive sense, as information technology management. That area of study should not be confused with computer science. IT service management is a practitioner-focused discipline. MIS has also some differences with Enterprise Resource Planning (ERP) as ERP incorporates elements that are not necessarily focused on decision support.

Background

A management information system (MIS) is a system or process that provides the information necessary to manage an organization effectively. MIS and the information it generates are generally considered essential components of prudent and reasonable business decisions.

The importance of maintaining a consistent approach to the development, use, and review of MIS systems within the institution must be an ongoing concern of both bank management and OCC examiners. MIS should have a clearly defined framework of guidelines, policies or practices, standards, and procedures for the organization. These should be followed throughout the institution in the development, maintenance, and use of all MIS.

MIS is viewed and used at many levels by management. It should be supportive of the institution's longer term strategic goals and objectives. To the other extreme it is also those everyday financial accounting systems that are used to ensure basic control is maintained over financial recordkeeping activities.

Financial accounting systems and subsystems are just one type of institutional MIS. Financial accounting systems are an important functional element or part of the total MIS structure. However, they are more narrowly focused on the internal balancing of an institution's books to the general ledger and other financial accounting subsystems. For example, accrual adjustments, reconciling and correcting entries used to reconcile the financial systems to the general ledger are not always immediately entered into other MIS systems.

Accordingly, although MIS and accounting reconcilement totals for related listings and activities should be similar, they may not necessarily balance.

An Institution's MIS Should be Designed to Achieve the following Goals:

- Enhance communication among employees.
- Deliver complex material throughout the institution.
- Provide an objective system for recording and aggregating information.
- Reduce expenses related to labour-intensive manual activities.
- Support the organization's strategic goals and direction.

Because MIS supplies decision makers with facts, it supports and enhances the overall decision making process. MIS also enhances job performance throughout an institution. At the most senior levels, it provides the data and information to help the board and management make strategic decisions. At other levels, MIS provides the means through which the institution's activities are monitored and information is distributed to management, employees, and customers.

Effective MIS should ensure the appropriate presentation formats and time frames required by operations and senior management are met. MIS can be maintained and developed by either manual or automated systems or a combination of both. It should always be sufficient to meet an institution's unique business goals and objectives.

The effective deliveries of an institution's products and services are supported by the MIS. These systems should be accessible and useable at all appropriate levels of the organization. MIS is a critical component of the institution's overall risk management strategy. MIS supports management's ability to perform such reviews. MIS should be used to recognize, monitor, measure, limit, and manage risks. Risk management involves four main elements:

- Policies or practices.
- Operational processes.
- Staff and management.
- Feedback devices.

Frequently, operational processes and feedback devices are intertwined and cannot easily be viewed separately. The most efficient and useable MIS should be both operational and informational. As such, management can use MIS to measure performance, manage resources, and help an institution comply with regulatory requirements. One example of this would be the managing and reporting of loans to insiders. MIS can also be used by management to provide feedback on the effectiveness of risk controls.

Controls are developed to support the proper management of risk through the institution's policies or practices, operational processes, and the assignment of duties and responsibilities to staff and managers.

Technology advances have increased both the availability and volume of information management and the directors have available for both planning and decision making. Correspondingly, technology also increases the potential for inaccurate reporting and flawed decision making. Because data can be extracted from many financial and transaction systems, appropriate control procedures must be set up to ensure that information is correct and relevant. In addition, since MIS often originates from multiple equipment platforms including main frames, minicomputers, and microcomputers, controls must ensure that systems on smaller computers have processing controls that are as well defined and as effective as those commonly found on the traditionally larger mainframe systems.

All institutions must set up a framework of sound fundamental principles that identify risk, establish controls, and provide for effective MIS review and monitoring systems throughout the organization. Commonly, an organization may choose to establish and express these sound principles in writing.

The OCC fully endorses and supports placing these principles in writing to enhance effective communications throughout the institution. If however, management follows sound fundamental principles and governs the risk in the MIS Review area, a written policy is not required by the OCC. If sound principles are not effectively practiced, the OCC may require management to establish written MIS policies to formally communicate risk parameters and controls in this area.

Sound fundamental principles for MIS review include proper internal controls, operating procedures and safeguards, and audit coverage. These principles are explained throughout this booklet.

Risks Associated With MIS

Risk reflects the potential, the likelihood, or the expectation of events that could adversely affect earnings or capital. Management uses MIS to help in the assessment of risk within an institution. Management decisions based upon ineffective, inaccurate, or incomplete MIS may increase risk in a number of areas such as credit quality, liquidity, market/pricing, interest rate, or foreign currency.

A flawed MIS causes operational risks and can adversely affect an organization's monitoring of its fiduciary, consumer, fair lending, Bank Secrecy Act, or other compliance-related activities.

Since management requires information to assess and monitor performance at all levels of the organization, MIS risk can extend to all levels of the operations. Additionally, poorly programmed or non-secure systems in which data can be manipulated and/or systems requiring ongoing repairs can easily disrupt routine work flow and can lead to incorrect decisions or impaired planning.

Assessing Vulnerability to MIS Risk

To function effectively as an interacting, interrelated, and interdependent feedback tool for management and staff, MIS must be "useable." The five elements of a useable MIS system are: timeliness, accuracy, consistency, completeness, and relevance. The usefulness of MIS is hindered whenever one or more of these elements is compromised.

Timeliness

To simplify prompt decision making, an institution's MIS should be capable of providing and distributing *current* information to appropriate users. Information systems should be designed to expedite reporting of information. The system should be able to quickly collect and edit data, summarize results, and be able to adjust and correct errors promptly.

Accuracy

A sound system of automated and manual internal controls must exist throughout all information systems processing activities. Information should receive appropriate editing, balancing, and internal control checks. A comprehensive internal and external audit program should be employed to ensure the adequacy of internal controls.

Consistency

To be reliable, data should be processed and compiled consistently and uniformly. Variations in how data is collected and reported can distort information and trend analysis. In addition, because data collection and reporting processes will change over time, management must establish sound procedures to allow for systems changes. These procedures should be well defined and documented, clearly communicated to appropriate employees, and should include an effective monitoring system.

Completeness

Decision makers need complete and pertinent information in a summarized form. Reports should be designed to eliminate clutter and voluminous detail, thereby avoiding "information overload."

Relevance

Information provided to management must be relevant. Information that is inappropriate, unnecessary, or too detailed for effective decision making has no value. MIS must be appropriate to support the management level using it.

The relevance and level of detail provided through MIS systems directly correlate to what is needed by the board of directors, executive management, departmental or area mid-level managers, etc. in the performance of their jobs.

Achieving Sound MIS

The development of sound MIS is the result of the development and enforcement of a culture of system ownership. An "owner" is a system user who knows current customer and constituent needs and also has budget authority to fund new projects. Building "ownership" promotes pride in institution processes and helps ensure accountability.

Although MIS does not necessarily reduce expenses, the development of meaningful systems, and their proper use, will lessen the probability that erroneous decisions will be made because of inaccurate or untimely information. Erroneous decisions invariably misallocate and/or waste resources. This may result in an adverse impact on earnings and/or capital.

MIS which meets the five elements of useability is a critical ingredient to an institution's short-and long-range planning efforts. To achieve sound MIS, the organization's planning process should include consideration of MIS needs at both the tactical and strategic levels. For example, at a tactical level MIS systems and report output should support the annual operating plan and budgetary processes. They should also be used in support of the long term strategic MIS and business planning initiatives. Without the development of an effective MIS, it is more difficult for management to measure and monitor the success of new initiatives and the progress of ongoing projects. Two common examples of this would be the management of mergers and acquisitions or the continuing development and the introduction of new products and services.

Management needs to ensure that MIS systems are developed according to a sound methodology that encompasses the following phases:

- Appropriate analysis of system alternatives, approval points as the system is developed or acquired, and task organization.

- Program development and negotiation of contracts with equipment and software vendors.
- Development of user instructions, training, and testing of the system.
- Installation and maintenance of the system.

Management should also consider use of "project management techniques" to monitor progress as the MIS system is being developed. Internal controls must be woven into the processes and periodically reviewed by auditors.

Management also should ensure that managers and staff receive initial and ongoing training in MIS. In addition, user manuals should be available and provide the following information:

- A brief description of the application or system.
- Input instructions, including collection points and times to send updated information.
- Balancing and reconciliation procedures.
- A complete listing of output reports, including samples.

Depending on the size and complexity of its MIS system, an institution may need to use different manuals for different users such as first-level users, unit managers, and programmers.

MIS Reviews

By its very nature, management information is designed to meet the unique needs of individual institutions. As a result, MIS requirements will vary depending on the size and complexity of the operations. For example, systems suitable for community sized institutions will not necessarily be adequate for larger institutions. However, basic information needs or requirements are similar in all financial institutions regardless of size. The complexity of the operations and/or activities, together with institution size, point to the need for MIS of varying degrees of complexity to support the decision-making processes. Examiners should base MIS reviews on an evaluation of whether the system(s) provide management and directors with the information necessary to guide operations, support timely decision making, and help management monitor progress toward reaching institutional goals and objectives. Although examiners should encourage management to develop sound information systems, they also should be reasonable in their expectations about what constitutes suitable MIS.

Examiner MIS reviews are normally focused on a specific area of activity, on a clearly identifiable departmental or functional basis, or as a part of the activity being examined within a larger department.

During the examination, the MIS review should occur at both a macro (big picture) level and also at the micro (functional/product oriented view of the business) level. The examiner-in-charge of the MIS-review program should look at the useability and effectiveness of the corporate-wide MIS structure.

The examiner should also collect MIS related observations and information from the examiners-in-charge of the other areas under review. It would be very difficult for one examiner to attempt to perform a detailed MIS review for all of an organization's functional and operational areas of activity. It is practical and reasonable, however, to have this lead examiner coordinate and consolidate the MIS reviews from the other examination areas. The MIS related feedback received from other area examiners provides important and practical input to the MIS review examiner.

The consolidation, coordination, and analysis of this MIS feedback can be used to reach supportable macrolevel conclusions and recommendations for corporate-wide MIS activities. MIS reviews in the functional or product review areas generally should be performed by an examiner who is considered to be a subject matter expert (SME) in the area of activities or operations that are being supported by the MIS systems or processes under review. The SME must have a thorough and complete understanding of the baseline "business" supported by the MIS system(s) under review. A solid understanding of the business is fundamental to the completion of a meaningful MIS review. The decision regarding the overall quality and effectiveness of MIS generally should be made by the SME for the area under review. The SME for each area where MIS is under review must subsequently communicate MIS related findings, conclusions, and opinions to the examiner charged with the responsibility for the complete MIS review work program at that examination. This is clearly a collaborative effort among area SMEs and the examiner charged with the responsibility for this area of review.

The examiner coordinating the overall MIS review program should be a commercial examiner with broad experience and understanding which covers many areas of organizational operations and activity. Alternatively, a bank information systems (BIS) examiner could serve in this capacity. BIS examiners should be consulted whenever there are questions, issues, or concerns surrounding the use of information systems (IS) or electronic data processing (EDP) technology or the effectiveness of MIS-related internal controls in any automated area of the organization's activities.

When performing MIS reviews, examiners should use the guidelines in this booklet to determine if management has:

- *Identified the institution's specific information requirements.* Examiners can focus on specific information needs related to issues such as asset quality, interest rate risk, regulatory reporting, and compliance. If possible, the MIS review should be concurrent with examinations of the commercial, consumer, fiduciary, and BIS activities. This would enhance interaction and communication among examiners.
- Established effective reporting mechanisms to guide decisions. This process includes reviewing controls that ensure that information is reliable, timely, accurate, and confidential.

Organizing as a Management Function

Managers who are efficient at organizing their workplaces will inspire employees and please clients. Organizing is continuous and very important in the workplace.

Planning, organizing, leading and controlling are the four basic functions of management. All managers will be performing these four functions at various times during their supervisory term. After a manager has crafted a plan for his or her workplace, the plan has to be put into action. The organizing function of management is the process of making sure the necessary resources are available to meet the goals of the organization.

Organizing Resources

Organizing resources can mean a variety of things. First, the manager is in charge of organizing human resources. For example, a manager will need to be sure the appropriate employees are hired. In addition, it is the manager's responsibility to ensure the employees have the skills necessary for the workplace. Organizing these employees, according to when they are needed and how they are utilized, is a critical part of the manager's position.

In a manufacturing facility, organizing as a management function also involves ordering parts and other components needed to produce products. A manager must be extremely organized to keep track of items needed, without having components too early or too late.

Organizing Occurs Continuously

Organizing is a daily, weekly and yearly task for most managers. In today's fast-paced business world, things change quickly and variations occur. Managers must remember that the organizational component is fluid and forever-changing. Flexible managers are able to change courses when necessary and still meet the client's needs.

Change is inevitable. For firms that experience change frequently, the organizing function is even more crucial. Organizational changes such as adding new positions or eliminating certain processes can change the organizational level and structure of the business.

Importance of Organization

People who are organized generally accomplish much more than disorganized individuals. The same is true of organized departments or businesses. Those managers who can master the organization function will enjoy a much smoother tenure in the management position.

For example, a construction business has to do a great deal of organizing to ensure a project goes well. The construction manager must organize each of the subcontractors and receipt of building materials. Scheduling a carpenter before the framing materials arrive is counterproductive and shows a lack of organization. In a construction situation, there is a particular order to the project; this is also true of projects in any other work scenario.

Employees who have an organized manager will emulate that behaviour and strive for organization as well. Managers who take the organizing function seriously and consistently update their plans accordingly will achieve success in the workplace.

Organizational Structure

An organizational structure is a mainly hierarchical concept of subordination of entities that collaborate and contribute to serve one common aim.

Organizations are a variant of clustered entities. An organization can be structured in many different ways and styles, depending on their objectives and ambiance. The structure of an organization will determine the modes in which it operates and performs.

Organizational structure allows the expressed allocation of responsibilities for different functions and processes to different entities such as the branch, department, workgroup and individual. Individuals in an organizational structure are normally hired under time-limited work contracts or work orders, or under permanent employment contracts or program orders.

Operational Organizations and Informal Organizations

The set organizational structure may not coincide with facts, evolving in operational action. Such divergence decreases performance, when growing. E.g. a wrong organizational structure may hamper cooperation and thus hinder the completion of orders in due time and within limits of resources and budgets. Organizational structures shall be adaptive to process requirements, aiming to optimize the ratio of effort and input to output.

An effective organizational structure shall facilitate working relationships between various entities in the organization and may improve the working efficiency within the organizational units. Organization shall retain a set order and control to enable monitoring the processes. Organization shall support command for coping with a mix of orders and a change of conditions while performing work. Organization shall allow for application of individual skills to enable high flexibility and apply creativity. When a business expands, the chain of command will lengthen and the spans of control will widen. When an organization comes to age, the flexibility will decrease and the creativity will fatigue. Therefore organizational structures shall be altered from time to time to enable recovery. If such alteration is prevented internally, the final escape is to turn down the organization to prepare for a re-launch in an entirely new set up.

Success Factors

Common success criteria for organizational structures are:

- Decentralized reporting
- Flat hierarchy
- High transient speed
- High transparency
- Low residual mass
- Permanent monitoring
- Rapid response
- Shared reliability
- Matrix hierarchy.

History

Organizational structures developed from the ancient times of hunters and collectors in tribal organizations through highly royal and clerical power structures to industrial structures and today's post-industrial structures.

Organizational Structure Types

Pre-bureaucratic Structures

Pre-bureaucratic (entrepreneurial) structures lack standardization of tasks. This structure is most common in smaller organizations and is best used to solve simple tasks. The structure is totally centralized. The strategic leader makes all key decisions and most communication is done by one on one conversations. It is particularly useful for new (entrepreneurial) business as it enables the founder to control growth and development. They are usually based on traditional domination or charismatic domination in the sense of Max Weber's tripartite classification of authority.

Bureaucratic Structures

Bureaucratic structures have a certain degree of standardization. They are better suited for more complex or larger scale organizations. They usually adopt a tall structure. Then tension between bureaucratic structures and non-bureaucratic is echoed in Burns and Stalker distinction between mechanistic and organic structures.

Post-bureaucratic

The term of post bureaucratic is used in two senses in the organizational literature: one generic and one much more specific. In the generic sense the term post bureaucratic is often used to describe a range of ideas developed since the 1980s that specifically contrast themselves with Weber's ideal type bureaucracy. This may include total quality management, culture management and matrix management, amongst others. None of these however has left behind the core tenets of Bureaucracy. Hierarchies still exist, authority is still Weber's rational, legal type, and the organization is still rule bound. Heckscher, arguing along these lines, describes them as cleaned up bureaucracies, rather than a fundamental shift away from bureaucracy. Gideon Kunda, in his classic study of culture management at 'Tech' argued that 'the essence of bureaucratic control-the formalisation, codification and enforcement of rules and regulations-does not change in principle.....it shifts focus from organizational structure to the organization's culture'.

Another smaller group of theorists have developed the theory of the Post-Bureaucratic Organization., provide a detailed discussion which attempts to describe an organization that is fundamentally not bureaucratic. Charles Heckscher has developed an ideal type, the post-bureaucratic organization, in which decisions are based on dialogue and consensus rather than authority and command, the organization is a network rather than a hierarchy, open at the boundaries (in direct contrast to culture management); there is an emphasis on meta-decision making rules rather than decision making rules. This sort of horizontal decision making by consensus model is often used in housing cooperatives, other cooperatives and when running a non-profit or community organization. It is used in order to encourage participation and help to empower people who normally experience oppression in groups.

Still other theorists are developing a resurgence of interest in complexity theory and organizations, and have focused on how simple structures can be used to engender organizational adaptations. For instance, Miner *et al.* (2000) studied how simple structures could be used to generate improvisational outcomes in product development. Their study makes links to simple structures and improviseal learning. Other scholars such as Jan Rivkin and Sigglekow, and Nelson Repenning revive an older interest in how structure and strategy relate in dynamic environments.

Functional Structure

Employees within the functional divisions of an organization tend to perform a specialized set of tasks, for instance the engineering department would be staffed only with engineers. This leads to operational efficiencies within that group. However it could also lead to a lack of communication between the functional groups within an organization, making the organization slow and inflexible.

As a whole, a functional organization is best suited as a producer of standardized goods and services at large volume and low cost. Coordination and specialization of tasks are centralized in a functional structure, which makes producing a limited amount of products or services efficient and predictable. Moreover, efficiencies can further be realized as functional organizations integrate their activities vertically so that products are sold and distributed quickly and at low cost. For instance, a small business could start making the components it requires for production of its products instead of procuring it from an external organization.

Divisional Structure

Also called a "product structure", the divisional structure groups each organizational function into a divisions. Each division within a divisional structure contains all the necessary resources and functions within it. Divisions can be categorized from different points of view. There can be made a distinction on geograpical basis (an US division and an EU division) or on product/service basis (different products for different customers: households or companies). Another example, an automobile company with a divisional structure might have one division for SUVs, another division for subcompact cars, and another division for sedans. Each division would have its own sales, engineering and marketing departments.

Matrix Structure

The matrix structure groups employees by both function and product. This structure can combine the best of both separate structures. A matrix organization frequently uses teams of employees to accomplish work, in order to take advantage of the strengths, as well as make up for the weaknesses, of functional and decentralized forms. An example would be a company that produces two products, "product a" and "product b". Using the matrix structure, this company would organize functions within the company as follows: "product a" sales department, "product a" customer service department, "product a" accounting, "product b" sales department, "product b" customer service department, "product b" accounting department. Matrix structure is amongst the purest of organizational structures, a simple lattice emulating order and regularity demonstrated in nature.

- Weak/Functional Matrix: A project manager with only limited authority is assigned to oversee the cross-functional aspects of the project. The functional managers maintain control over their resources and project areas.
- Balanced/Functional Matrix: A project manager is assigned to oversee the project. Power is shared equally between the project manager and the functional managers. It brings the best aspects of functional and projectized organizations. However, this is the most difficult system to maintain as the sharing power is delicate proposition.
- Strong/Project Matrix: A project manager is primarily responsible for the project. Functional managers provide technical expertise and assign resources as needed.

Among these matrixes, there is no best format; implementation success always depends on organization's purpose and function.

Organizational Circle: Moving Fack to Flat

The flat structure is common in enterpreneurial start-ups, university spin offs or small companies in general. As the company grows, however, it becomes more complex and hierarchical, which leads to an expanded structure, with more levels and departments.

Often, it would result in bureaucracy, the most prevalent structure in the past. It is still, however, relevant in former Soviet Republics and China, as well as in most governmental organizations all over the world. Shell Group used to represent the typical bureaucracy: top-heavy and hierarchical. It featured multiple levels of command and duplicate service companies existing in different regions. All this made Shell apprehensive to market changes, leading to its incapacity to grow and develop further. The failure of this structure became the main reason for the company restructuring into a matrix.

Starbucks is one of the numerous large organizations that successfully developed the matrix structure supporting their focused strategy. Its design combines functional and product based divisions, with employees reporting to two heads. Creating a team spirit, the company empowers employees to make their own decisions and train them to develop both hard and soft skills. That makes Starbucks one of the best at customer service.

Some experts also mention the multinational design, common in global companies, such as Procter & Gamble, Toyota and Unilever. This structure can be seen as a complex form of the matrix, as it maintains coordination among products, functions and geographic areas.

In general, over the last decade, it has become increasingly clear that through the forces of globalization, competition and more demanding customers, the structure of many companies has become flatter, less hierarchical, more fluid and even virtual.

Team

One of the newest organizational structures developed in the 20th century is *team*. In small businesses, the team structure can define the entire organization. Teams can be both horizontal and vertical. While an organization is constituted as a set of people who synergise individual competencies to achieve newer dimensions, the quality of organizational structure revolves around the competencies of teams in totality. For example, every one of the Whole Foods Market stores, the largest natural-foods grocer in the US developing a focused strategy, is an autonomous profit centre composed of an average of 10 self-managed teams, while team leaders in each store and each region are also a team. Larger bureaucratic organizations can benefit from the flexibility of teams as well. Xerox, Motorola, and Daimler Chrysler are all among the companies that actively use teams to perform tasks.

Network

Another modern structure is network. While business giants risk becoming *too clumsy to proact, act and react efficiently*, the new network organizations contract out any business function, that can be done better or more cheaply. In essence, managers in network structures spend most of their time coordinating and controlling external relations, usually by electronic means. H&M is outsourcing its clothing to a network of 700 suppliers, more than two-thirds of which are based in low-cost Asian countries. Not owning any factories, H&M can be more flexible than many other retailers in lowering its costs, which aligns with its low-cost strategy. The potential management opportunities offered by recent advances in complex networks theory have been demonstrated including applications to product design and development, and innovation problem in markets and industries.

Boundaryless Structure

The most radical concept in today's organizational design is the concept of *boundarylessness*, which seeks to overcome traditional boundaries between layers of management (vertical), functional areas (horizontal), as well as geographic boundaries. Some claim the boundaryless structure is a combination of team and network structures, with the addition of *temporariness*. Ikea, the world's largest furniture manufacture, has been successful in implementing the boundaryless structure. The company works closely with suppliers by providing technical assistance, leasing them equipment, and giving advice. It also refined the role of the customer, putting responsibility on them to cart the furniture home and assemble it themselves. As a result, the company can offer lower prices, which supports its low-cost focused strategy.

Virtual

A special form of boundaryless organization is *virtual*. It works in a network of external alliances, using the Internet. This means while the core of the organization can be small but still the company can operate globally be a market leader in its niche. According to Anderson, because of the unlimited shelf space of the Web, the cost of reaching niche goods is falling dramatically. Although none sell in huge numbers, there are so many niche products that collectively they make a significant profit, and that is what made highly innovative Amazon.com so successful.

As we can see, organizations develop, modify and change their structures so that they align with their strategies. And the main trend for the last decades seems to be coming back to flatter structures. Although this structure seems suitable for small companies only, large organizations can take elements of it in harder times. Being at risk of losing profits or even going bankrupt due to the major financial downturn today, a lot of companies are moving to flatter structures. Not only are they unable to maintain multiple management levels any more, they are also in need of a more flexible structure to cope with new threats.

Organizational Structure Types and Design Strategy

Welcome to Organizationalstructure.net. Starting a new organization can be a hard task, no matter how big or small it may be. Whether you are starting a new company, business, or you're a school board member, your organization needs a good structure to keep it going. On our site, you can find information on strategies, designs, and the implementation of different types of organizational structure. We can offer examples for businesses, companies, corporations, schools, restaurants, and more.

The structure of your business will act as the backbone and support concerning decision making and other processes. Deciding early what type of organizational system you want to implement will help to ease the stress of the initial start-up. If each person in the organization knows what he or she is supposed to be doing, there is less room for confusion and poor judgment. Perhaps setting up a management team would work the best for your organization, or perhaps a hierarchy of decision makers would work better. Either way, setting up a definite structure before important shots are called makes a difference.

Organizational Structure Corporate Theory

The first step is determining what type of organizational structure you would like to design and implement. Some examples of structures would be, functional and hierarchical. Next, you should develop a strategy to start organizing your business, company, or group. How do you want it to run? From the top down, or by a matrix of different people, such as a management department is a big decision. Once you have a few options picked out, you can decide which option will be optimal to produce the results you desire.

On this site, you can find assistance on the topics above. Available to you are designs, models, alternative ideas, and strategy examples for setting up the structure of your business. Also available are different theories and opinions surrounding some strategies discussed. As for smaller organizations, we can offer some public resources to help you in your specific area. Additionally, simple versions of structures can be found.

If you choose the options that best fit your organization then you're more likely to succeed in your market. By having the right people in the right place, it can lead to better networking opportunities, higher sales, increased interest in your organization, and overall success.

Define or Definition

OS can be defined as the way or method through use of a hierarchy that a group, business, organization, people or objects collaborate to achieve success on one common goal.

A New or Small Business Startup Structure

A new business or determined entrepreneur lacks the structure and development to succeed at first. Typically in a small business start-up the team lacks a set standard in structure that will actually work for them. The standards are yet to be set in place and in turn end up hurting company growth, progress and even revenue. However, most new startups all go through this phase because there isn't a set standard in design for every company. So that being said most companies have different types of organizational structure. Sometimes it takes weeks, months, and even years to get a structural plan in place that works best for a company.

A new business owner will call all the shots and make all the decisions, so it's somewhat impossible to think about proper organizational structure until a company has reached a certain point in revenue, employees, and business. Before any business can proceed from a start up, it must have the one boss calling all the shots, and in most cases would be the CEO or co-founders. All the decisions and support come straight from the top in one centralized region of the company. The founder or co-founders take all the serious matters and address them appropriately until the company can grow enough to have people put into place to achieve this for them. When they can a proper hierarchy can put set in place.

In a retail start-up situation, it would be the group of people in charge of the books, and getting the business of the ground would address solutions on a personal basis. Most big companies like Dell,

McDonalds, or even Wal-Mart surely had to start in the phase at one point in time.

Hierarchy of Organizational Structure

All large companies have a design in their structure that works best for them. Most large companies follow the basis of what any other large organization would. Such as School, Military, Police, or even a Government, they all have their own set in standard way of hierarchy. This can be mirrored of what a fortune 500 company would use. Of course you have your owner, VP's, and then comes the managers.

- CEO
- Vice Presidents
- Lawyers
- Decision Support
- Management
- Employees.

In this typical layout, it can be spread across any number of product lines or services a company offers. For instance if a company offers five different product lines then there is usually going to be a Vice President put in place to represent one of each sections, then would come the decision support for those sections and of course followed by its own management structure. Fortune 500 companies like Verizon, Comcast, or even Staples must have achieved this successful design and strategy to allow them to grow so rapidly and become so large. The divisional way of doing things can be seen like a matrix, where any given employee can have anywhere from two managers to dozens.

Decisions on a Company Networking Basis

Some companies opt to use a different approach in their organizational structure. It's an approach that doesn't rely on just straight forward management and the chain of command. Although it does not always benefit and work out for companies to operate this way, it sometimes allows them to perform even better financially. This type of organizational structure is a networking type feel. It takes all employees big or small, old and new into consideration when making decisions at the moment. Of course there's a penalty to poor decision making by a bad employee, but sometimes it does more good than bad.

For instance it would work on a checks and balances type set up where a organization would collaborate like ideas to perform the best decision making. Each important decision would rely on a set of employees which in turn would collaborate with other employees throughout the company specialized in different fields. Their expertise in their respective fields would cover all aspects in any given decision opportunity.

Functional Structure Design Example

Let's say there's a decision whether to cut spending in the call centre department of company XYZ. This would require employees from different areas such as a manager in the customer service department, an actual call centre employee, an accounting representative, and a decision support specialist in company growth.

On a much larger scale these individuals would collaborate to implement the best approach in the spending depletion. Whether it is the financial spending that needs to be in a certain range, or not cut at all, this would allow them to make the best possible decision. It would then typically be confirmed through another set of managers or vice presidents before put into place.

Organizational Structure Charts and Diagrams

Here you will find various organizational structure charts, diagrams, and visual representations to help you gain a better understanding of what the hierarchy should look like. This page will be updated periodically with new charts and diagrams as we come across them. If you would like to submit a organizational chart of your own please feel free to contact us.

As you may know, there are three main types of organizational structure: functional structure, Divisional structure and Matrix structure. Each structure has its own strong and weak points.

In the functional structure, above, the employees are working in departments based on what they are doing i.e. we have engineering department, maintenance department, finance department, research department, Warehouse department, purchasing department. This structure enhances the experience of each function. For example, all the maintenance engineers are working in the same department and thus they will exchange knowledge and support each other. This structure saves us money because of the economies of scale. This structure makes the coordination between different department more difficult than other structures. It also does not allow for flexibility because of the centralization.

Divisional structure divides, shown above, the employees based on the product/customer segment/geographical location. For example, each division is responsible for certain product and has its own resources such as finance, marketing, warehouse, maintnenace..etc.

Accordingly, this structures is a decentralized structure and thus allows for flexibility and quick response to environmental changes. It also enhances innovation and differention strategies. On the other hand, this structure results in duplication of resources because, for ex., we need to have warehouse for each division. Obviuosly, it does not support the exchange of knowledge between people working in the same profession because part of them are working in one division and the others are working in other divisions.

Matrix structure, shown above, combines both structures. For example, we can have a functional structure and then assign a manager for each product. Some employees will have two managers: functional manager and product manager. This type of structure tries to get the benefits of functional structure and also of divisional structure; however, it is not easy to implement because of the dual authority. This structure is very useful for multinational companies.

It is important to keep in mind that each managerial decision has its pros and cons. Sometimes, writers will convince you that divisional or matrix structure are the recent trends and that you need to reengineer your structure tomorrow morning. Obviuosly, this is not true. Many organizations still has functional structure and is doing very well. It is very important to select the structure that best service your condition. What is your strategy? How many products do you have? What type of technology are you using? How big is your company/organization?

Management should take necessary actions to decrease the disadvantages of the chosen structure and to enhance its the positive effects. For example, if we think the divisional structure is the best type for our condition then we should have tools to exchange knowledge between engineers working in different divisions. These tools can include forums on the LAN and conferences to exchange knowledge. Conversely, if we adopt functional structure, we can form teams from different functions to solve problems and develop our products.

Developing countries suffer from the lack of research. Most of research on organization structure based on studying Japanes, American and European compoanies but it is rare to find a research based on a sample of african companies.

That is a challenge for managers working in developing countries because the research does not really tell them what to do and what to expect. The differences in cultures can affect the results of adopting certain structure in certain part of the world. Sometimes, you deal with the same organization in different parts of the world and get very different standard of service. This shows that this multinational organization failed to reach the same results in the developing country.

Management should not think they are going to double their profits because they adopted flat structure (less number of management layers). If this structure reengineering is not part of a certain strategy, it will not work.

For example, if we adopt flat structure and then transfer the authorities of the middle management to the top management then we are increasing centralization and decreasing our flexibility. Similarly, if we adopt functional structure and allow for the duplication of resources, then we will get the disadvantages of the functional structure and will lose one of its main advantages which is economies of scale.

Many companies have combination between functional, divisional and matrix structure. Many of the decentralized companies will have one or two department centralized such as human resources or marketing.

Whatever structure you have, the results are the most important. The results are not your perception that you are the best. Measure yourself compared with similar companies. Do you need one week to take a decision that they make in one hour? Are your employees motivated more than those in other companies? Are you developing new products and services faster than other companies? Are you achieving your main strategy?

Bureaucratic Organization

Every organization has a certain objective to achieve. However, members of the organizations do not necessarily share the same objectives, and therefore, a need for control over their activities arises so that the company is able to meet their objectives. Authority therefore is needed to advance and achieve the objective of an organization.

Bureaucracy is a form of authority using structures and sets of regulation in place to control activity. It is represented by standardized procedure (rule-following) that dictates the execution of most or all process within the body. It is one of the most efficient and fair way of control over an organization, but however, is often accused of wiping out individual responsibility of the members in the organization.

Bureaucratic Organization

Max Weber is one of the most influential proponents of bureaucracy. He sees bureaucracy as technically superior over other organizational forms in precision, speed, lack of ambiguity, continuity, unity & uniformity, effective discipline & objectivity. As he described:

"The decisive reason for the advance of bureaucratic organization has always been its purely technical superiority over any other form of organization. The fully developed bureaucratic mechanism compares with other organizations exactly as does the machine with the non-mechanical modes of production."

He formed certain ideas on what an ideal bureaucracy would be like and defined. In this section, we shall discuss about Weber's idea on the basic elements of the bureaucratic organization.

Basic Elements of Bureaucracy

The basic elements of the bureaucratic organizations are Written rights & responsibility, Hierarchical Order of Authority, Formal Appointment/Promotion, Expert/Technical Training, Fixed Monetary Salaries, Administration as a Full-time Occupation and the separation of Office & Person.

Written Rights & Responsibility

In a bureaucratic organization, rules & guidelines are all written down on paper, and employees are expected to work within the confines of this rules & guidelines. Job & departmental responsibilities are also stated clearly, and employees are to work within their specified areas. It is a cardinal principal that the incumbent in this position should never overstep the bounds of his authority.

Hierarchical Order of Authority

The organization has a order of hierarchy and the division of power involves the ranking of offices to provide a clear chain of command. In bureaucracies, the hierarchy is also typically complex leading to many levels providing a highly differentiated structure of authority.

Formal Appointment/Promotion

Appointments & Promotion of officers are formal, with specific titles and power which come from the office assigned to them.

Expert/Technical Training

Employees are employed base on their technical competency in their position of employment. Factors like luck, favouritism or personal connection should play no part in the position the officials attains; advancement should be decided by expertise and ability alone.

Fixed Monetary Salaries

Employees are paid on a pre-agreed salary between the employer and employee. Salaries are tied to a pay grade system, with all employees in a certain pay grade drawing similar amount of salary. As they are promoted, they move forward in the pay grade, drawing a fixed salary for that particular position.

Administration as a Full-time Occupation

Labour in the organization is divided into various portions, with a group of people doing fully administrative work.

Separation of Office and Person

All dealings within the bureaucracy and with clients should be conducted on the basis of equal treatment according to procedural routine. The objective conduct of business should be free from any personal feelings.

A Bureaucratic Officer

With the above elements of a bureaucratic organization spelled out, we can draw out that an ideal bureaucratic officer is personally free and appointed to his position on the basis of conduct & his technical qualification for the job. He exercises the authority delegated to him in accordance with impersonal rules, and his or her loyalty is enlisted on behalf of the faithful execution of his official duties.

Administrative work would be his full-time career and work is rewarded by a regular salary and prospects of advancement in a lifetime career. A bureaucratic officer need to exercise his own judgment and skills, but his duty is to be place these at the service of a higher bureaucratic officer, who follows the same rule, place the product of his judgment and skills to the next higher officer and so on.

Accusation: Wiping out Individual Responsibility of Employee

Bureaucracy has often been accused of wiping out individual responsibility of employee. We shall first examine the various critique of bureaucracy and then on practical observation of bureaucracy at work.

In my approach to this accusation of bureaucracy, we will first explore how bureaucracy dehumanize employees, how the core bureaucratic believe of rationality makes irrational people and finally, how bureaucracy causes goal displacement.

Dehumanization

According to the philosopher, Immanuel Kant, rationality lies in daring to know, in having the courage to use one's own reason rather than rely upon the authority of others.

However, rationality according to bureaucracy seems to be the exact opposite of how it is defined above.

For an organization to be rational, it must eradicate irrational behaviour that humans are likely to succumb to, and to do that, they would have to prohibit the capacity for discretion by ascertaining certain rules for people to follow. It is deemed important for a bureaucratic organization to maintain their structure, using rules to take out unpredictability of individual human beings. Human are not seen as individuals, they are like machines, predictability working together in harmony to achieve the goal of the organization. With everything recorded and written down, everyone following rules and regulation set out by the organization, it does rob people away from their responsibility, their freedom to use their own reasoning to work out situation placed upon them in the organization.

In bureaucracy, there is also a sharp divide in the division of labour. Information is also not fully available to all (due to the enormousity of organization or management control of information), and most people working in it will never see the full picture of the organization, and how certain decision made at one end of the organization will affect the other end of the organization, more so with globalization where the top management is usually far away from the production workers of the product. With many of the managers having insufficient information, how could they be responsible for certain actions that they carry out? This, too rob employees of their responsibility.

Formal & Substantive Rationality

Rationality, could also be seen as a dichotomy – Formal or Substantive rationality. The issue here is that whether we question the ends it serve, or the means to the ends. An example of this would be the Nazi Holocaust. The Nazi represents the extreme application of bureaucratic logic. With a system of rules, they are able to register and monitor the population of the Jews and other categories of people who they opposed to. They are able to systematically transport people from 1 camp to another, and then to exterminate them systematically. Are they Substantively Rational? According to my view, and I believe the ground soldiers carrying out this orders, they are not. Are they formally rational? Yes, with this systematic way of doing things, they are very efficient in what they do.

Many modern organizations are formally rational, but some of them could be substantively irrational. As we move away from the extreme case, it would be very difficult to define what is substantively rational.

Moving back to the discussion on individual responsibility of employees, the requirement for formal rationality could means that sometimes, they have to do things that seems substantively irrational to them. Take for example the recent case in•Melamine poisoning of milk in China. In order to make milk to appear to have more protein in certain analysis test done by the regulatory body, they added in Melamine to make the milk appear to have a higher protein concentration. This is formally rational, as they could dilute the milk so as to sell more of it.

However, looking at the number of babies that died, it is substantively irrational to everyone else. Knowing of the consequences to the consumer, substantively, the people involved in the whole production of the milk should raise the alarm and alert the authority of this misdeed.

However, given that the workers are formally rational, they would prefer to keep their jobs and their belly filled then watch the company go down. It took great courage & moral standing for the executive in Fonterra, Sanlu business partner to blow the whistle on this. Is it substantively rational for them to do that? Yes. Formally rational? No, they lose their investment when the company goes down.

In the light of formal rationality, it does affect employees on their decision, looking at the consequences they would face if they were to stand up to their ethics and morals. If they do not voice out, nothing will happen to them as it is not them who make the decision, it is always someone higher up in the hierarchy that makes it. Thus in this modern case that we see, bureaucracy does rob employee of their personal responsibility, where many people choose to do nothing at an apparent wrong doing their organization is committing.

Other then Sanlu, there are various other organization that faces the same dichotomy, Nike & their sweatshops, Shell & their ties with Nigerian militant and DeBeers & their blood diamonds. For Sanlu, the "responsible" people have been punished, but for Nike, Shell & Debeers, no one is responsible for anything.

Goal Displacement

Merton (1940) argues that bureaucracy has an inbuilt tendency to focus on means and not ends, to degenerate to the situation where the means becomes an end in itself. Suppose a security guard at a factory is suppose to follow a rule, that no one without a pass could enter the factory. The purpose of this rule is to protect the factory, and the means is the security guard checking passes. One day, the Managing Director arrived early for a meeting.

The factory is in trouble and the MD is supposed to meet the creditor on that day. The security guard recognized the MD, but will not let her enter without a pass. Rules are rules, he says. So the MD fails to make the meeting and the factory closes down. The security guard's goal of protecting the factory has been displaced, so that the means of checking passes has become an end to itself.

Many employees would never see the goal of their job, but more of the description, the means of the organization which they are employed to carry out. If they employee are contracted to work in accordance to a set of rules, how could they be responsible for their actions if they work within the confine of the rules? This again robs employees of their responsibility.

We can see that Bureaucracy is an effective means of organization, but however, it does and is robbing people working in them of their responsibility by dehumanizing the employee by seeing them as part of the machine suppose to achieve a specific task, by having formal rationality being seen as more important as substantive responsibility, and by goal displacement, where employees see the means, but not the goals of the organization.

Modern organizations however are changing, and many are moving into Human Relations Theory & Job Redesign to empower their employees. Bureaucracy is a crude, ugly machine that is able to churn out products achieving goals of the organization. As it is seen and is already the way to manage organization, it is time to start beautifying and improving on the piece of machinery, to add in certain variable one at a time to see whether it will improve to be a better tool of management.

The Eight Major Characteristics of the Bureaucratic Organization

There are eight major characteristics of what is called the "bureaucratic form." Your organization likely uses most of these. Virtually all organizations that use the bureaucratic form seem to suffer the same suffocating and immobilizing symptoms that people call "bureaucracy." The characteristics of the bureaucratic organization are:

1. Most employees blame their organization's "bureaucracy" on senior management. They assume that management must want it, or it wouldn't be tolerated.
2. Senior managers don't want or like "bureaucracy" any more than the rest of the employees. The detestable effects of bureaucracy victimize everyone, regardless of level. Senior managers haven't known what to do to get rid of it. Executives have tried many things to eliminate "bureaucracy," but the "program-of-the-year" approach generally hasn't worked, because they have been fighting symptoms, not the root cause.
3. The root cause of "bureaucracy" is the organizing model, the "bureaucratic form." Yet, the bureaucratic form is so pervasive that its destructive nature is seldom questioned.
4. If you were starting a new enterprise today, you could avoid "bureaucracy" by using a new organizing model called the "mission-driven" model.
5. Existing bureaucratic organizations can reduce the amount of "bureaucracy" by changing one or more of the basic organizing principles, either temporarily or permanently. The steps for de-bureaucratizing by changing basic organizing principles are:
   a. Make an assessment of the present state of the organization to learn how much permission to change and commitment to change is available from stakeholders and senior management.
   b. Depending on the amount of available commitment, choose the optimal goal state: a modest goal, a moderate goal, or an ambitious goal.
   c. The goal state will suggest the strategy for changing the organization. The strategy will range from a minimum effort based mostly on training to a maximum effort based on reorganization and a new way of managing called "continuous improvement."
   d. Continuous improvement is an entirely new way of operating in which the people closest to the product or

customer, working in teams, are empowered to continuously improve the organization's quality, service, or both. Continuous improvement requires three things:

i. A "shadow" organization chartered to make the changes necessary in the existing organization to achieve the desired goal state.

ii. New forms of qualitative customer feedback from internal and external customers to be used to drive changes in quality, service, or both.

iii. Training for employees enabling them to work in teams, to accept the offered empowerment, to identify and prioritize root causes of problems, and to find solutions they will use to continuously improve quality, service, or both.

6. Management people in the existing organization will need to learn and use new ways of managing. They will need to learn what they have been doing that adds to the "bureaucracy" in the organization. They will need to learn new ways of doing their jobs that diminish the amount of bureaucracy within the organization. Most importantly, they will need to provide empowerment for those who work for them, and protection and coaching to those who accept and act upon the offered empowerment.

7. People in the organization who currently aren't managing will play a vital new role in the de-bureaucratized organization. The labour/management war, if it exists in your organization, must end. Everyone in the organization will need to act as one unified team, driven by a common mission, and aligned by a common vision of the new organization. People who today are not formally managing will be grouped into teams in which the brainpower, skills, talents, and experience of the individuals will be harnessed to continuously improve the organization's quality, service, or both.

   People who are presently not in managerial positions will be drawn to enroll in the change effort because their new, expanded role offers less bureaucracy and more opportunity for motivation through personal growth, achievement, responsibility, recognition and more interesting work.

8. Inally, the vision of what your organization might look like, and be like, when you have achieved your desired goal state is outlined in detail in "Busting Bureaucracy." You will discover the rewards that come from working in an organization of empowered people who are satisfying or even dazzling their customers, and are doing so with few, if any, of the immobilizing and suffocating effects of bureaucracy.

The foremost theorist of bureaucracy is the German sociologist Max Weber (1864–1920), who described the ideal characteristics of bureaucracies and offered an explanation for the historical emergence of bureaucratic institutions.

According to Weber, the defining features of bureaucracy sharply distinguish it from other types of organization based on nonlegal forms of authority. Weber observed that the advantage of bureaucracy was that it was the most technically proficient form of organization, possessing specialized expertise, certainty, continuity, and unity. Bureaucracy's emergence as a preferred form of organization occurred with the rise of a money-based economy (which ultimately resulted in the development of capitalism) and the attendant need to ensure impersonal, rational-legal transactions.

Instrumental organizations (e.g., public-stock business firms) soon arose because their bureaucratic organization equipped them to handle the various demands of capitalist production more efficiently than small-scale producers.

Contemporary stereotypes of bureaucracy tend to portray it as unresponsive, lethargic, undemocratic, and incompetent. Weber's theory of bureaucracy, however, emphasizes not only its comparative technical and proficiency advantages but also attributes its dominance as a form of organization to the diminution of caste systems (such as feudalism) and other forms of inequitable social relations based upon a person's status.

In the pure form of bureaucratic organization universalized rules and procedures would dominate, rendering personal status or connections irrelevant. In this form, bureaucracy is the epitome of universalized standards under which similar cases are treated similarly as codified by law and rules, and under which the individual tastes and discretion of the administrator are constrained by due process rules. Despite the widespread derogatory stereotypes of bureaucracy, a system of government grounded in law requires bureaucracy to function.

Nevertheless, the words *bureaucracy* and *bureaucrat* are typically thought of and used pejoratively. They convey images of red tape, excessive rules and regulations, unimaginativeness, a lack of individual discretion, central control, and an absence of accountability. Far from being conceived as proficient, popular contemporary portrayals often paint bureaucracies as inefficient and lacking in adaptability. Because the characteristics that define the organizational advantages of bureaucracy also contain within them the possibilities of organizational dysfunction, both the flattering and unflattering depictions of bureaucracy can be accurate. Thus, the characteristics that make bureaucracies proficient paradoxically also may produce organizational pathologies.

8

Levels of Organization

Power and Influence

The term 'power' is often considered as synonymous to authority. Really there is a difference between two terms. Power refers to the ability or capacity to influence the behaviour or attitudes of other individuals. A manager's power may be considered as his ability to cause subordinates to do what the manager wishes them to do.

Power, like authority, is a means of exercising influence on the behaviour of people. But power is stronger than influence. Influence is a psychological force while power is a personal force that enables a person to change the behaviour of others. Influence also differs from authority. Authority is one means to exert influence.

Formal and Informal Organization

Formal organization refers to the planned structure of jobs and positions with clearly defined objectives and functions. It is deliberately or consciously created by top management for the accomplishment of enterprise objectives. It is made up of official relationships and channels of communication. Formal structure is governed by established rules and procedures.

Informal organization arises from the personal and social relations of people. It is not formally designed but develops interactions between persons. It is influenced by personal attitudes, like and dislikes. Informal relations cut across formal channels. For example, a superior may take advice from the sales manager instead of from the production manager who is his boss.

Decision-Making

Decision-making is the process of choosing a course of action from available alternatives. This process involves understanding the problem, collecting information, developing and evaluating alternative, choice of a solution and its evaluation. Decision-making is an integral part of every manager's job. Every manager is a decision-maker and spends a major portion of his time in taking decisions. It is not the monopoly of top management alone. All managers take decisions though the quality and type and decisions taken may differ from one level of management to another. Decision-making is inherent in all managerial functions and embraces all the areas of business. Management of an organization has to take a series of decisions. The business executive is by profession a decision-maker. Decision-making is a pervasive function of management. Therefore, management is essentially a decision-making process and managers are called decision-makers. Managerial job is perpetually a decision making challenge. It is through decision-making that plans and policies are translated into concrete choice. Decision-making is the vehicle for carrying managerial workload and discharging managerial responsibilities.

Strategy

The term 'strategy' began to be used in business with increase in competition and complexity of operations. A strategy may be defined as gamesmanship or an administrative course of action designed to achieve success in the face of difficulties. It is an overall plan prepared for meeting the challenge posed by the activities of competitors and other environmental forces. Strategy is the complex plan for bringing the organization from a given posture to a desired position in a future period of time. For example, if the management anticipates price-cut by competitors, it may decide upon a strategy of launching an advertising campaign to educate the customers and to convince them of the superiority of its products. In order to formulate, an effective strategy management must anticipate accurately the plans of competitors and look at them from the viewpoint of rival firms.

Distinction Between Management Fundamentals and Management Techniques

Management fundamentals-theory and principle-should be defined clearly and must be distinguished from management techniques. A specific technique or approach of management may differ from the culture to culture or from the country to country, but management fundamentals are universally applicable. Identical concepts, theories and principles apply with equal force in widely different environment. Variations in cultures may affect the application of management fundamentals but the fundamentals are having universality of application. Techniques may vary under different cultures but the fundamentals themselves do not. While practices and applications will vary widely from one situation to another, fundamental concepts and principles of management and of human relations will remain much the same even when they take effect in different combinations.

Coordination & Controlling

Coordination refers to harmonizing and integrating the activities and efforts of different individuals into teamwork. It requires unification of diverse and specialized activities towards the achievement of common goals. Through coordination, a manager secures unity of action in the pursuit of common purpose. A manager's job may be compared with that of the conductor of an orchestra. The conductor interprets the composer's score and harmonizes the efforts of different instrumentalists to assure rhythm in the orchestra team. Similarly, a manager interprets and explains the goals and policies of the organization to his subordinates. He integrates the efforts of different employees to ensure that they work as a team. Controlling is the process of ensuring that the organization is moving in the desired direction and that progress is being made towards the achievement of goals.

Directing & Motivating

Directing is the managerial function of guiding, supervising, motivating and leading people towards the attainment of planned targets of performance. In the process of directing, his subordinates, a manager takes active steps to ensure that the employees accomplish their tasks according to the established plans. Directing is the executive function of management because it is concerned with the execution of plans and policies. Motivating is an important element in the process of directing. It is the process of inspiring people to strive for the accomplishment of common goals by providing stimuli that satisfy their needs and motives. Motivation is an important determinant of job performance.

Managerial Functions and Managerial Levels

Though the managerial functions are necessary at all levels of organization, the relative significance of different may not be the same at all levels of management. The time spent on various functions differs from one level to another. In general, planning and organizing are more significant at higher levels of management. Lower level executives spend comparatively a greater part of their time on direction and controlling functions. A middle level manager is likely to divide his time more evenly among the different functions. At higher levels, planning is long term and strategic while at lower levels it tends to be short term and operational planning.

Importance of Management

The success of group depends upon mutual co-operation among the members of the group. Management creates teamwork and coordination among specialized efforts. Management is indispensible in all organizations whether businesses firm, a government, a hospital, a college, a club, etc. Management is a creative force which helps in the optimum utilization of resources. Competent managerial leadership alone can convert the disorganized resources of men, money, materials and machinery into a productive enterprise. In the absence of management, an organization is merely a collection of men, money, materials and machinery. Managers can do much to improve the work environment, to stimulate people to do better work and to achieve progress. Management is the dynamic life-giving element in every business. Without it, the resources of production, remain resources and never become production.

The Management of a Large Organization may have three Levels

1. Senior management (or "top management" or "upper management")
2. Middle management
3. Low-level management, such as supervisors or team-leaders
4. Foreman
5. Rank and File.

Top-level Management

- Require an extensive knowledge of management roles and skills.

- They have to be very aware of external factors such as markets.
- Their decisions are generally of a long-term nature
- Their decisions are made using analytic, directive, conceptual and/or behavioural/participative processes
- They are responsible for strategic decisions.
- They have to chalk out the plan and see that plan may be effective in the future.
- They are executive in nature.

Middle Management

- Mid-level managers have a specialized understanding of certain managerial tasks.
- They are responsible for carrying out the decisions made by top-level management.

Lower Management

- This level of management ensures that the decisions and plans taken by the other two are carried out.
- Lower-level managers' decisions are generally short-term ones.

Foreman/Lead Hand

- They are people who have direct supervision over the working force in office factory, sales field or other workgroup or areas of activity.

Rank and File

- The responsibilities of the persons belonging to this group are even more restricted and more specific than those of the foreman.

Departmentation

Departmentation is a process of breaking an enterprise into smaller groups and levels. There are a number of ways to break the enterprise. A widely accepted practice is by functions of the enterprise, viz., Marketing, Production, Finance, Personnel, Materials, etc. The second method is based on geographic area distribution. This method is resorted to when the distances are long, the activities are many and the decision making is decentralized. Many organizations have divisions, branches and territories through which the business operations are conducted.

The third method to departmentalize is by way of the product or the services the organization is providing.

Organization Structure By Departmentation

Organization Structure – Department

1. Departmentation by organization enterprise functions.
2. Departmentation by Geography/territory.
3. Departmentation by customer services.
4. Departmentation by product.

Dept. by Products

Grouping of activities according to product/product lines especially on multilines enterprises.

Meeting needs profitably-> market.

Product is a set of tangible and intangible attributes that a customer is ready to buy.

Product linement essentially for a similar use.e.g. Produce

The all variety of tea in the land of Unilever is called product.

Other variety which they have called product range.

Dept. by customers

Grouping of activities that reflect primary interest in customers.e.g.

It's all activities base on customer services.

Dept. by territory/geography

Grouping of activities by area/territory in enterprise operating over wide areas. Functional departmentation is useful where there is production of single product or similar kind of product, for example TV Computer monitor or TFT.

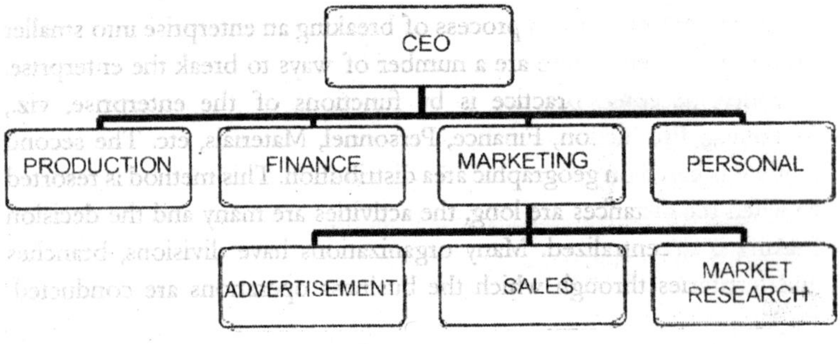

Advantages

- Advantage of specialization
- Easy control over functions
- Pinpointing training needs of manager
- It is very simple process of grouping activities.

Disadvantages

- Lack of responsibility for the end result
- Overspecialization or lack of general management
- It leads to increase conflicts and coordination problems among departments.

Products: When grouping of activities and departments formed are given name on the basis of products manufactured in an organization, it is called products departmentation. It is applied where there is a large range of products are manufactured. When there are several product lines and each product line consists of a variety of items, functional classification fails to give balanced emphasis on each product. Apart form this use; product or services may be made the basis of major divisions by a departmental store, a banking concern and an insurance company. Again, manufacturing an marketing departments may subdivide their activities on the basis of products.

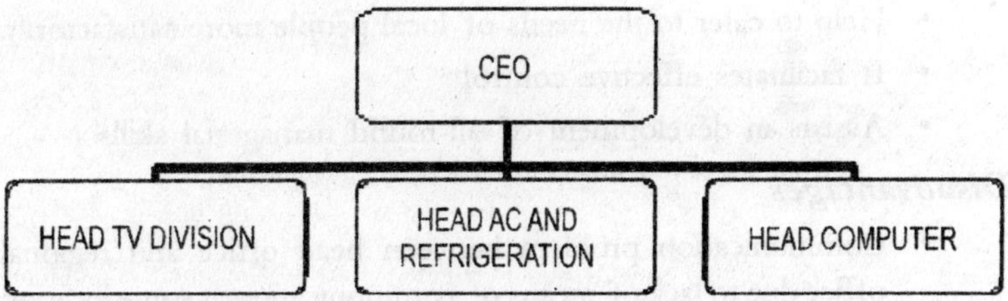

Advantages

- It ensures better customer service
- Unprofitable products may be easily determined
- It assists in development of all around managerial talent
- Makes control effective
- It is flexible and new product line can be added easily.

Disadvantages

- It is expensive as duplication of service functions occurs in various product divisions
- Customers and dealers have to deal with different persons for complaint and information of different products.

Territories: Like the products basis, geographical regions are adopted for main division as well as for subdivision purposes. When activities of an organization are physically dispersed in different locations territorial departmentation is adopted. Units that are located at different areas are made so many self-contained divisions of the organization. Marketing activities are very often subdivided on the basis of geographical areas. This form of departmentation can be useful where business is on national or international level. For eg. Indian railways, insurance company use territorial departmentation.

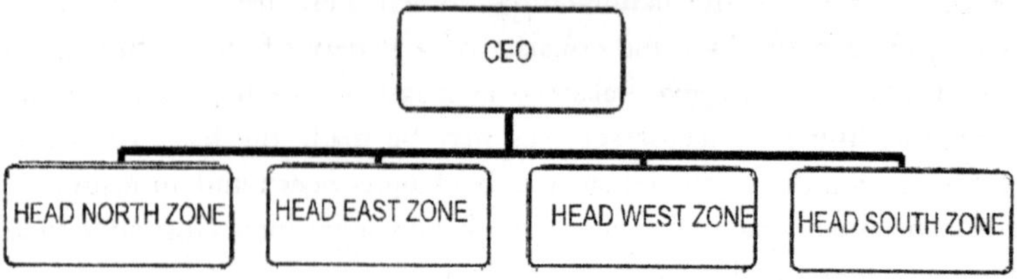

Advantages

- Help to cater to the needs of local people more satisfactorily.
- It facilitates effective control
- Assists in development of all-round managerial skills

Disadvantages

- Communication problem between head office and regional office due to lack of means of communication at some location
- Coordination between various divisions may become difficult.
- Distance between policy framers and executors
- It leads to duplication of activities which may cost higher.

Customers: When departments are formed to cater different kind of customers it is known as customer departmentation this basis of classification is widely followed in subdividing activities of the marketing department. When the products are offered to market through various channels and outlets, it has the special merit of supplying goods in accordance with the peculiar needs of customers. Customers may be classified according to buying capacity or nature like whole sale, retail and export or government or general public. Most departmental stores may attempt reach customers preferring low price or higher price

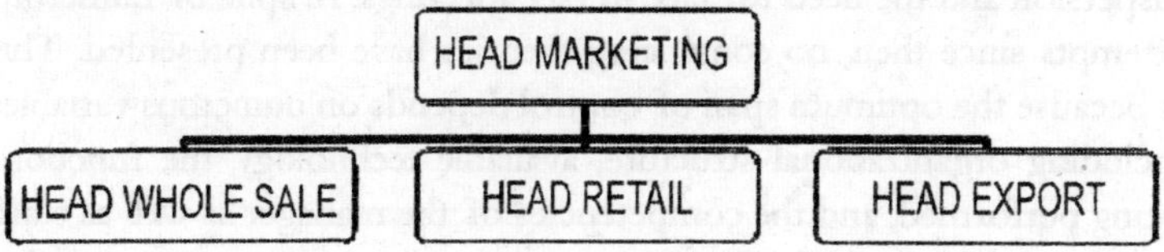

Advantages

- It focused on customers who are ultimate suppliers of money
- Better service to customer having different needs and tastes
- Development in general managerial skills

Disadvantages

- Sales being the exclusive field of its application, co-ordination may appear difficult between sales function and other enterprise functions.
- Specialized sales staff may become idle with the downward movement of sales to any specified group of customers.

Span-of-Control

Span of control is a term originating in military organization theory, but now used more commonly in business management, particularly human resource management. Span of control refers to the number of subordinates a supervisor has.

In the hierarchical business organization of the past it was not uncommon to see average spans of 1 to 10 or even less. That is, one manager supervised ten employees on average. In the 1980s corporate leaders flattened many organizational structures causing average spans to move closer to 1 to 100. That was made possible primarily by the development of inexpensive information technology. As information technology was developed capable of easing many middle manager tasks – tasks like collecting, manipulating and presenting operational information – upper managers found they could hire fewer middle managers to do more work managing more subordinates for less money.

The current shift to self-directed cross-functional teams and other forms of non-hierarchical structures, have made the concept of span of control less salient. Theories about the optimum span of control go back to V. A. Graicunas. In 1933 he used assumptions about mental capacity and attention span to develop a set of practical heuristics. Lyndall Urwick (1956) developed a theory based on geographical dispersion and the need for face to face meetings. In spite of numerous attempts since then, no convincing theories have been presented. This is because the optimum span of control depends on numerous variables including organizational structure, available technology, the functions being performed, and the competencies of the manager as well as staff.

Factors Affecting Span of Control

(a) Geographical Location, if the branches of a business are widely dispersed, then the manager will find it difficult to supervise each of them, as such the span on control will be smaller.

(b) Capability of workers, if workers are highly capable, and do not require much supervision and can be left on their own, eg: Theory Y type of people, need not be supervised much as they are motivated and take initiative to work, as such the span of control will be smaller.

(c) Similarity of task, if the task that the subordinates are performing are similar, then the span of control can be wider, as the manager can supervise them all at the same time. However, of course the capability of the supervisor has to also be taken into consideration.

Theoretical Considerations

The first to develop a more general theory of management was Henri Fayol, who had gathered empirical experience during his time as general manager of a coal and steel company, the Commentary-Fourchambault Company. He was first to add a managerial perspective to the problem of organizational governance. The rationale for defining a strict hierarchy of communication channels is found in the need for vertical integration of activities, imposed by management's need for control and information.

However, exercising control over activities performed by subordinates and monitoring their communication, the nodes at the upper hierarchical levels would be suffering from information overload, since all communication to other branches of the organizational structure would be routed through them. In addition, a larger number of subordinates also requires supervisors to monitor a high number of interactions below their own level, i.e. that information overload and span of control are positively correlated.

The sum of these three types of interactions is the number of potential relationships of a supervisor. Graicunas showed with these formulas, that each additional subordinate increases the number of potential interactions significantly. It appears natural, that no organization can afford to maintain a control structure of a dimension being required for implementing a scalar chain under the unity of command condition. Therefore, other mechanisms had to be found for dealing with the dilemma of maintaining managerial control, while keeping cost and time at a reasonable level, thus making the span of control a critical figure for the organization. Consequently, for a long time, finding the optimum span of control has been a major challenge to organization design. As Mackenzie (1978, p 121) describes it:

> *"One could argue that with larger spans, the costs of supervision would tend to be reduced, because a smaller percentage of the members of the organization are supervisors. On the other hand, if the span of control is too large, the supervisor may not have the capacity to supervise effectively such large numbers of immediate subordinates. Thus, there is a possible trade-off to be made in an attempt to balance these possibly opposing tendencies."*

Fayol proposed that subordinate employees should be allowed to communicate directly with each other, given that their superiors had agreed upon this procedure. This principle became known under the name of Fayol's bridge.

The use of Fayol's bridge resulted in a number of other aspects needing to be taken into consideration. In order to put this system to work, Taylor's functional foremanship has to be abandoned, and unity of command needs to be established. At the same time, decision power is distributed to individuals on lower levels in the organization, and only decisions that exceed the pre-defined decision scope of an employee are referred upwards. This, in turn, strengthens the co-equality of authority and responsibility. Since a Fayol bridge is not limited to a certain functional area within the organization, but can span over functional boundaries, e.g. from purchasing to manufacturing, it can be considered as a first attempt to create a horizontal integration of related activities under a certain level of self-management, an early business process.

Mackenzie and others (Massie 1965, Pugh et al., 1972) also noted that there is no generally applicable optimum span of control. There are instead several factors influencing the balance between the desired level of control, and the manageability of the organization.

Firstly, it depends on the capabilities of the organizational members, managers and workers. It was assumed, that no manager would be capable of supervising more than 5-6 direct subordinates. However, this conclusion built on the assumption, that the superior must actively monitor the work of all subordinates. Later on, this statement was diversified, and Davis (1951) divided managerial work into two categories, one requiring the attention to physical work, the other one requiring mental activity. Depending on the type of supervision, a span of 3-8 subordinates for managers at higher levels was considered adequate, while first level supervisors, i.e. those supervising shop floor personnel could have up to 30 subordinates.

The neoclassical theorists have developed a different solution. They assumed that a considerable amount of decisions could be delegated to organizational members at lower organizational levels. This solution would be equivalent to the application of Fayol's bridge combined with the principle of employee initiative that he proposed. As a result, the need for supervision would be reduced from direct control to exception handling. According to this assumption, they considered the opportunity of having access to a supervising manager would be sufficient to satisfy the need for control in standard situations. Peter Drucker (1954) refers to this principle as the span of managerial responsibility.

Management :Authority and Responsibility

How can people be influenced to make commitments to the goals of the organization? In part, this question can be answered by how managers define and use power, influence, and authority. Deciding what type of authority system to create is part of the managerial responsibility of organizing. Compare, for example, two managers. One accepts or rejects all ideas generated at lower levels. The other gives the authority for making some decisions to employees at the level where these decisions will most likely affect those employees. How managers use their power, influence, and authority can determine their effectiveness in meeting the goals of the organization.

Responsibility

Responsibility is the obligation to accomplish the goals related to the position and the organization. Managers, at no matter what level of the organization, typically have the same basic responsibilities when it comes to managing the work force: Direct employees toward objectives, oversee the work effort of employees, deal with immediate problems, and report on the progress of work to their superiors. Managers' primary responsibilities are to examine tasks, problems, or opportunities in relationship to the company's short-and long-range goals. They must be quick to identify areas of potential problems, continually search for solutions, and be alert to new opportunities and ways to take advantage of the best ones. How effectively goals and objectives are accomplished depends on how well the company goals are broken down into jobs and assignments and how well these are identified and communicated throughout the organization.

Influence and Power

Formal job definitions and coordinating strategies are not enough to get the work done. Managers must somehow use influence to encourage workers to action. If they are to succeed, managers must possess the ability to influence organization members. Influence is the ability to bring about change and produce results; people derive influence from interpersonal power and authority. Interpersonal power allows organization members to exert influence over others.

Power stems from a variety of sources: reward power, coercive power, information power, resource power, expert power, referent power, and legitimate power. *Reward power* exists if managers provide or withhold rewards, such as money or recognition, from those they wish to influence. *Coercive power* depends on the manager's ability to punish others who do not engage in the desired behaviour. A few examples of coercion include reprimands, criticisms, and negative performance appraisals. Power can also result from controlling access to important *information* about daily operations and future plans. Also, having access to and deciding to limit or share the *resources* and materials that are critical to accomplishing objectives can provide a manager with a source of power. Managers usually have access to such information and resources and must use discretion over how much or how little is disseminated to employees. *Expert power* is based on the amount of expertise a person possesses that is valued by others. For example, some people may be considered experts with computers if they are able to use several software programs proficiently and can navigate the Internet with ease. Those who do not have the expert knowledge or experience need the expert's help and, therefore, are willing to be influenced by the expert's power. When people are admired or liked by others, *referent power* may result because others feel friendly toward them and are more likely to follow their directions and demonstrate loyalty toward them. People are drawn to others for a variety of reasons, including physical or social attractiveness, charisma, or prestige. Such politicians as John F. Kennedy were able to use their referent power to effectively influence others. *Legitimate power* stems from the belief that a person has the right to influence others by virtue of holding a position of authority, such as the authority of a manager over a subordinate or of a teacher over a student.

In some respects, everyone has power—the power to either push forward or obstruct the goals of the organization by making decisions, delegating decisions, delaying decisions, rejecting decisions, or supporting decisions. However, the effective use of power does not mean control. Power can be detrimental to the goals of the organization if held by those who use it to enhance their own positions and thereby prevent the advancement of the goals of the organization.

Truly successful managers are able to use power ethically, efficiently, and effectively by sharing it. Power can be used to influence people to do things they might not otherwise do. When that influence encourages people to do things that have no or little relationship to the organization's goals, that power is abused. Abuses of power raise ethical questions. For example, asking a subordinate to submit supposed business-trip expenses for reimbursement for what was actually a family vacation or asking a subordinate to run personal errands is an abuse of power. People who acquire power are ethically obligated to consider the impact their actions will have on others and on the organization.

Employees may desire a greater balance of power or a redistribution of authority within the existing formal authority structure. People can share power in a variety of ways: by providing information, by sharing responsibility, by giving authority, by providing resources, by granting access, by giving reasons, and by extending emotional support. The act of sharing information is powerful. When people don't share information, the need to know still exists; therefore, the blanks are filled in with gossip and innuendo. When people are asked to take on more responsibility, they should be provided with tasks that provide a challenge, not just with more things to increase their workload that don't really matter. People need the legitimate power to make decisions without having to clear everything first with someone higher up in the organization. People who have power must also have the necessary range of resources and tools to succeed. Access to people outside as well as inside the organization should be provided and encouraged. People should be told why an assignment is important and why they were chosen to do it. Emotional support can come in the form of mentoring, appreciation, listening, and possibly helping out.

Sharing power or redistributing authority does not necessarily mean moving people into positions of power; instead, it can mean letting people have power over the work they do, which means that people can exercise personal power without moving into a formal leadership role. The ability to influence organization members is an important resource for effective managers. Relying on the title "boss" is seldom powerful enough to achieve adequate influence.

Authority

Authority is seen as the legitimate right of a person to exercise influence or the legitimate right to make decisions, to carry out actions, and to direct others. For example, managers expect to have the authority to assign work, hire employees, or order merchandise and supplies.

As part of their structure, organizations have a formal authority system that depicts the authority relationships between people and their work. Different types of authority are found in this structure: line, staff, and functional authority. Line authority is represented by the chain of command; an individual positioned above another in the hierarchy has the right to make decisions, issue directives, and expect compliance from lower-level employees. Staff authority is advisory authority; it takes the form of counsel, advice, and recommendation. People with staff authority derive their power from their expert knowledge and the legitimacy established in their relationships with line managers. Functional authority allows managers to direct specific processes, practices, or policies affecting people in other departments; functional authority cuts across the hierarchical structure. For example, the human resources department may create policies and procedures related to promoting and hiring employees throughout the entire organization.

Authority can also be viewed as arising from interpersonal relationships rather than a formal hierarchy. Authority is sometimes equated with legitimate power. Authority and power and how these elements are interrelated can explain the elements of managing and their effectiveness. What is critical is how subordinates perceive a manager's legitimacy. Legitimate authority occurs when people use power for good and have acquired power by proper and honest means. When people perceive an attempt at influence as legitimate, they recognize it and willingly comply. Power acquired through improper means, such as lying, withholding information, gossip, or manipulation, is seen as illegitimate. When people perceive the authority of others as illegitimate, they are less likely to willingly comply.

Delegation

In order for managers to achieve goals in an efficient manner, part of their work may be assigned to others. When work is delegated, tasks and authority are transferred from one position to another within an organization. The key to effective delegation of tasks is the transference of decision-making authority and responsibility from one level of the organization to the level to which the tasks have been delegated. In order to effectively delegate work, some guidelines should be followed: Determine what each worker can most effectively accomplish; decide whether the worker should just identify a problem or also propose a solution; consider whether the person can handle the challenge of the task; be clear in the objectives of the task; encourage questions; explain why the task is important; determine if the person has the appropriate resources—time, budget, data, or equipment—to get the job done on a deadline; create progress reviews as part of the project planning; and be prepared to live with less than perfect results. Authority should be delegated in terms of expected results. Generally, the more specific the goal, the easier it is to determine how much authority someone needs.

Some employees resist delegation for a variety of reasons. Initiative and responsibility involve risk that some people try to avoid. People tend to play it safe if risk results in criticism. Those who feel they already have more work than they can do avoid new assignments. Some people doubt their own abilities and lack the self-confidence to tackle new assignments. Delegation is an excellent professional development tool so long as it expands a worker's expertise and growth. Delegation can also compensate for a manager's weakness. A successful team is developed by building on the strengths of its members.

People develop most when stimulated to broaden themselves—when challenged. More authority can add challenge; too much challenge, however, can frustrate people and cause them to avoid new responsibilities. Delegation should involve acceptable challenge—enough to motivate but not so much as to frustrate.

In today's workplace, managers are compelled to rely more on persuasion, which is based on expert and referent power rather than reward, coercive, or inappropriate use of power. A manager who shares power and authority will be the one with the greatest ability to influence others to work toward the goals of the organization.

Directing

There are effective ways of overcoming problems set by change. One adapts to change by seeing what is changing and how it is changing. One estimates what is likely to happen, plans ahead and acts accordingly.

Planning includes evaluating alternative strategies to find the best strategy. It is this best strategy which then becomes part of our forward plan. This process has been developed to the point where it is both practical and straightforward.

And employees may be expected to work to targets which are set annually. The way targets are agreed, progress monitored and individuals rewarded is crucial for the success of the organisation or enterprise. Where attempts are made to introduce a system of procedures and reports to take the place of responsible person-to-person management and delegated work, where attempts are made to impose a system of tougher management direction and control in terms of employment, then costs are high and benefits uncertain and even unlikely.

Success depends to a large extent on commitment of employees towards the organisation's aims and on cooperation between them. This means identifying with the company. What benefits the company needs to be seen and felt by the employees as also benefiting them. To achieve commitment of employees toward's the organisation's aims, appraisal and target-setting meetings can be carried out in accordance with the proved and effective technique described in this report.

We see how important the style of management is in achieving results. It affects in a fundamental way the interview between manager and subordinate when they agree the targets for the subordinate. And this report is one of a series of seven reports which cover, and underlie, the field of General Management, for middle, senior and top management.

1. Directing and Managing Change

   Includes: Adapting to Change, Deciding What Needs to be Done;

   Planning Ahead, Getting Results, Evaluating Progress;

   Appraisal Interviews and Target-setting Meetings.
2. Style of Management and Leadership
3. Organising
4. Work and Pay, Incomes and Differentials: Employer, Employee, Community
5. The Will to Work: What People Struggle to Achieve Includes: Remuneration, Job Satisfaction and Motivation
6. Inflation, Balance of Payments and Currency Exchange Rates
7. Social Responsibility, Profits and Social Accountability.

Directing

Directing is something all of us do throughout our lives. We all make decisions which affect ourselves and our family, which affect the people with whom we come in contact, the community in which we live, the enterprise which employs us. They are often extremely important decisions. What kind of an education, what kind of school, what kind of trade or profession, whom to marry, choosing between alternative medical treatments such as drugs or surgery, whether to change one's job, indeed the country in which we wish to live and the kind of government we prefer, all these are decisions which we make and which have to be made again and again as we direct the course of our lives within the choices open to us.

Here we are discussing the work of managers and administrators, starting with those who direct their own companies and larger organisations. The decisions taken, by those who head enterprises and by those who govern, affect more people and greater resources than do those taken by ourselves in the course of our daily and private lives, but there is much common ground. Very basic is an understanding of what is going on, of what is happening, of the problems of the day.

So we begin by having a look at the sort of things which are taking place all around us.

The World in Which we Live

Some illnesses have disappeared, our life span has increased considerably within living memory but each year something like 100,000 people are admitted to our hospitals for diseases caused by drugs which should have cured.

There is inflation accompanied by confrontation between those who work and those who manage. While people are safeguarded against extreme poverty and hardship by extensive social security legislation and by the national health service, there is much unemployment, frustration and unrest.

Some established norms have been questioned. People's behaviour is being affected and there has been an increase in permissiveness (promiscuity), delinquency and crime, there is the younger age of those involved. There are social problems of oneparent families, there is increasing loneliness. There is increasing vandalism and callousness towards other people. There is use of violence (terrorism) against people for political ends.

The planet has become much smaller, meaning by this that we speak each other's languages, that we communicate all around the planet in a matter of seconds, that we travel anywhere in a matter of hours. The market now spans the entire planet, competition is tough and international.

There is the impact of technology, of laser applications, of electronic calculators, desk computers, computer-based automatic operations and control, microprocessors, and much more. But while on the one hand our space ships explore our planetary system and we have landed on the moon, on the other hand a country like Russia uses psychiatric hospitals in an attempt to break the resistance of those who stand up for individual freedom by disagreeing with the dictates of the state.

A few years have seen far reaching changes take place in the wealth of countries and individuals, a vast transfer of wealth towards largely Arab oil producing countries, with other countries struggling to maintain their standard of living. In addition there is an enormous and speedily increasing gap in living standards between the underdeveloped world and developed countries. A very high proportion of those living on the planet are permanently hungry, undernourished, starving, illiterate, deprived.

It used to be that costs and overheads were estimated and a customary percentage added for profit. This gave one the price at which the article was sold. Now we tend to assess what quantities can be sold at each of a number of different prices. The price tends to be what the market will bear and one has to produce and sell accordingly. Under such conditions the price is the maximum one can persuade people to pay for what one can persuade them to buy. The way in which oil prices were pushed up by the oil producing and exporting countries is a case in point. This is 'marketing'. When marketing replaces selling this affects the internal organisation of the company in different ways. There is increasing consumer awareness and interest in products, prices and company operations. Much is happening. These are after all only some developments and trends and there is much else.

But there is one word which sums up what is taking place in all the many different areas. That word is 'change'.

Change is taking place and things are changing more quickly. We now live in a time of change, we live in a time of accelerating change. This is how our life today differs from life but a few years ago.

Yet pick up almost any textbook on management written but a few years ago and somewhere in it you are likely to find the phrase that people do not like change, that people will resist change <1>. Yet we live in a time of accelerating change and have to live with it, indeed have to overcome the resulting problems. There are effective ways of overcoming the problems set by change {1} and we now look at how this can be done.

Adapting to Change

Consider a man walking as quickly as he can along a jungle path. He turns a corner and there a few yards ahead and facing him is a tiger. He immediately starts climbing the nearest tree. It happens quickly but much has gone on in his mind in that split second between seeing the tiger and starting to climb.

He sees the tiger. What can I do? Draw my pistol and shoot? Have I got it with me? Is there time to draw it? Is the tiger hungry? Is there a half-eaten animal nearby? How long will it be before the rest of the party get here? Are there any climbable trees nearby? Can I climb it? Start climbing!

What he did was to assess the situation and then act accordingly.

One survives in the jungle by adapting to it. To survive in a time of change, one must adapt to change. One adapts by assessing the situation and then acting accordingly. We see what is changing and how it is changing, estimate what is likely to happen and then act first. We forecast change and plan accordingly.

Forecasting and Planning

The experts see what is changing and how it is changing, and then estimate what things will be like at some time in the future. Such estimates are no more than qualified guesses made on the basis of the best available information at the time the guess is made. But such looking ahead into the distance is very necessary.

It is rather like driving a car. If we looked immediately in front of the bonnet we would have no time to react, would oversteer. Events would take us by surprise with what could easily be disastrous consequences. In driving a car we look into the distance and so are able to observe and correct small deviations from the straight course we intend to follow.

It is very difficult to look ahead thirty years with any degree of reliability. You may indeed find yourself getting lost in some fundamental and fascinating questions such as "Will we still be here?" or "Will we be nationalized wholly or in part?" but will you be getting your money's worth out of the exercise? What you will get will be an appreciation of some long-term trends, some idea of the kind of basic and fundamental problems which we may possibly have to cope with in the not-too-distant future.

You may well conclude that the gap between underdeveloped and developing people (countries) will continue to increase, that there will be such a shortage of food that the developing countries may be buying as many arms as they can so as to fight each other and us for what little food there may be. Or you may conclude that the developed countries will be able to produce large excess quantities of naturally grown or artificially produced foodstuffs for export to the starving underdeveloped countries.

You may then conclude that in the light of conditions existing at the time of the forecast, and in the light of information available at the time the forecast was made, that it would be good business to develop your interests in the armaments industry or to concentrate on food production, or you may indeed try both. Or you may find that there may be an increasing demand for insurance, or that telecommunications is likely to be the growth industry of the near future.

But you will need to remember that a forecast is no more than a considered opinion about the relative importance and interaction of trends. The far-away picture may change drastically at any time. For example, sudden success in developing a rice variety which crops twice as heavily as before would considerably change the long-term conclusions.

In other words, if you need to make the kind of decisions mentioned here then these are the kind of forecasts required. Much work may be required, the exercise is expensive and the results are uncertain. In any case you need to be sure to assess the underlying often academic or political assumptions which at times may not even be directly stated, which may only be implied.

Looking at this in 1960 we might decide to accept his estimate for the first five years up to year 1965, as illustrat. From this five-year trend we can estimate other likely changes which affect us such as energy requirements, new houses to be constructed, food to be produced, likely available labour force, possible effect on sales, number of hospital beds and doctors required, and so on.

We are at least forced to consider the kind of problems that are likely to arise. For example, one forecast I saw before 1980 made some simple striking points:

1. The population of the planet is increasing steadily.
2. For associated reasons the amount of agricultural land is shrinking steadily.

3. By the year 2000 the available agricultural land would just about still feed the growing population. After that the shortage of food would increase rapidly.
4. One of the assumptions made was that the productivity of the land remained unchanged.

Double the productivity of the land and you gain no more than about twenty-five years. Quadruple it and you gain perhaps no more than another twenty years.

Here are some other forecasts made about 1970 about the kind of breakthroughs likely to have taken place by about the year 2000, as follows:

1. New organs through transplanting.
2. Primitive artificial life.
3. Direct link between brain and computer.
4. Life span increased by another fifty years.

So-called 'genetic engineering' attempts to produce entirely novel microbes. Just one of the risks is (2) that experiments could endow a disease producing streptococcus with the capacity to resist penicillin and that it would obviously be a disaster if such a strain got loose on the population.

In different ways much work being done now is highly dangerous. It would be highly dangerous even in a responsible society as there is a very high degree of risk both to the workers involved and to the community at large.

I have selected the forecasts mentioned here because they are thought-provoking and much else could have been mentioned.

There is great need for people and governments as well as managers to become aware of the factors which are likely to be affecting our lives, for people in responsible positions to look ahead, to prepare us for what is likely to be in store so as to enable us to survive. We need to assess what is changing and how it is changing and plan accordingly.

Deciding Policy

We decide policy when we decide what is to be achieved. A knowledge of the way the environment is changing, and for that matter of the way in which our own affairs are changing, is only one of the aspects which need to be considered. In essence, we also need to consider where we wish to go in relation to where we are, need to consider existing opportunities in relation to the strengths and weaknesses of our enterprise.

We then evaluate alternative strategies so as to find the best strategy. It is this best strategy which then becomes part of our forward plan.

Systematic Approach For Deciding And Implementing Policy

Deciding Policy

1. State aims (both long-term and short-term).
2. State present position.
3. Evaluate opportunities.
4. Review strengths and weaknesses.
5. Derive alternative strategies (different ways of getting from 'present position' to 'aims').
6. Decide best strategy (ies).

Setting Targets

7. List best strategy (ies).
8. Prepare forward plan (quantified and timed).
9. Institute controls.
10. Feedback.

It is seen that we first look at what we wish to achieve in the long-term and in the immediate future. We then evaluate our present position. We look for and evaluate opportunities and review our strengths and weaknesses. Having developed our own appreciation and knowledge of the position in each area, we then continue by developing a number of different ways of getting from where we are to where we wish to be, that is we develop alternative strategies. We can then derive the best strategy or strategies.

When using the system we at least ensure that we have considered the relevant factors to the best of our knowledge and in the light of the information available to us at the time. And what we have done is that we have decided what to do, that is the direction in which we wish to move and the required speed. We have decided policy.

Once completed for the first time those concerned are usually so impressed with the usefulness of what they have done, that they continue to take stock and plan ahead in this way at regular intervals of either one or two years.

There are different kinds of plan dependent on the period which they cover. There is the long range policy statement which covers a period of between five and ten years. Then there is the intermediate or medium range plan which covers a period between three and six years. It is more precise and specific and enables people to plan ahead in outline. Then there is the annual short range or forward plan for the organisation which covers the work to be achieved during the coming year.

It is customary for such plans to be reviewed and revised once a year. However, once the annual plan has been accepted it becomes the forward plan for the whole organisation and indeed the organisation has agreed to commit itself to it and achieve it.

Implementing Policy

We have now decided what we wish to achieve, the direction in which the organisation is to move, the speed at which we wish to progress. This forward policy now has to be passed on to the whole organisation in a way which enables those who work in it to cooperate with each other to achieve our aims.

During a time of rapidly increasing change the company has to think ahead and move with the times and indeed the whole organisation has to work together to achieve the policy aims set by those who lead.

But this means that individuals instead of sitting at a desk and doing the same job again and again all their lives, instead of having a job, are now employed to achieve the company's or organisation's aims which may change from year to year at least in emphasis. We are now accordingly expecting people to think about the work they are doing and about the way in which they are doing it in relation to what the enterprise is attempting to achieve. We are now expecting people to work to targets which are set annually.

Effect of Style of Management

None of this is really different from the management process which goes on in any case. A manager will delegate certain work to his subordinates, he will discuss progress with them, he will advise, he will help, he will evaluate the extent to which their performance is affected by their own limitations, by their own lack of experience, or by circumstances outside their control. And above all he will ask them for comments and suggestions about how the work could be improved, about how the company can meet its targets more effectively. And this can and does work very well indeed if the manager is good and if he knows what he is doing.

It is here again that good management counts and bad management loses. Experience tells that the system does not work well if targets are simply imposed from the top downwards, if routine procedure and form-filling take the place of what may well have been good management, if what used to be secure employment becomes an annually renegotiated contract when the individual has to sign that he will within one year achieve certain objectives which his superior tells him must be achieved, or else. Where the opportunity is taken by management to introduce what is in effect an annually renegotiated contract of employment against specific targets determined by top management, where the individual's security is affected by the achievement of his targets, then this is likely to upset the organisation to the point where formal target setting procedures have to be abandoned. Authoritarian organisations have similar problems which are discussed in more detail in the report on style of management.

Very little relevant cost data is available on the changeover from just working at doing one's job and the organisation working together to achieve the forward policy of its leadership. However, we do know that where attempts are made to introduce a system of procedures and reports to take the place of person to person responsible management and of delegated work, where attempts are made to impose a system of tougher direction in terms of employment, being imposed down the line from the top, that costs are high and benefits uncertain. This agrees with our previous findings that authoritarian managements are on the whole now known to be less effective.

Where gains are made, they are made because the subordinates are asked for their opinion as to how their job could be done better and the company then proceeds to use their ideas. I put it to you that this is common good practice anyway. In companies which are well run, a manager will in any case ask his subordinates how their job could be improved, how they could do their work better. If the subordinates are at all interested, it is they who will be able to improve their own work and the way in which it is done because after all that is what they know best.

Large gains are made in this way, large savings and much progress results.

Setting Targets

There may be much that we would like to change. Morale may be low, there may be an external threat from a new foreign competitor who is establishing a factory in our own country. Much effort may be wasted, our organisation may not be as effective as we think it should be. There could be lack of dedication and effort by those who work in the company or organisation, by those who support it, by those on whom we rely to achieve our aims.

It simply would not achieve much to express our aims in vague general terms such as that we wish to increase morale, that we wish to reduce labour turnover, that we need to increase sales, that we need to diversify. What is needed are specific, clear aims so that those who work with us and for us know what we expect of them, know what we are asking them to achieve.

What is needed are clear, quantified and timed aims, that is 'targets', such as:

1. We are aiming to reduce labour turnover from 60 percent to 45 percent within one year and to 30 percent at the end of two years from now.
2. Sales have to increase from 2,000 units to 2,800 units within one year from now.

Time limits for completion fulfil a similar purpose when work is not readily quantified.

Having stated our policies in such precise terms, we are then able to divide the work among different divisions, departments or managers in such a way that each knows his share, knows the part he has to play so that the policies can be achieved.

Targets convey clearly what one would like to achieve. They also enable us to provide those doing the work with the information they require to assess whether their progress is better or worse than planned.

In other words we can readily control events by instituting some kind of reporting back at regular intervals. In this way we enable the manager concerned to see how well he is progressing so that he may take appropriate action or feed information up the line asking for assistance or modification to the overall plan.

Agreeing Targets

The same system can be used badly or it can be used well, as illustrated by the following example:

An engineer in his middle forties was told that the company would soon be using new and involved computer software for design purposes and that he did not have the required knowledge or skill to use it, that he was too old, that he would have to find other work. Events have overtaken him, technological change has knocked him out, he is redundant, unlikely to find other employment at the same sort of level.

But his manager could have said:

"Jim, you know as well as I do that life is competitive. We are working to tougher margins, we must get our tenders out more quickly. To do this we are going to design and cost much of the work we do by using advanced computer software.

Your many years experience in the industry and with us are invaluable, you know how the company works, you know our methods, you have come across most of the snags before. So we would like you to assist with and perhaps run this part of our activity, we would like you to make sure that what we get is what we need and want.

You do not have to tell me that this is a new field for you. The company is making available some short courses for people like you and me at the software supplier's place, and their experts will be here during the change-over.

If you are interested then we would be only too pleased if you could go to these courses and develop the necessary knowledge and skills.

The company expects a lot from this development and we think that you are the right man to make sure that we do not make the kind of mistakes other people made when they tried the same thing. Let me know in two or three days what you think about it and whether you are prepared to tackle it."

The manager who is able to meet both his organisation's requirements as well as look after the needs of the employees in such a manner gains much from his team and for the company. Shipping lines used to provide fast passenger transport across the Atlantic. The advent of regular, frequent plane services changed this. Passenger traffic is carried by planes. The impact was felt by the shipping lines. They had to adjust and had little time to do so. The passenger carrying boats which now cross the Atlantic are in the holiday and entertainment business, provide cruises and on-board entertainment instead of transport. The work changed, staffing changed, routes changed.

Here also we see the importance of making use of one's knowledge of what one wishes to achieve during the coming year and beyond by giving one's staff the opportunity to develop their skills, functional as well as managerial, so as to make sure that the company's experience and resources are fully utilised in meeting the company's changing requirements. On the other hand, a man's performance now depends on him preparing himself for the kind of work the company expects him to do in the future.

It is 'targets' which state what has to be done and can be done so as to achieve the overall target of the higher level. The target itself is broken down into component targets for the next lower level.

The way in which targets are determined and the way in which the work is passed down the line is crucial to the success of the plan. It does not matter whether the work consists of well-known work tasks or of parts of the forward plan (targets). The manager in either case distributes work and coordinates effort, has agreed with his subordinate just what he expects him to do and by when. The subordinate has to monitor his own progress and keep the manager informed of any difficulties so that appropriate action can be taken if and when required. Allowing for circumstances outside the subordinate's control, the manager assesses the subordinate's performance and the reward will to some extent be determined by this.

Tasks imposed from above are most unlikely to be done either willingly or well. Employees do not really care and effort is withdrawn. If in addition one's income, bonus, promotion or security of employment depend purely on the achievement of imposed targets regardless of other considerations, then much can and does go wrong.

In one place some time ago scientists had to submit their research plans in advance. Their grant for the following year was then made to depend on the extent to which they had successfully completed their planned research programme for the previous year.

So they had a problem. Most research is highly unpredictable and if their research was not successful then their grant would be reduced. What were they to do? Their way out was to keep back the results of successful research and state in their forward plan that they would do in the following year the research they had already successfully completed. Hence they always met their targets and always got their grants but of course publication of the results of the research was delayed by at least a year and probably at times by at least two years. This defeated the aims of the original planners.

Another example is that of the department which found that one or two months before the end of the year it had used up the allocated amount of paper but found that a certain high quality expensive paper reserved for senior management was not covered by any target. The manager of the department did not want to exceed his target and so they used the more expensive paper for the rest of the year. On the one hand they had met their target but on the other it had cost the company a good deal more than had been anticipated.

Sometimes people have to work under threat when survival and progress depend on completing the targets on time. People then find ways of reducing effort, of playing it safe, of ensuring that they meet their targets. Under such conditions the completion of individual targets becomes more important than the aims of the company or the cost to the company as a whole. People work against instead of with each other.

We see how important the style of management is in achieving results. It also affects in a very fundamental way the interview between manager and subordinate when they agree the targets for the subordinate.

When targets are imposed from above, when the manager insists on having his specific targets accepted as a norm, when sanctions such as loss of promotion or even the possibility of dismissal are implied, then cooperation is replaced by confrontation and negotiation.

The subordinates know as does the manager that the subordinates' performance in achieving their targets is likely to affect their appraisal, their performance rating, the increase they are likely to get, their future prospects. They can play it safe and hold out for easy targets which means that the company now aims rather lower and achieves less. Or the manager cán tell them that they must accept his targets and they may have no option but to agree, knowing right from the beginning that the targets cannot be achieved. Other employees who depend on the achievement of these targets if they are to achieve theirs, are defeated before they even start.

Any subsequent appraisal of progress has to sort out why a particular target is not being achieved or has not been achieved. It could be because of circumstances outside the employee's control, it could be because he did not do his work well enough or because he did not pull his weight.

Clearly the way in which targets are agreed, progress controlled and individuals rewarded, is of the utmost importance if the company is to succeed. This depends to a large extent on commitment of employees towards the organisation's aims and on cooperation between them. This means identification with the company. What benefits the company needs to be seen and felt by the employees as also benefitting them. This is discussed in more detail in the reports on the style of management {3} and on the will to work {4}, but here consider the question of appraisal. What manager and subordinate are trying to sort out between them is the extent to which failure to achieve targets is due to either

a. circumstances beyond the control of the employee (such as unrealistic targets, inadequate support, unexpected external change, etc.), or

b. the employee's lack of skill, or

c. inadequate performance (for example due to employee, manager, style of management, etc.)

One can of course take an appraisal form, complete it in the security of one's private office, send it to Personnel Department without the subordinate knowing that he has been appraised. In due course he will be told the increase he has been awarded as a result of his work. In practice he is likely to know quite unofficially about the whole procedure and is left to guess what you really think about him by comparing his increase with that of others.

I developed a different system of appraisal way back about twenty years ago. We have used it and recommended it since then. I think it works well. It is effective and straightforward. All the manager does is to give a copy of the rating form to the subordinate and ask him to take it and rate himself at home, returning it after two days. The manager completes his copy of the form on his own and when they meet they can now discuss the employee's performance by comparing notes.

Although one points out that the whole exercise is in complete confidence, most employees have to be encouraged to rate themselves. The results are of value. The manager becomes aware of the simple fact that the employee generally knows the manager's opinion of him and has a pretty shrewd and clear idea of his shortcomings, that he would like to overcome them but does not really know how. Employees generally rate themselves below the opinion of their manager.

The result is that in about 80 percent of cases the manager becomes aware that the employee knows his opinion and in effect stops criticising, from then on concentrating on helping his subordinates to overcome their weaknesses and utilise their strengths. The employee finds out that the manager thinks more highly of his work and ability than he does himself, a considerable boost to the way in which he views himself and his work.

The overall result is increased cooperation between them and increased committal towards the company's aims and dedication towards achieving personal targets.

Similar considerations apply to the process of determining and agreeing targets. One needs to find out what is possible and the circumstances under which it is possible.

The organisation has at least to be given a chance to weld itself into a solid team which supports the leadership, which moves the organisation in the direction indicated by the leadership at the speed at which it is supposed to move.

The target setting process amounts to discussions between managers at the same level or at different levels looking at what one would like to do and who between them are deciding what can be done to achieve the targets. In other words, the overall targets need to be passed down the line and discussed at the various levels and need to be returned, coordinated and with comments, to senior management. It is now that an overall consistent and practicable plan can be prepared and put into effect.

We saw earlier on that such discussions can generate a wealth of suggestions about how work can be done better and ideas about opportunities. Some time ago I saw a cartoon which illustrates this point. The Post Office was continually making large losses and the cartoon showed a Post office employee whose suggestion was: "Why don't we misprint some stamps and make up the loss that way?" You may not agree with this particular suggestion but it does illustrate that there are plenty of ideas, one only has to listen.

Managers at different levels have been able to consider what can be done and how the work for which they would be responsible would fit in with work done by others elsewhere. Hence senior managers now know what, in the opinion of those who work for them, can be achieved and are also aware of reservations which have been made and of points to watch. Improvements have been suggested, opportunities have been pointed out.

Evaluating Performance

To plan well and to have work done effectively requires both sound organisation and a clear appreciation of what each employee has to achieve.

Continuous discussion brings out again and again the fact that too many managers are not really aware of what they are supposed to achieve, what their own managers want them to do, just what the important parts of their work are in the eyes of their own manager and of the organisation.

In many ways the discussion between manager and subordinate about their targets helps to define the job of the subordinate and helps to give him a clear idea of what he is supposed to achieve. This is something every manager wants to know and wants to be sure of.

We have already seen that the way of planning ahead described here can assist managers to prepare themselves for the work the company wants them to do in the future. Another result is that managers do not optimise something that is not really needed but a manager may tend to regard as less important and thus tend to neglect that part of his work which is not targeted.

Because performance is measured more readily, reward seems to be more easily related to results. However, the manager still has to assess the effect of circumstances outside the employee's control and deal with those situations and remove those obstacles which block progress.

Managers at all levels become more aware of what is taking place and generally do the best they can to achieve the plan, to feed information to others so as to get assistance, to overcome circumstances outside their control or to have the plan revised.

At the beginning of the year we may have estimated or budgeted for regularly increasing production. This does nor mean that it is bound to happen. A plan is no more than a statement of what we wish to achieve and considered practicable at the time the plan was made. If results are not according to plan, that is are not as expected, then the plan has fulfilled a very good purpose. Becoming aware of the difference between expected and actual results enables us to take appropriate action either to achieve the plan or else to feed information back so that the plan can be brought up to date.

What we have covered in this report is the need for planning and how to plan, the need for establishing priorities and for agreeing quantified and timed targets, the need to monitor progress.

There are certain sensitive and important areas such as the agreeing of clear targets, staff appraisal and the reviewing of performance. It is also important to use the control data to take appropriate action before it is too late.

The way of working described here, if applied well, can do much to increase the will to work.

Bibliography

Anindya Bakrie & Morendy Octora.: *Schooling, Experience, and Earnings*, New York, Singapore National University, Columbia University Press 2002.

Baran, Paul A.: *The Political Economy of Growth,* New York, Modern Reader Paperbacks, 1975.

Bardsley, N., Cubitt: *Assessing Experimental Economics*, Princeton, Princeton University Press, 2009.

Basu, Kaushik. *Analytical Development Economics, The Less Developed Economy Revisited,* Cambridge, Mass.: MIT Press, 1997.

Bazilevskii, Y. Y.: *The Theory of Mathematical Machines*, Pergamon Press, Macmillan Co., New York, 1963.

Benería, Lourdes. *Gender, Development, and Globalization, Economics as if All People Mattered,* New York and London, Routledge, 2003.

Borcherding, K., : *Contemporary Issues in Decision Making,* Amsterdam, North-Holland, 1990.

Burke, Frank M., *Valuation and Valuation Planning for Closely Held Businesses*, Englewood Cliffs, NJ, Prentice Hall, 1981.

Caplin, A. and Schotter, A.: *The Foundations of Positive and Normative Economics*, New York, Oxford University Press, 2008.

Caviglioni O. : *Mapwise: Accelerated Learning Through Visible Thinking*, Network Educational Press, 2000.

Cohen, Lizabeth, *Making a New Deal, Industrial Workers in Chicago, 1919-1939* Cambridge University Press, 1991.

Commons, J. R., *Institutional Economics-Its Place in Political Economy*, The University of Wisconsin Press, Madison, Wisconsin, 1934.

Cootner, Paul : *The Random Character of Stock Market Prices*, MIT Press, 1964.

Copeland, Tom, Tim Koller, and Jack Murrin, *Valuation: Measuring and Managing the Value of Companies,* New York, Wiley, 1994.

Damasio, AR.: *Descarte's Error: Emotion, Reason and the Human Brain*, New York, 1994.

Daniel Kahneman, Amos Tversky.: *Choice, Values, Frames*, The Cambridge University Press, 2000.

Desmond, Glenn, and John A, Marcell, *Handbook of Small Business Valuation Formulas and Rules of Thumb*, Valuation Press, 1993.

Dimson, Elroy: *Stock Market Anomalies*, Cambridge University Press, 1988.

Fraser, Steven, *Labor Will Rule, Sidney Hillman and the Rise of American Labor*, Reprint ed. Ithaca, N.Y.: Cornell University Press, 1993.

Fruhan, W. E.: *Financial Strategy, Studies in the Creation, Transfer and Destruction of Shareholder Value*. Homewood, 1979.

Goleman D.: *Emotional Intelligence*, New York: Bantam, 1995.

Gowdy, J., *Coevolution Economics: The Economy, Society and the Environment*, Kluwer, Boston, 1994.

Granger, Clive W. J.: *Empirical Modeling in Economics, Specification and Evaluation*, London, Cambridge University Press, 1999.

Guala, F.: *The Methodology of Experimental Economics*, New York, Cambridge University Press, 2005.

Guarti, Luigi, *The Valuation of Firms*, Blackwell Publishing, 1994.

Gul, F. and Pesendorfer, W.: *The Foundations of Positive and Normative Economics*, New York, Oxford University Press 2008.

Harrigan, K. R.: *Strategies for Declining Businesses*. Lexington, MA: Heath, 1980

Hausman, D. M.: *The Inexact and Separate Science of Economics*, Cambridge, Cambridge University Press, 1992.

Hayek, F. A. *Individualism and Economic Order*, The University of Chicago Press, Chicago, 1948.

Hunt, E. K. *History of Economic Thought, A Critical Perspective*, New York, HarperCollins, 1992.

Janis, I. L., & Mann, L.: *Decision Making, A Psychological Analysis of Conflict, Choice and Commitment*. New York, Free Press, 1977.

Kasper, Larry J.: *Business Valuations, Advanced Topics*, Westport, CT, Quorum Books, 1997.

Knapp, C. L.: *Commercial Damages, A Guide to Remedies in Business Litigation*, Matthew Bender, 1993.

Lindblom, C. E.: *A Strategy of Decision: Policy Evaluation as a Social Process*, New York, The Free Press, 1970.

Link, Albert N.: *Evaluating Economic Damages, A Handbook for Attorneys*, Westport, CT, Quorum Books, 1992.

Lipsitz, George. *Rainbow at Midnight, Labor and Culture in the 1940s*, Urbana, Ill.: University of Illinois Press, 1994.

Loomes, G.: *Current Issues in Microeconomics*, New York: St. Martin's Press, 1989.

Magnussen, L., *Evolutionary and Neo-Schumpeterian Approaches to Economics*, Kluwer, Boston, 1994.

March, J. G.: *A Behavioural Theory of the Firm*, Englewood-Cliffs, Prentice Hall, 1963.

Marris, R. L., and Wood, A.: *The Corporate Economy*, London: Macmillan, 1971.

Martin, Gerald D.: *Determining Economic Damages*, Santa Ana, CA: James Publishing, 1995.

Meyer, M. W.: *Theory of Organizational Structure*, Indianapolis, 1977.

Mooney, J. D., and Reiley, A. C.: *Onward Industry*, New York, 1931.

Nelson, Judy A.: *Feminism, Objectivity and Economics*, London and New York, Routledge, 1996.

Peirson, G., Bird, R., Brown, R., & Howard, P.: *Business Finance*, Roseville, 1990

Pennings, J. M.: *Decision Making, An Organizational Behaviour Approach*, New York, Markus Wiener Publishing, 1983.

Pfeffer, J., and Salancik, G. R.: *The External Control of Organizations, A Resource Dependence Perspective*, New York, 1978.

Plous, S.: *The Psychology of Judgement and Decision Making*, New York, McGraw-Hill, 1993

Rappaport, A.: *Creating Shareholder Value, The New Standard for Business Performance*, New York, Free Press, 1986.

Ross, D.: *Economic Theory and Cognitive Science*, Cambridge, Mass., MIT Press, 2006.

Roth, A. E.: *The Handbook of Experimental Economics*, Princeton, Princeton University Press, 1995.

Santos, A.C.: *The Social Epistemology of Experimental Economics*, London, Routledge 2009.

Schumpeter, J. A., *The Theory of Economic Development*, Harvard University Press,Cambridge, Massachusetts, 1934.

Scott, W. R.: *Organizations: Rational, Natural, and Open Systems*, Englewood Cliffs, 1981.

Selznick, P.: *Leadership in Administration, A Sociological Interpretation*, New York, Harper & Row, 1957.

Smith, Gordon V., and Russell Parr, *Valuation of Intellectual Property and Intangible Assets,* New York: Wiley, 1994.

Smith, V. L.: *Papers in Experimental Economics*, Cambridge, Cambridge University Press, 1991.

Taylor, F. W.: *The Principles of Scientific Management*, New York, 1917.

Throsby, David, *Economics and Culture*, Cambridge University Press, 2001.

Tietenberg, Tom, *Environmental Economics and Policy,* New York, HarperCollins, 1994

Tinbergen, Jan.: *On the Theory of Economic Policy*, Amsterdam, North-Holland 1952.

Towse, Ruth ed.: *A Handbook of Cultural Economics*, Edward Elgar, 2003.

Trugman, Gary R., *Guide to Conducting a Valuation of a Closely Held Business*, New York, American Institute of Certified Public Accountants, 1993.

Ullman, D. G.: *Making Robust Decisions,* Trafford, 2006.

Warwick, D. P.: *A Theory of Public Bureaucracy*, Cambridge, MA: Harvard University Press, 1975.

Weber, M.: *The Theory of Social and Economic Organizations*, New York, Oxford University Press, 1947.

Weibull, J. W.: *Advances in Understanding Strategic Behaviour*, New York, Palgrave, 2004.

West, Thomas L.: and Jeffrey D. Jones: *Handbook of Business Valuation*, New York: Wiley, 1992.

Woodward, J.: *The Oxford Handbook of Philosophy of Economics*, New York, Oxford University Press, 2009.

Yegge, Wilbur M., *A Basic Guide for Valuing a Company*, New York, Wiley, 1996.

Zipp, Alan S., *Business Valuation Methods* New York, American Institute of Certified Public Accountants, 1990.

Index

F

G

H

I

L

M

O

P

R

S

T

W

□□□